MAIN STREET FESTIVALS

DOWNTOWN WASHINGTON, INC.
P. O. Box 144
Washington, MO 63090

MAIN STREET FESTIVALS

TRADITIONAL AND UNIQUE EVENTS ON AMERICA'S MAIN STREETS

Amanda B. West

The National Main Street Center of the
National Trust for Historic Preservation

Preservation Press

JOHN WILEY & SONS, INC.

NEW YORK   CHICHESTER   WEINHEIM   BRISBANE   SINGAPORE   TORONTO

A cooperative publication with the National Trust for Historic Preservation, Washington, D.C., chartered by Congress in 1949 to encourage the preservation of sites, buildings, and communities significant in American history and culture.

This book is printed on acid-free paper. ∞

Published by John Wiley & Sons, Inc.
Published simultaneously in Canada.

This publication is designed to provide accurate and authoritative information in regard to the subject matter covered. It is sold with the understanding that the publisher is not engaged in rendering professional services. If professional advice or other expert assistance is required, the services of a competent professional person should be sought.

Designed by Brian Noyes

LIBRARY OF CONGRESS CATALOGING-IN-PUBLICATION DATA
West, Amanda

    Main Street Festivals : traditional and unique events on America's
main streets / Amanda West (National Main Street Center).
      p. cm.
    Includes indexes.
    ISBN 0-471-19290-2 (acid-free paper)
    1. United States — Guidebooks. 2. Festivals — United States — Guidebooks. I. National Main Street
Center (U.S.) II. Title.
    E158.W46 1998   97-33058
    917.304'929—dc21

Printed in the United States of America
10 9 8 7 6 5 4 3 2 1

DEDICATED TO THOSE who recognize
that the hearts of their communities are worth saving,
and who work tirelessly to revitalize them.

THE AUTHOR WOULD LIKE TO THANK the outstanding staff of the National Main Street Center of the National Trust for Historic Preservation for supporting this book in its evolution from a road-trip brainstorm to a reality. Thanks go as well to all the participating Main Street communities who provided the information about their events without which this book would have been impossible.

CONTENTS

INTRODUCTION

COMING BACK TO MAIN STREET FOR FUN

ALL OVER AMERICA, in the face of homogenizing sprawl development and loss of the local sense of place, Americans have turned back to their Main Streets for identity, rolling up their sleeves and going to work in the process of revitalizing the hearts of their communities—their downtowns and neighborhood Main Streets. Likewise, travelers nationwide are clamoring for the real, the authentic, and the original, recognizing that back-road America is where to find the true character of our country, rather than along monotonous, lifeless interstates. This guide highlights those communities participating in the National Trust for Historic Preservation's Main Street Program that have developed downtown festivals as part of their revitalization process. Reaching deep into their community's identity, Main Street programs have created wonderful and original themes for festivals, which could not have come from anywhere else but the community's rich heritage. The festivals they organize celebrate local history, agriculture, music, food, and culture and reflect citizens' new pride in their downtown and love for their community.

In this book, the traveler will find the weird and wacky, the tasteful and tasteless, the flavorful and fun—all happening downtown. Many Main Street festivals are developed with a heavy dose of humor. Lebanon, Kentucky goes whole-hog for its Country Ham Days, featuring pig pen relays, a pig pusher race, and the ever-popular hog slopping contest. Frankfort, Indiana, uses its high school mascots, the Fighting Hot Dogs, as the theme for its annual Hot Dog Festival, which has a four-mile Bun Run, a Parade of Pooches, and the Every Dog Has a Flea Market. Part of Evansville, Indiana's Riverfest is the wacky Office Olympics, pitting more than 80 teams from local businesses in the Office Chair Roll-Off and the Post-It Note Stick competitions.

Food is one of the most popular themes for festivals, and you'll find it in abundance at most celebrations. Food-based events are an adventure in eating: the Okrafest in Checotah, Oklahoma, presents okra in many ways: okra grits, okra quesadillas, okra sausage, and okra pecan pie. The cooking competitions are usually intense, such as the Perfect Perogie Cookoff at Pittsburgh's South Side Summer Street Spectacular, the Ardmoredillo Chili Cookoff Festival of Ardmore, Oklahoma, in which teams vie in a special "showmanship" category, and barbeque competitions such as Lexington, North Carolina's Barbecue Festival, where 20,000 barbecue sandwiches are served.

Local industry and agriculture are apparent in many events, such as Black Dirt Days in Conrad, Iowa, which celebrates its farming economy with plowing contests, the Farmer Olympics, and Cow Patty Bingo. The Shrimp and Petroleum Festival of

Morgan City, Louisiana, successfully combines, with gusto, the two economic mainstays of the community. Vidalia, Georgia, celebrates its famous sweet onions with onion eating contests, the Little Miss Vidalia Onion Pageant, an onion rodeo, a 10k onion run, and other activities not onion related.

Music is a part of most festivals, and many communities celebrate a musical form linked to their heritage. The King Biscuit Blues Festival, developed around its history of a local blues radio show, has grown to become a nationally known blues showcase. Fine arts and crafts are also popular at Main Street festivals, such as the Crosstie Arts Festival in Cleveland, Mississippi, that showcases local artisans in traditional and untraditional media. Paint the Town, in Morrison, Illinois, turns downtown sidewalks into 3- by 4-foot canvases for children and adults, armed with chalk, to create their own masterpieces.

For many travelers, festivals provide a glimpse of history they would never normally get just by passing through town. At the Railway Festival in Manassas, Virginia, in a demonstration of manual rail straightening, one can hear the cadences once used by "bar gangs." Visitors can witness tin smithing and listen to the sounds of the dulcimer in Appalachian folk music at the Historic Constitution Square Festival in Danville, Kentucky. Golconda, Illinois, remembers the 1838 Cherokee Trail of Tears that passed nearby with an event featuring members of the Cherokee Nation demonstrating their traditional dance, skills, and language. Sometimes a festival itself is part of a town's history, such as in Ogden, Iowa, where Fun Days dates back to the Depression, when it was developed with an agenda of simple games to pick up people's spirits, and continues to do the same today.

WHAT IS THE MAIN STREET PROGRAM?

THE MAIN STREET PROGRAM is a methodology for downtown revitalization that combines historic preservation and economic development, initiated and promoted by the National Trust for Historic Preservation's National Main Street Center. This is not a grant program; local Main Street programs are self-funded nonprofits or city agencies headed by a full-time director, with activities fueled by an army of volunteers.

The Main Street Approach to commercial district revitalization has been successful because it brings together many players that have a stake in their community centers: city government, businesses, civic groups, historic preservationists, historians, and residents. All recognize the need to save the city center as the heart of the community, and through consensus building and partnerships the local Main Street organization is able to bring participants together to develop a vision for the downtown's—and the community's—future. Main Street is successful because it takes that vision and puts it into a workplan to make change happen. Because of this approach, many community members affiliated with local Main Street programs feel both a new sense of direction and empowerment to shape their community into a vibrant place to live, despite the obstacles to success.

And the obstacles to revitalizing a downtown can be enormous: aggressive development on the outskirts of town, dilapidated buildings, local petty politics, lack of funding, hidden agendas, bad public image, apathetic city government, "white elephant" buildings, and zoning laws that penalize downtown development and encourage strip development. Bringing partners to the table, the Main Street program identifies these obstacles as well as goals for the community's future, both long- and short-term. Developing a realistic workplan and keeping an eye on their goals and mission, programs work methodically toward their objectives while facing and resolving new problems along the way. Their activities may be as simple as asking merchants to keep their sidewalks swept clean or as elaborate as putting together a complex partnership of financing with the city and local developers to rehabilitate a downtown building. The kinds of projects these programs take on depend on their goals, which may be revised along the way, as well as their experience and capacity to handle the work. In all cases, there is no quick fix to revitalizing a downtown–it's a low-gimmick, labor-intensive, community-involved process that is measured in terms of years, not months. The road to revitalization is a long one, but it does lead to *real* economic and community health. And although the hard work of maintaining a commercial district's health never truly ends, leaders and volunteers claim the new pride, vitality and sense of place in their communities is well worth it.

WHAT MAIN STREET PROGRAMS DO

Revitalization Through Historic Preservation

THE KINDS OF ACCOMPLISHMENTS achieved by Main Street programs are many and varied, but all lead to the revitalization of the traditional community core. Historic preservation and the rehabilitation of structures is a central focus of Main Street program activities. Programs encourage preservation projects through direct design assistance to building owners, which includes providing drawings of proposed improvements to their buildings and working with owners to plan improvements in stages compatible with their financial constraints. Many programs develop low interest loan pools or grants for building and sign improvements that enable rehabilitations that otherwise would not be possible. Main Street programs also work to find solutions for difficult-to-reuse buildings, known as "white elephants," such as movie theaters, hotel buildings, and department store buildings, which may be costly or overwhelming for one owner to improve. By recruiting partners for redevelopment, such as the city and private investors who are able to use the Federal Rehabilitation Tax Credit, programs are able to creatively find new uses for structures that may have sat empty for years.

Improving the Economy Downtown

IMPROVING a downtown economy by strengthening existing businesses and filling vacancies is another primary goal of Main Street programs. The reason is not hard to see: a strong Main Street creates demand for the reuse of buildings, which fuels historic preservation; building owners feel confident in investing in the rehabilitation of their structures when their business tenants are doing well and tenant occupancy is secure. Viewing the downtown as a destination market, a Main Street program evaluates the market and demographics of its area, targets business opportunities, and configures a retail and business mix for the downtown. It then sets out to assist existing businesses, sometimes by suggesting new product or service tactics based on its market research, sometimes by holding workshops or seminars on better business practices or trends. Many businesses have been saved by the one-on-one relationships built by Main Street programs that identify problem areas, help them react to changes in the market, or find new owners when they wish to retire or sell their businesses. In many cases, communities had never fully examined their business market comprensively nor did businesses have anyone to turn to when times got rough, so they simply closed. A local Main Street program's market research also enables it to effectively recruit new businesses that complement existing downtown businesses and take advantage of market opportunties.

Building a New Image

IN MANY CASES, a poor public image has stymied business recruitment efforts and investment by the public and private sector. Image derives from many sources, ranging from a perceived lack of parking, to trash-ridden flower boxes, to a consumer's not being able to find what he or she needs. Identifying problems with downtown's image is part of the Main Street Approach, and programs must take these problems head-on in order to create change downtown. Changing image involves providing solutions to image-damaging factors, such as recruiting garden club members to maintain the flower boxes or providing better signs for existing parking areas to improve parking availability. It also involves creating a positive image to counteract the negative one through direct communications, use of media, and one-on-one experiences. Developing festivals and other events based on local history, agriculture, or just plain fun is an excellent way to bring people back to the downtown to see the new businesses and rehabilitated buildings. It is a successful Main Street tactic for changing the image of what downtown is—and what it can be. But the festivals listed in this book go far beyond tactics of building a better downtown economy; they are reflections of a community's identity, which, like the Main Street program itself, have kindled community pride and the sense of place that has been lacking for many years.

Building Effective Partnerships for Change

THE MAIN STREET PROGRAM, in many cases, is the primary advocate for the downtown. Bringing together different elements of the community to create change is at the center of the Main Street Approach's success. But often it must work over a period of years to change attitudes and build partnerships. Likewise, there may be a history of mistrust or bad experiences between businesses, city hall, and even civic groups such as the chamber of commerce and the historical society—that has prevented them from working together. Main Street's job is to place those groups in the position of being partners, rather than threats, eventually changing suspicion to cooperation in creating a plan for the downtown's renewal. Many local governments have adopted downtown-damaging policies in land use planning, building codes, and business recruitment incentives that make it hard to build downtown and encourage strip development outside town. Removing city hall from downtown to the strip, instead of adding on to an existing downtown structure, is a decision made by well-meaning governments that fails to consider either the damage to the core of the community or the hidden costs of encouraging sprawl and its expensive infrastructure. It is through building a relationship and credibility with government that a local Main Street program can change the minds of officials to make decisions and plans that consider the long-term impact on the entire community and its character. Finally, the Main Street organization must face challenges of its own: funding in the midst of a lean economy and complacent merchants; keeping its volunteer board members energized in the face of sometimes overwhelming tasks; and strengthening its downtown merchants despite constant pressure from national mega-retail "category killers" and superstores.

All of these elements—*historic preservation, economic development, image development,* and *organization and partnership building*—are interrelated, affecting each other and combining to produce a well-balanced downtown revitalization effort that is firmly based on community consensus. They are part of a successful approach that has been cultivated by the National Main Street Center and reaffirmed by the hundreds of Main Street communities across the nation over the last 17 years.

THE FINANCIAL SUCCESS OF MAIN STREET

THE BENEFITS OF REVITALIZATION can be enormous: higher tax base, renewed sense of community, preservation of local heritage, increased retail sales, higher tourist visitation, and sense of community pride. And the economic benefits have been documented: the average amount of reinvestment in a Main Street Program community is $30.72 for every $1 spent on the operation of the program. More than 1,250 communities across the nation have seen over $7 billion in reinvestment, 39,700 net new businesses, and 143,000 net new jobs. Main Street has proven that historic preservation *equals* economic development.

WHAT HAPPENED TO AMERICA'S MAIN STREETS?

BEFORE WORLD WAR II, Main Street was a community's primary commercial hub. Downtown buildings usually had several tenants—typically, a ground-floor retailer and, frequently, several upper-floor offices or apartments; together, these tenants provided enough rent for property owners to keep their buildings in good condition. The presence of a post office, library, banks, and local government offices added to the steady flow of people downtown. Not only was Main Street the center of the community's commercial life, it was also an important part of its social life; people thronged the streets on Saturday nights to meet friends, see a movie, and window-shop.

In the past 40 years, America's downtowns have changed drastically. The creation of the interstate highway system and subsequent growth of suburban communities transformed the ways in which Americans live, work, and spend leisure time. With improved transportation routes, people found it easier to travel longer distances to work or shop. Roads that once connected neighborhoods to downtown now carried residents to outlying shopping strips and regional malls. Throughout the nation, in town after town, the story repeated itself. Downtown businesses closed or moved to the mall, the number of shoppers dwindled, property values and sales tax revenues dropped. Some downtowns sank under the weight of their own apathy. Neglected buildings, boarded-up storefronts, and empty, trash-strewn streets gradually reinforced the public's perception that nothing was happening downtown, that nothing was worth saving there. People forgot how important their downtown and its historic commercial buildings were in reflecting their community's unique heritage.

In many communities downtown merchants and property owners tried to halt this spiral of decline by imitating their competition—the shopping mall. Their attempts to modernize downtown took the forms of pedestrian malls, covering traditional building fronts with aluminum slipcovers and attaching huge, oversized signs on their buildings to attract attention. These well-meaning but usually ineffective methods did not stabilize the downtown's decline, mostly because they did not address the fundamental problem—that businesses did not change when the market did, and that people did not see the downtown as a destination for shopping anymore. With the economic boom of the 1980s, Main Street also saw increased development occurring outside traditional areas, and the problem of "sprawl," with its uncontrolled growth and cookie cutter architecture that reflected neither a sense of place nor a sense of pride, became an issue that most communities contend with today.

Facing these issues, more than 1,200 communities have adopted the Main Street approach in the past 17 years, looking again at Main Street, the heart of the community, to save its historic buildings, to revive its commercial core, to strengthen business, to control community-eroding sprawl, and to keep a sense of place and community life in America.

WHAT IS THE NATIONAL MAIN STREET CENTER?

THE NATIONAL MAIN STREET CENTER is a program of the National Trust for Historic Preservation. Since 1980, the National Main Street Center has worked with local communities to build successful downtown revitalization organizations based on historic preservation. Providing technical assistance, the Center has guided them through the maze of possibilities and pitfalls of enacting change based on its experience in hundreds of other communities. In many cases partnering with state governments, the Center works with local nonprofit and city-based Main Street organizations to provide guidance. The Center also produces a myriad of publications and training tools for communities to use in training themselves in the Main Street Approach and applying it to their community. It serves as the nation's clearinghouse for information, technical assistance, research, and advocacy for preservation-based commercial district revitalization and the Main Street program. It offers membership in the National Main Street Network, sponsors the Great American Main Street Awards, and coordinates the annual National Town Meeting on Main Street conference, which brings together revitalizationists from across the country.

ABOUT THE NATIONAL TRUST FOR HISTORIC PRESERVATION

THE NATIONAL TRUST, a private, nonprofit corporation, encourages public participation in the preservation of sites, buildings, and objects significant in American history and culture. The National Trust acts as a clearinghouse of information on all aspects of preservation, assists in coordinating the efforts of preservation groups, provides professional advice on preservation, conducts conferences and seminars, maintains 20 historical sites as museums, administers grant and loan programs, and issues a variety of publications. Six regional offices provide localized preservation advisory services. Financial support for National Trust programs comes from membership dues, endowment funds, contributions, and matching grants from federal agencies, including the U.S. Department of the Interior, National Park Service. The main telephone number for the National Trust is 202/588-6000.

FOR MORE INFORMATION ABOUT
THE MAIN STREET PROGRAM, CONTACT:

The National Main Street Center
National Trust for Historic Preservation
1785 Massachusetts Avenue N.W.
Washington, DC 20036
202/588-6219
http://www.mainst.org
e-mail: mainst@nthp.org

USING THIS BOOK

WHETHER DAY TRIPPING or planning a cross country trek, this book and the events listed can bring interstate-weary travelers closer to the people and culture of the land they are visiting. The festivals and events are listed by state. Each entry provides a brief description of the events, along with information about the community's history, local sites of interest, and the progress and achievements of the Main Street organization. There is also a local contact for further information: *It is strongly advised that you call ahead to confirm event dates and times.* The contact listed for each town or city should be able to provide accurate information about each event and about lodging and directions. For a chronological listing, see the index at the back of this book.

Even if you're not arriving in town on the magical day of a festival, you can still enjoy a stroll through town with a walking tour or visit the local museum or soda fountain. To make the most of your visit, be sure to stop at the local tourist or visitor office to obtain information.

ABOUT THE COMMUNITIES IN THIS BOOK

UPON ARRIVING IN ONE OF THE COMMUNITIES listed in this book, you'll see notable buildings that have been rehabilitated and are being used for new purposes, streets that have been improved with new lighting and benches, and other projects that reflect the efforts and determination of the community to revitalize its traditional commercial area. The communities described in this book are participants in the Main Street Program, but by no means do they constitute an exhaustive list of the more than 1,200 programs nationwide. Being a "Main Street community" is more than just a designation, it signifies a community having an active organization, pursuing its downtown's revitalization through historic preservation efforts, and espousing the Main Street Approach. *Main Street activities go way beyond festival coordination:* programs work behind the scenes to make downtown revitalization a reality (see "What Is a Main Street Program?") in a huge range of activities, from the simple to the complex.

NORTHEASTERN AND
MID-ATLANTIC STATES

Connecticut

Delaware

Massachusetts

Pennsylvania

Vermont

Virginia

West Virginia

Connecticut

EAST HARTFORD, CONNECTICUT

The Podunk Bluegrass Music Festival

The Podunk Bluegrass Music Festival is a two-day celebration of this original American musical form. It features nationally known bluegrass performers on a specially constructed "longhouse-style" stage amid the trees and hills of the new Town Green. Additional attractions include music workshops, foods and crafts, Native American exhibits, and sports activities.

> ADMISSION: *Friday night concert is free; Saturday festivities are $5 general admission*
> DATES: *Fourth Friday and Saturday in July*

Red Hot Blues and Chili Cookoff

Sponsored by the Connecticut Blues Society and the International Chili Society, this event brings together blues competitions, a chili cook-off, and a classic Corvette show. A variety of people are drawn to downtown East Hartford for this combination of entertainments, as well as for crafts exhibits, beer tasting, and fun.

> ADMISSION: *$6 Adults; $3 Children*
> DATE: *First Sunday in August*

Civil War Reenactment

The annual Civil War reenactment held in Wickham Park in East Hartford is widely regarded as a "mini Gettysburg." It features daily battle reenacts and living history events, period characters such as Mary Todd and Abraham Lincoln, and memorabilia shows and sales. The battles are waged rain or shine, and proceeds benefit the restoration of East Hartford's Civil War Monument of 1868.

> ADMISSION: *$5 Adults; $3 Children 6–12, under 6, free*
> DATE: *Fourth Saturday and Sunday in August*

About East Hartford

LOCATED ON THE BANKS of the Connecticut River, East Hartford was established in 1631 and incorporated in 1783. By 1923 its tobacco farming and small manufacturing economy began to give way to commercial aircraft and defense industry manufacturing. In recent years, downsizing and competition from two regional malls have forced the community, and especially the downtown, to redefine itself. Main Street Plus has been a partner in public and private efforts to revitalize the downtown neighborhood, building on its strength as a community meeting place and working to develop a niche in arts and culture. Initiatives include the rehabilitation of a 1917 high school as a facility with artists' studios, classrooms, and auditorium.

WHAT TO EXPLORE WHILE IN TOWN: A major portion of the downtown area was recently named to the National Register of Historic Places, and 80 percent of the properties in the downtown are cited as contributing to its historic character. There is a varied and interesting mix of architecture in East Hartford; a walking-tour guide is available from the Center Cemetery, a prerevolutionary burial ground located in the midst of downtown, as well as from the Main Street Plus office, 914 Main Street. Notable buildings include the Community Cultural Center, formerly a 1917 high school, the Starlite Playhouse, a 1941 movie theater now housing live theater; the Sage-Allen Building, an Art Moderne department store now put to new commercial use; and the 1880 Hose Company No. 1, the original and oldest fire company in East Hartford. For fine architectural examples, be sure to see the 1835 First Congregational Church and Parish House, the most outstanding example of Greek Revival style in East Hartford, as well as St. John's Episcopal Church and Corning Hall, a High Gothic Revival church built 1867-1869. Other attractions include the Vintage Radio & Communications Museum, housing radio, television, and motion picture memorabilia, and the King Museum of Tobacco and Aviation located at the Raymond Library, chronicling these industries in East Hartford.

Reenactors prepare for battle.

GETTING THERE: East Hartford, located at the juncture of Interstates 91 and 84 on US-5, is just across the river from Hartford.

FOR MORE INFORMATION: Main Street Plus, 914 Main Street, Suite 208, East Hartford, CT 06108, 860/282-7577

Delaware

DOVER, DELAWARE

Old Dover Days

Old Dover Days celebrates the architectural and historical heritage of Colonial Dover. Its featured events reflect the colonial theme with maypole dancing, games, and colonial craft demonstrations. Additional, events include a juried art show, house and museum tours, concerts, food, and games for kids. Old Dover Days takes place on the historic town green, surrounded by buildings from the colonial period, and is a family-oriented event that can be as educational as it is fun.

ADMISSION: *None*
DATE: *First weekend in May*

First Night

First Night Dover is a community-wide, alcohol-free family event celebrating the arrival of the New Year through the arts. Held in downtown Dover, it features entertainment from mid-afternoon until after the clock strikes midnight, signaling the new year. The early evening ushers in a procession of giant puppets, colorful banners, and artists, dancers, and musicians, who encourage everyone to participate in the fun. In addition, ice sculptures, storytelling, and hands-on activities entertain children for hours. A fireworks display caps off the evening before the "ball" drops: a balloon that contains hundreds of resolutions from community members. The admission fee buys a pin that gains you entry to all events.

ADMISSION: *$5 prior to December 25, $8 after; Children under 10 free (with adult)*
DATE: *December 31*

About Dover

DOVER, THE CAPITAL OF DELAWARE, has a downtown rich in colonial and Victorian architecture, extending from its historic central green. The green was the gathering place of colonial troops marching from Dover to aid General Washington, the location of the reading of the Declaration of Independence to cheering citizens, and the site of Delaware's ratification of the new Constitution. With the coming of the railroad, Dover boomed and much of the current commercial building stock was constructed. Downtown Dover suffered a decline with the coming of the age of the strip mall in the 1970s and early 1980s, but has recently regained its sense of pride and community heart with its participation in the first Main Street program in Delaware. The historic Bayard Hotel was saved through the efforts of Main Street Dover and its partnerships.

WHAT TO EXPLORE WHILE IN TOWN: The extensive collection of colonial buildings in downtown Dover surrounding the central green are reason enough to pay a visit; a walking tour booklet describing these buildings can be picked up at the Delaware State Visitors Center at 406 Federal Street. Other places of note are the Biggs Museum of American Art on Federal Street, the Johnson Victrola Museum, the Meeting House Galleries, and Woodburn, the governor's house on Kings Highway.

GETTING THERE: Dover is located in central Delaware and is accessible by US Highways 113 and 13.

FOR MORE INFORMATION: Main Street Dover, 155 South Bradford Street, Dover, DE 19903, 302/678-9112

Massachusetts

IPSWICH, MASSACHUSETTS

Ipswich River Festival

The town of Ipswich understands the significance of the Ipswich River in its settlement and development and celebrates that appreciation every year with the River Festival. Environmentalists, sportsmen, historians, and all who enjoy the river gather each year for a day of activities including bird walks, boating, canoeing, fly fishing, music, art exhibits, and more. Past events have also included storytelling, kite making, and discussions on water ecology.

ADMISSION: *None*
DATE: *Third Saturday in June*

About Ipswich

KNOWN AS AGAWAM by the Native Americans, Ipswich was settled in 1633, three years after the founding of the Massachusetts Bay Colony. The early settlement took place on the Ipswich River, a navigable waterway emptying into the Atlantic. In colonial times Ipswich was one of the most properous Massachusetts communities, second only to Boston. When in 1687 Reverend John Wise, a local churchman, denounced "taxation without representation" and encouraged a furor in the community, Ipswich became known as the birthplace of American Independence. Because of its early settlement, Ipswich has the largest collection of First Period homes (1625–1725) in the nation. Over the years the Ipswich River was a conduit for trade, and in the nineteenth century water-powered mills were built on its banks. An old mill in town has recently been renovated to house a CD ROM publisher, taking Ipswich into the twenty-first century.

WHAT TO EXPLORE WHILE IN TOWN: In addition to its rare accumulation of early colonial architecture, Ipswich has canoeing and kayaking, and Crane Beach and antique shops are nearby. Also of note are the 1640s Hart House and other local restaurants serving the famous Ipswich clam; a local brewery gives tours. Visitor information can be found at the Hall-Haskell Visitor Center.

GETTING THERE: Ipswich is situated on the northern coast of Massachusetts in a scenic inlet of the Ipswich River, which empties into the Atlantic. The nearest Interstate is 95; take exit 52, then head east for 10 miles.

FOR MORE INFORMATION: Ipswich Partnership, 2 North Main Street, Ipswich, MA 01938, 508/356-6161

Pennsylvania

CARLISLE, PENNSYLVANIA

Arts Festival, Octubafest, and Eighteenth Century Encampment

This one-day festival is actually three events in one, celebrating music, history, and arts and family fun. Hundreds of tuba enthusiasts come together to make beautiful music. An eighteenth-century encampment features life in colonial times, offering educational "vignettes." Visitors are treated to a street battle with soldiers in full regalia. The arts festival includes more than 240 juried exhibitions, a Kids Alley with children's activities, scarecrow making, and a food court.

ADMISSION: *None*
DATE: *Second Saturday in October*

About Carlisle

CARLISLE WAS FOUNDED IN 1751 and has enjoyed a rich history, but was plagued in the mid-1980s with the onset of urban renewal and the migration of several businesses to nearby shopping malls and centers. In 1984, Carlisle began a Main Street program, producing a chronicle of successful development and reinvestment in the downtown area. In fact, the Main Street program, the Downtown Carlisle Association, is one of the longest-running Main Street programs in Pennsylvania.

Soldiers from the eighteenth-century encampment.

WHAT TO EXPLORE WHILE IN TOWN: The Cumberland County Historical Society Museum and the seventeenth-century Two Mile House can fill you in on local history. There are many lovingly restored eighteenth- and nineteenth-century buildings throughout the historic district, some developed through the assistance of the Main Street program. The majestic 1939 Comerford Theater, which has been redeveloped from a movie house to a regional performing arts center, is worth a look. A walking tour brochure is available from the Downtown Carlisle Association at 6 North Hanover Street.

GETTING THERE: Carlisle is located 20 miles west of Harrisburg, situated at the junction of Interstate 81 and the Pennsylvania Turnpike.

FOR MORE INFORMATION: Downtown Carlisle Association, 6 North Hanover Street, Carlisle, PA 17013, 717/245-2648

SOUTH SIDE, PITTSBURGH, PENNSYLVANIA

South Side Summer Street Spectacular

The South Side Summer Street Spectacular has become the city's largest community event. This is a celebration that promotes the South Side neighborhood of Pittsburgh, as well as the ethnic communities that live within the area. A highlight of the week is the "Perfect Pierogie Cook-off," which invites local groups and restaurants to sell this Pittsburgh specialty to benefit local charities. Other features include live music, Pittsburgh's Longest Sidewalk Sale, a juried crafters' market, and a classic car show.

ADMISSION: *None*
DATE: *First full week after the Fourth of July*

About South Side

SOUTH SIDE'S BEGINNINGS can be traced back to 1752, when John Ormsby, a major in the British Army, was awarded 2,000 acres of land on the southern banks of the Monongahela River. In the early 1800s the land was named Birmingham, and industrialization grew. By 1870, 68 glass factories were producing half of the nation's supply. As Birmingham's reputation for factory work spread worldwide, immigrants from eastern Europe and the British Isles came in huge numbers, bringing with them customs and beliefs that endure to this day. The strong sense of community that exists in the South Side and the community's ethnic heritage has been preserved over the years. Recognized as a National Register Historic District, and a city historic district, South Side has the largest collection of Victorian architecture in the county and is appreciated as Pittsburgh's alternative cultural district. Since its inception, the Main Street program on East Carson has helped to generate more than 160 storefront renovations and $25 million in public and private investment.

South Side's eastern European heritage is alive at the Summer Street Spectacular.

WHAT TO EXPLORE WHILE IN TOWN: There are lots of places to visit in this funky area of Pittsburgh that reflects the city's history: the City Theater, an abandoned church that was rehabilitated by a local theater group; Market House in Bedford Square, one of two remaining market houses in Pittsburgh, unusually situated in the middle of a square; the Bedford School House-Birmingham Number One, a Greek Revival schoolhouse, possibly the oldest schoolhouse in Pittsburgh; and St. John the Baptist Ukranian Catholic Church—this landmark church with eight onion domes that shape the skyline, is indicative of the Eastern European immigration and presence in the neighborhood.

GETTING THERE: South Side, Pittsburgh, is located in western Pennsylvania. It is accessible by many major Interstates, including 79, 70, and the Pennsylvania Turnpike (I-76).

FOR MORE INFORMATION: South Side Local Development Company, 1417 East Carson Street, Pittsburgh, PA 15203, 412/481-0651

Vermont

RANDOLPH, VERMONT

Randolph's Fourth of July Celebration

Recognized as one of the best in Vermont, Randolph's Fourth of July celebration is held over a three-day period, beginning July 3. Festivities start with an impressive fireworks display, courtesy of the Randolph Fire Department. The community theater presents a lavishly staged Broadway musical in one of the town's true historic treasures, Chandler Music Hall. The centerpiece of the event is the large and lively parade on the Fourth. Bands, floats, marching Scouts, and local celebrities travel Main Street and wind through neighborhoods. The Vermont Agricultural Museum holds its annual Field Days with antique demonstrations, exhibits, and contests, and the Randolph Mountain Bike Classic is held on the back roads just outside town.

ADMISSION: *None*
DATES: *July 3 through July 5*

New World Festival at Chandler

The New World Festival celebrates Vermont's Celtic and French-Canadian roots with the traditional song, music, and dance of the "New World" that has survived and has entertained generations. The music and interpretation are authentic here, with workshops on instruments such as accordian, fiddle, and drum; response songs from the French-Canadian culture and even "called dancing" from the New England, French, and Irish traditions. The festival runs from noon until midnight in downtown Randolph. The main stage is Chandler Music Hall and Cultural Center, built in 1906 and now on the National Register of Historic Places. Four other continuous stages offer top performances in music, dance, and storytelling. There's a children's play area, as well as an exploration of French-American and Irish-American cultural heritage.

Traditional musicians at the New World Festival.

ADMISSION: *Adults $12 all day; Children under 12, $3*
DATE: *Sunday of Labor Day weekend*

RANDOLPH WAS FIRST SETTLED IN 1776, but settlement was slow because of Indian skirmishes. An early resident, Justin Morgan, developed the famous Morgan Horse stock that is recognized as America's first horse breed. Endowed with fertile, well-situated agricultural lands, Randolph became an important farming area. An abundance of timber led to the beginning of lumbering and wood industries. The coming of the railroad in 1848 made distant markets available to farm products and manufactured goods, which spurred growth and prosperity. Today Randolph is a lively community, offering a downtown listed on the National Register of Historic Places. Randolph's Main Street program and its parent organization, the Randolph Community Development Corporation, have facilitated the rebirth of the downtown following three devastating fires in 1991 and 1992. Current accomplishments include a new transportation center in the renovated railroad freight house, a new downtown Amtrak stop, and streetscape amenities downtown.

WHAT TO EXPLORE WHILE IN TOWN: Visitors to Randolph should see the Chandler Music Hall and Gallery. Built in 1906 and restored in the 1970s, the Hall is renowned for its accoustical excellence and is on the National Register. Classic Victorian architecture is prevalent in Randolph, and during the summer months the Randolph Historical Museum displays a complete turn-of-the-century drug store and barber shop. Visitor information is available at the Randolph Chamber of Commerce on Route 66.

GETTING THERE: Randolph is at the geographic center of Vermont, 3 miles from exit 4 of Interstate 89. Amtrak's Vermonter passenger train stops in downtown Randolph.

FOR MORE INFORMATION: Randolph's Main Street Program, Randolph Community Development Corporation, P.O. Box 409, Randolph, VT 05060, 802/728-4305, http://www.vermontsite.com

RUTLAND, VERMONT

Rutland Region Ethnic Festival

This festival recognizes Rutland's diverse ethnic traditions, derived from French-Canadian, Italian, Irish, Polish, Welsh, and Scandinavian immigrants. But it also acknowledges the greater global society and celebrates cultures from around the world. Ethnic food, entertainment, and art are used to encourage cultural appreciation. Authentic ethnic entertainment is offered all day, more than 25 food vendors sell delicacies from around the world, and ethnic cooking demonstrations are presented by the Vermont Folklife Center. Hands-on crafts activities and entertainment are available for children. This festival is the result of a year of planning and the involvement of more than 60 volunteers, and is an expression of community pride.

ADMISSION: *None; donation requested*
DATE: *Third Sunday of June*

About Rutland

SETTLED IN THE 1790s, Rutland became the political, commercial, and social center of Vermont during the nineteenth century. As a transportation hub, Rutland was able to serve the booming logging, marble, slate, and machinery industries that provided jobs for locals as well as new immigrants from many lands. Following the decline of these industries and the termination of railroad service, Rutland's economy sagged, and only during the past six years has significant downtown revitalization occurred. Successful efforts have been made to attract new businesses, service the existing ones, and provide promotional and cultural activities downtown. These initiatives have recently culminated in the renovation of a large downtown shopping plaza and the arrival of Amtrak service direct to New York City.

WHAT TO EXPLORE WHILE IN TOWN: Guided walking tours are offered in the summertime through the chamber of commerce, as well as a brochure for self-guided tours, for a small fee. Other information such as maps, guides, and events schedules are also available at the chamber, located at 256 N. Main Street.

GETTING THERE: Rutland is located in central southern Vermont, on US-7 and US-4. It is also accessible by Amtrak, which makes a stop here.

FOR MORE INFORMATION: The Rutland Partnership, 103 Wales Street, Rutland, VT 05701, 802/773-9380

Virginia

CLIFTON FORGE, VIRGINIA

Clifton Forge Fall Foliage Festival

This annual event brings many visitors to downtown Clifton Forge for a good cause: all proceeds go to support Shriners Hospitals. The festival features crafts, craft demonstrations, local entertainment, flea markets, and a wide variety of food vendors. But the real star of the show is the beautiful autumn color that graces the trees of Clifton

Forge and the surrounding mountains at this time of the year.

ADMISSION: *None*
DATE: *Third weekend in October*

About Clifton Forge

CLIFTON FORGE'S ORIGINS AND ITS NAME derived from a charcoal furnace and iron forge that operated in the early 1800s. The city incorporated in 1884, after the incoming Chesapeake and Ohio (C&O) railroad named its new depot at the east end of town, "Clifton Forge." The town's main economy was the railroad until the 1960s, and vestiges of this industry still remain. Since its inception, the Main Street program has worked to improve the sagging economy and the appearance of the downtown area. Visitors to the downtown can see the restored businesses and buildings that have become Main Street's "pride and joy." The once near-dead historic district is now a viable business area for the entire Allegheny Highlands of southern Virginia.

WHAT TO EXPLORE WHILE IN TOWN: The Allegheny Highlands Arts and Crafts Center is a unique arts center that offers juried art and crafts works from the surrounding area. The Center is located in the heart of downtown. The C & O Historical Society Museum houses railroad memorabilia. One of the Main Street Program's successes is a mini-mall, housed in a Spanish Style building that was once painted orange but is now restored to its former glory. Visitors can find information and a walking tour guide at the Main Street office on Ridgeway Street, or at the Arts and Crafts Center.

GETTING THERE: Clifton Forge is located in southwest Virginia, on US-220 just off Interstate 64.

FOR MORE INFORMATION: Clifton Forge Main Street, 501 East Ridgeway Street, Clifton Forge, VA 24422, 540/862-2000

CULPEPER, VIRGINIA

Fourth of July Celebration

This day-long celebration is Culpeper's largest festival of the year, drawing many visitors from afar. Activities include arts and crafts exhibitions, games, entertainment, hot air balloons, live music, a parade, and a variety of food and fun. The celebration closes with a spectacular round of evening fireworks.

ADMISSION: *None*
DATE: *July 4*

African-American Cultural Day

This annual event is designed to share with community members the historical and cultural heritage of African-Americans. There will be lots of home-cooked soul food, games to play, prizes to win, raffles and cakewalks, and live entertainment. Black history exhibits and an arts and crafts exhibition round out the roster of activities.

ADMISSION: *None*
DATE: *Second Saturday in September*

Culpeper Music Fest

Celebrate the fall with a day of music, food, and fun. This event features local musicians from the Culpeper area; performances are held downtown at the East Davis Street parking area. A variety of music styles are presented—gospel, bluegrass, country, blues, and rock—including many original compositions. Local civic groups will be selling food and drink with proceeds going to community projects.

ADMISSION: *None*
DATE: *First Saturday in October*

Downtown Culpeper Holiday Open House

Holiday Open House ushers in the holiday season amid an afternoon of festivities. See demonstrations of the old-world skills of rug hooking, needlework, quilting, blacksmithing, chair caning, and sausage making. This event features Civil War reenactments and carriage rides. Kids can have their photos taken with Santa and listen to storytelling. Strollling carolers provide a Christmas atmosphere as merchants host open houses that include refreshments.

ADMISSION: *None*
DATE: *Sunday before Thanksgiving*

Christmas on Old South East Street

This is a time to enjoy Southern hospitality and the holiday season on Culpeper's historic old South East Street. Many private homes, rich and diverse in architectural history and all dressed up for the holiday season, will be open for touring. Walk back into history and find excitement at the authentic Civil War campsite reenactment. Choral singing and strolling musicians put you in the Christmas spirit as you walk through the charming neighborhoods. Take a ride in an antique horse-drawn carriage, join in the community carol sing, or watch a candle-lit play. Experience a small-town Christmas in historic Culpeper.

ADMISSION: *$12 for tour of homes; other events free*
DATE: *Second Saturday in December*

About Culpeper

CULPEPER, ORIGINALLY called Fairfax, was established in 1759 and renamed in 1870. This small town, nestled in the foothills of the Blue Ridge Mountains, has a wealth of history. A railroad head for a regional rail line, Culpeper was frequently in the path of both Northern and Southern armies that shifted east and west during the Civil War. Several commercial buildings were used as hospitals for wounded soldiers, and both Union and Confederate soldiers are buried in downtown cemeteries. Competing with three shopping centers and a Wal-Mart has been challenging for downtown merchants. The Main Street program, named Culpeper Renaissance Inc., has led the revitalization effort over the last several years, resulting in a thriving downtown. It has established low-interest loans for property owners to improve their facades, sponsored business seminars to strengthen local businesses, obtained grants for rehab of the local train depot, and organized special events to draw people to the downtown as the center of the community.

WHAT TO EXPLORE WHILE IN TOWN: The Museum of Culpeper History at 140 East Davis Street has everything on Culpeper history from dinosaur tracks to Civil War memorabilia. Ace's Books and Antiques on West Culpeper Street has thousands of used books. Antioch Baptist Church at 202 South West Street is the oldest Black church in the area, organized in 1865. Throughout the downtown are music, book, and antique furniture stores just made for browsing. A walking tour guide and other materials are available from Culpeper Renaissance at 117 South Main, retail stores, and the Museum of Culpeper History.

GETTING THERE: Culpeper is located in central northern Virginia, at the junction of US-522, US-15, and US-29.

FOR MORE INFORMATION: Culpeper Renaissance, Inc., 117 South Main Street, P.O. Box 1071, Culpeper, VA 22701, 540/825-4416

FRANKLIN, VIRGINIA

Franklin Fall Festival

This three-day festival has become an extremely popular event. Diverse in its offerings, Fall Festival offers visitors nationally known entertainment, extravagant fireworks, an all-day downtown craft fair, a car show, and fishing and horseshoe tournaments. As if that weren't enough, there are a whole array of family stage shows, dance exhibitions, and a gospel sing. The fall foliage provides a colorful setting for this festival in charming downtown Franklin.

ADMISSION: *None*
DATE: *First weekend in October*

About Franklin

FRANKLIN WAS SETTLED as a railroad community in 1834. The town continued to prosper as a western Tidewater commercial center throughout the nineteenth century and well into the next. Like many communities, it faced the threat of strip shopping centers built on the outskirts of town that began to draw business away from downtown. Community leaders organized and founded Franklin Downtown Development, which eventually joined the Virginia Main Street program in 1985. It has worked tirelessly over the years to revitalize the downtown area—and has succeeded: downtown now boasts a 3 percent vacancy rate. This organization has developed loan and grant programs to assist new and existing businesses with facade and interior improvements to their buildings, and, perhaps most impressive, it has generated more than $21 million in reinvestment in the downtown area—not bad for a little community of 8,000.

Entertaining the crowds at the Franklin Fall Festival.

WHAT TO EXPLORE WHILE IN TOWN: The downtown of Franklin is a National Register Historic District, and Franklin Downtown Development has worked to make it a nice place to visit, where you can still get an old-fashioned soda or dine in a fine restaurant. Outside the downtown area, you may want to tour the local paper mill, Union Camp Corporation. Additional information can be found at the Franklin Downtown Development offices in city hall at 207 West Second Avenue, Third Floor.

GETTING THERE: Franklin is located in southeastern Virginia, 45 miles west of Norfolk on US-58. It is also accessible via Interstate 95 by taking exit 11 and heading east on US-58 for 35 miles.

FOR MORE INFORMATION: Franklin Downtown Development, 207 West Second Avenue, P.O. Box 179, Franklin, VA 23851, 757/562-8511

LEXINGTON, VIRGINIA

Fourth of July Bike Parade

This is a parade made up of area youngsters on bicycles, tricycles, and in strollers, held on the morning of the Fourth. Children gather at the local library parking lot to begin decorating their vehicles with streamers, balloons, and flags. All decked out, the procession begins down Main Street to Hopkins Green. The Green is the site for watermelon and refreshments, face painting, hat making, and other children's activities. This event is small-town America at its best.

ADMISSION: *None*
DATE: *Fourth of July*

Candlelight Procession and Community Tree Lighting

Held the day after Thanksgiving, this event kicks off the holiday season. Each of the participants is given a candle and a song sheet, and the carolers proceed down Main Street, led by a horse-drawn carriage. As the procession passes the downtown businesses, business owners illuminate their decorations, signaling the start of the holidays in Lexington. Upon reaching Hopkins Green, the caroling continues, culminating in the lighting of the community tree.

ADMISSION: *None*
DATE: *The day after Thanksgiving*

Downtown Lexington Holiday Parade

This annual holiday parade is a community celebration that traditionally takes place on the second Friday after Thanksgiving. More than one hundred entries participate, including the Virginia Military Institute Corps of Cadets and marching bands from local schools, heralding the arrival of Santa Claus at the end of the parade.

ADMISSION: *None*
DATE: *The second Friday after Thanksgiving*

About Lexington

LEXINGTON IS A SMALL COMMUNITY of 7,000 people, nestled in the foothills of the Blue Ridge Mountains in the Shenandoah Valley of Virginia. Founded in 1777, the area has numerous historical sites, many associated with the famous Confederate generals Robert E. Lee and Thomas J. "Stonewall" Jackson. These sites, as well as Washington and Lee University and Virginia Military Institute, plus the natural beauty of the valley, attract more than 80,000 visitors annually. The Lexington Downtown Development Association, founded in 1985, has been instrumental in preserving the unique architectural and historical features of the vibrant downtown that now boasts many shops and restaurants. The Association has initi-

Kids are the stars of the Fourth of July Bike Parade down Main Street.

ated a facade and sign grant program that has helped fund many of the unique and decorative signs that line the downtown streets. Working with the Virginia Main Street Program, it has provided free facade design assistance that has resulted in a number of improvements, including Pete's Bar-B-Que, which reused an old gas station.

WHAT TO EXPLORE WHILE IN TOWN: Lexington is home to many noteworthy historical sites, including the grave of general Thomas J. "Stonewall" Jackson at the Stonewall Jackson Cemetery on Main Street. His home has been preserved as a museum and is open for tours. Robert E. Lee and his family are interred beneath the Lee Chapel on Washington and Lee's campus. The entire campus of Virginia Military Institute and the colonnade at Washington and Lee are on the National Register of Historic Places. One interesting rehabilitation project is the former Rockbridge County Jail, which now houses the national headquarters of the Kappa Alpha Order fraternity. Carriage tours of the historic district are offered daily, April through October. The Lexington Visitors Center, located at 106 East Washington, offers maps, walking tour guides, accommodation information, and any other service needed by the traveler.

GETTING THERE: Lexington is located in western Virginia, along the Blue Ridge Mountains' spine, which runs down the length of the state. The city is just off the intersection of Interstates 81 and 64.

FOR MORE INFORMATION: Lexington Downtown Development Association, 101 South Main Street, P.O. Box 1078, Lexington, VA 24450, 540/463-7191

MANASSAS, VIRGINIA

Railway Festival

Celebrate America's love affair with the railroad! Railway history comes alive during a day filled with memorabilia, exhibits, living history and folklore, music, children's amusements, great food, and fun. Enthusiasts are able to get close to a working engine, which is on display and open for viewing. "Bar gangs" reenact the call and response cadences once used when railroad workers straightened rails by hand. And because a visit wouldn't be complete without a ride on a real train, the Virginia Railway Express runs rail excursions during the event.

ADMISSION: *None*
DATE: *First Saturday in June*

Annual Fall Jubilee

For a day of community spirit and family fun, the street of Old Town will be closed to traffic and filled with top-notch artists and crafters from several states. Local performers entertain crowds with performances of line dancing, clogging, and theater. Each year offers something new, with talented professionals booked to amuse adults and children alike. The children's corner is packed with theatrical face painting, hands-on activities, puppets, and storytellers. Fabulous food, children's rides, and seasonal fall weather complete the day. This event stems from the original 1911 Manassas National Peace Jubilee, which celebrated 50 years of peace following the Civil War and the first Battle of Manassas. The original event culminated in emotional exchanges of handshakes between former Confederate and Union soldiers on the courthouse lawn in Old Town Manassas.

ADMISSION: *None*
DATE: *First Saturday in October*

About Manassas

ALTHOUGH MANASSAS IS PERHAPS best known for its association with the famous Civil War battles, the city also has a fine collection of historic architecture, most of which dates from the late nineteenth to the early twentieth century. Thirty minutes from Washington, D.C., Old Town Manassas has four galleries of fine art, a live jazz club, retail offerings, fine restaurants, and cozy cafes. The Main Street program, in operation since 1988, has worked to revitalize Old Town by promoting the preservation of historic buildings and supporting the revitalization of the business district. The popular annual festivals and events sponsored by the Main Street program continue to revive community spirit.

Bar gangs demonstrate call and response cadences developed when rails were straightened by hand.

WHAT TO EXPLORE WHILE IN TOWN: A visitors center at 9431 West Street can provide maps, walking and driving tour booklets, restaurant guides, and further information for visitors. It even has relocation packets for persons considering a move to the area. The Manassas Museum chronicles the history of the Northern Virginia Piedmont area with items reflecting the rich past of the community. In addition, there are also the Rohr's Museum and the Fire Museum. Visitors to this area will be especially interested in seeing Manassas National Battlefield Park, about two miles outside town.

GETTING THERE: Manassas is located in northern Virginia, at the junction of Virginia State Roads 28 and 234. The town is five miles south of Interstate 66.

FOR MORE INFORMATION: Historic Manassas Inc., 9025 Center Street, Manassas, VA 20110, 703/361-6599

Marion Downtown! Independence Day Chili Championship

This chili cook-off, held in Marion's downtown district, draws thousands each year as teams from local businesses compete for the title "Best Chili in Town." Sanctioned by the International Chili Society, it offers cash prizes and trophies for the top teams. Other awards are made for People's Choice Chili, Showmanship, Most Creative Costume, and, for the weakest concoction, the ever-popular "Chili Wimp" award. Live music, celebrity auctions, children's activities, and more make this a traditional small-town celebration to be remembered.

ADMISSION: *None; chili-taster tickets are $.25 each*
DATE: *July 4*

About Marion

LOCATED IN FAR SOUTHWESTERN VIRGINIA, near Mount Rogers, is Marion. Settled in 1755 and incorporated in 1849, it is named for "Swamp Fox" General Francis Marion of Revolutionary War fame. The town is also home to Mountain Dew; the popular soft drink was formulated by a local businessman. The economy of Marion has traditionally been divided between agriculture and manufacturing. With the downsizing of both industries, Marion found its downtown in a state of decay. Through the efforts of the Marion Downtown Revitalization Association, first-floor vacancies in the downtown district have dropped from a high of nearly 35 percent in 1994 to its current level of well under 5 percent. In 1995, Marion's downtown district saw over $2.5 million in private funds reinvested in this area. Improvements include renovation of a old warehouse to a church fellowship hall, reuse of a long-empty factory building as a bread and pastries store and warehouse, and the construction of a new downtown post office. Many of the buildings downtown have undergone improvements as a result of this program.

WHAT TO EXPLORE WHILE IN TOWN: Visit the City Drug Store, which had its ghastly aluminum false front removed and its historic facade renewed. Downtown Marion features an eclectic blend of architectural styles, ranging from the Federal Style old post office building to the Italianate arches of the Bank of Marion building. But Marion is best known for its Art Deco and Art Moderne structures. Visit the former Marion Drug Company building, now Hayden's World. Maps and downtown business guides are available at the Main Street office at 138 West Main Street.

GETTING THERE: Marion is located in southwestern Virginia, on US-11 just off Interstate 81. The city is near Hungry Mother State Park, to the north, and Mount Rogers National Recreation Area, just 7 miles to the south.

FOR MORE INFORMATION: Marion Downtown!, 138 West Main Street, P.O.

Box 915, Marion, VA 24354-0915, 540/783-4190, e-mail: 1005@netva.com, http://www.area-net.com

WARRENTON, VIRGINIA

Kids and Pets Fourth of July Parade

This is the youngest parade in Virginia: a kids parade, with no motorized vehicles allowed. Kids and pets walk, march, bicycle, skateboard, ride in baby carriages and wagons, in horse-drawn carts— you name it—down Main Street to the sounds of hundreds of plastic musical instruments. Bags of decorating material for bicycles and other vehicles are provided to the participants. Ice cream, popcorn, and dog biscuits are handed out at the end of the parade. The street is closed to traffic for a half-hour following the parade so that children can experience bicycling downtown. Every child is awarded a participant ribbon.

Kids, pets, and bikes don red, white, and blue on the Fourth.

ADMISSION: *None*
DATE: *July 4*

An Evening Under the Stars

This award-winning event features food from top area restaurants and caterers and dancing to a 1930s-style big band. A silent auction of items gathered from around the state of Virginia is part of the gala evening. The event is staged on Main Street with the Old Courthouse as the backdrop. This is a fundraiser for the Partnership for Warrenton. All the nearby storefronts are decorated with the theme of the evening and lit with white lights.

ADMISSION: *$30*
DATE: *Third Saturday in September*

The Children's Christmas Shop at Gumdrop Square

The Christmas Shop is a children's Christmas fantasyland; it includes toy trains, doll houses, Christmas trees, and Santa, with more than 250 pounds of gumdrops used in decorations. It's a special shop, for kids only, where "elves" help little ones shop for Christmas gifts for their families. The items for sale are provided by downtown merchants and are very low in cost. This event also involves area high school students, who donate more than 2,000 hours in decorating and assisting as elves.

ADMISSION: *None*
DATE: *First Friday in December, and every weekend until Christmas*

About Warrenton

THE TOWN OF WARRENTON was incorporated in the early 1800s and named after General Warren, a hero of the Battle of Bunker Hill. The lengendary "Gray Ghost" of the Civil War, Colonel John S. Mosby, is buried here, and Warrenton is also where Chief Justice John Marshall first practiced law. Located in the heart of Virginia hunt country, the town is recognized for its historic buildings and fine architecture. In the 1960s, Warrenton was impacted by the emergence of nearby shopping centers. The Main Street program, Partnership for Warrenton, has worked on building improvements and historic rehabilitation projects, as well as the development of community events. The organization has successfully filled Main Street storefront vacancies with traditional retailers such as a bakery and jewelry store, preserving the character of the downtown as a genuine working community. The rehabilitated buildings, snappy storefront signs, and planters along the street are all results of the Main Street program's efforts. The downtown again has become the center of commerce and social activity in Warrenton.

WHAT TO EXPLORE WHILE IN TOWN: The Old Jail Museum, circa 1808, located next to the Old Courthouse on Main Street, is worth visiting for some local history. The Old Warren Green Hotel at 10 Hotel Street is where, in 1862, General George McClellan made his farewell address to his officers after being removed from his command by President Lincoln. The town's first confectionary shop at 58 Main Street was originally owned by Thomas Marshall, son of Chief Justice John Marshall. The "old pharmacy building" at 15 Main Street was recently restored, having been a pharmacy from 1820 until 1995. A walking tour guide is available at the Information Center at 43 Main Street.

GETTING THERE: Warrenton is located in the northern Virginia Piedmont, at the junction of US-15/29 and US-211. It is about 15 miles south of Interstate 66.

FOR MORE INFORMATION: The Partnership for Warrenton Foundation, P.O. Box 3528, Warrenton, VA 20188, 540/349-8606

West Virginia

BECKLEY, WEST VIRGINIA

Kids Classic Festival

This is an event made just for kids, with events lined up for a full day of fun. Features include a parade with children participating on their nonmotorized vehicles of choice and a fair with games, entertainment, demonstrations, fun food, contests, and a bike race. One of the highlights is a hot air balloon race in which contestants give tethered balloon rides to kids. The festival ends with fireworks at night.

ADMISSION: *None*
DATE: *Third weekend in September*

Chili Night

Heat up a cool night by dancing under the stars and sampling spicy chili during this annual event held the first Saturday in October. This chili cook-off features spicy concoctions prepared by area restaurants and organizations and judged by a panel of local chili connoisseurs. This event is a fundraiser for the Beckley Main Street program.

ADMISSION: *$5*
DATE: *First Saturday in October*

About Beckley

ESTABLISHED IN THE 1830s, Beckley has developed from a county seat and Civil War camp to the center of commerce for the coalfields of the early 1900s. The central business district experienced a loss of business during the 1980s with the development of shopping centers. But with the help of the Main Street program and a progressive city government, Beckley is becoming a hub of governmental, social, and commercial activity. The central business district, called the "uptown" area, has been designated as a National Register Historic District. The Main Street program has coordinated successful promotions, developed incentive programs for rehabilitation and businesses, and organized successful partnerships with the city.

WHAT TO EXPLORE WHILE IN TOWN: Beckley Main Street has produced a walking tour brochure as well as a brochure highlighting downtown businesses, galleries, and restaurants. It is available from Beckley Main Street at 409 S. Kanawha Street, next to city hall. Soldiers Memorial Theater and Arts Center frequently offers a coffee house with entertainment; inquire at the Main Street office. Nearby attractions include TAMA-RACK—the Best of West Virginia, which is a highly respected arts and crafts gallery showcasing West Virginia artisans, and the Beckley Exhibition Coal Mine, revisiting the history of the region's coal mines. The New River Gorge, providing white-water rafting opportunities, is also nearby.

GETTING THERE: Beckley is located in southern West Virginia at the intersection of Interstates 64 and 77.

FOR MORE INFORMATION: Beckley Main Street, 409 South Kanawha Street, P.O. Box 821, Beckley, WV 25802, 304/256-1776

CHARLES TOWN, WEST VIRGINIA

Harvest Days Celebration

This two-day festival in October celebrates the beautiful autumn season in West Virginia. Participants can enjoy a variety of crafts, multiple entertainers, and contests for adults and youngsters alike. Hayrides, scarecrow making, and pumpkin carving are enjoyed by all. There are also a crafts exhibition and a golf tournament. The festivities end with the Harvest Ball, held at a local restaurant.

ADMISSION: *None, except for Harvest Ball (cost varies from year to year)*
DATE: *Second weekend in October*

Christmas in Charles Town

This two-week gala is a citywide celebration, beginning with a tree lighting at the courthouse. Attendees enjoy roasted chestnuts, hayrides, and bonfires. Civil War reenactors are on hand to give a living history of the area. The annual Christmas parade is held on the first Saturday, with more than 100 units participating. On the second Sunday there is a unique parade of horses.

ADMISSION: *None*
DATE: *First two weeks of December*

About Charles Town

CHARLES TOWN, NAMED for Charles Washington, George Washington's youngest brother, was laid out in 1780 on a site owned by George Washington. In 1859, John Brown was tried for treason in the Jefferson County Courthouse and hanged in Charles Town. In 1896, William L. Wilson, a U.S. postmaster general from Charles Town, started the first rural free delivery. A major focal point of modern Charles Town is the Charles Town Horse Races, a local institution that has been newly revived and employs many people. The Charles Town Main Street program is focusing on the renovation of the Fire Hall as a community center and also offers low-interest loans to building owners for rehabilitation projects.

WHAT TO EXPLORE WHILE IN TOWN: The Charles Washington Inn is a wonderful old building—and is said to be haunted. An old Woolworth's building has been converted to a cafe and art gallery. A walking tour brochure is available at the Visitors Center at 200 West Washington Street, at the antique center.

GETTING THERE: Charles Town is located in the eastern panhandle of West Virginia on US-340. It is easily accessible by Interstates 66 and 81.

FOR MORE INFORMATION: Charles Town Main Street, Inc., P.O. Box 205, Charles Town, WV 25414, 304/725-5477

HUNTINGTON, WEST VIRGINIA

Chilifest—The West Virginia State Chili Championship

Chilifest is the West Virginia State Chili Championship, sanctioned by the International Chili Society. The winner of this "much heated" event qualifies to represent West Virginia at the World Chili Championship in Reno, Nevada. Cooks come from far and  wide to downtown Huntington, with their pots, spices, secret ingredients, and chili lore, as they gear up for this spirited competition. Prizes are awarded not only for chili, but for showmanship and booth design as well. Other competitions include a jalepeño eating contest (the record now stands at 39 in two minutes—pass the Tums). There are street performers, jugglers, and the much heralded West Virginia Sumo Wrestling Contest, which you'll just have to see to believe. Sample tickets buy you "tastes" of each chili.

ADMISSION: *None, but sample tickets are $.50 each*
DATE: *Second or third Saturday in September*

About Huntington

HUNTINGTON, ON THE BANKS of the Ohio River, was founded in 1871 as a terminus for Collis P. Huntington's Chesapeake and Ohio Railway, and the linkage of the river and rail transport has been important to Huntington's history. In the 1970s downtown Huntington experienced a major retail exodus after the state's largest mall opened in a nearby community. However, since the Main Street program was launched in 1989, dramatic changes have taken place. The downtown now pulsates with activity generated by new restaurants, shops, and other businesses, all located in rehabilitated commercial structures. The improved appearance of the downtown is due to Huntington Main Street, which has developed a low-interest loan program for building-owners, and has worked with them to plan improvements.

WHAT TO EXPLORE WHILE IN TOWN: A walking-tour guide is available from the visitor's center and the Huntington Main Street office at 404 Ninth Street, Suite 202. Area points of interest include Heritage Village, a former Baltimore and Ohio (B&O) Railroad station now housing restaurants and shops; the Museum of Radio and Technology; the Huntington Museum of Art; and Blenko Glass Company, makers of handmade glassware.

GETTING THERE: Huntington is located on the Ohio River, in western West Virginia, on the border with Ohio. It is just off of Interstate 64 at exits 6 through 11.

FOR MORE INFORMATION: Huntington Main Street Inc., 404 Ninth Street, Suite 202, Huntington, WV 25701, 304/529-0053

KINGWOOD, WEST VIRGINIA

Preston County Buckwheat Festival

This festival celebrates the locally grown grain, buckwheat, as well as the importance of agriculture to the region around Kingwood. Events include the crowning of Queen Ceres and King Buckwheat, carnival rides, entertainment, parades, and bike races. Eat your fill of their world-famous buckwheat cakes and "whole-hog sausage." Listen to the competition at the banjo and fiddlers contest, then see the Grand champion lambs, hogs, and steers raised by local youth at the agricultural displays and livestock competitions. The flavor of rural, agricultural West Virginia is alive at this special weekend event.

Queen Ceres and King Buckwheat at the Buckwheat Festival.

ADMISSION: *None*
DATE: *Last Thursday through Sunday in September*

About Kingwood

AS SETTLERS MOVED WEST through the Appalchian frontier after the American Revolution, they stopped near a spring and large grove of trees and named the spot "King Woods." In 1811, the Virginia legislature established the community of Kingwood. Its residents were strong supporters of the Union during the Civil War and played an integral role in the formation of West Virginia. After the war, Kingwood became the economic center of the booming coal, limestone, and timber industries. With the demise of these once-thriving extractive industries, Main Street Kingwood formed to improve the economic and aesthetic conditions of the city. The organization has raised funds to retain a local tourist railroad, restore local historic sites, and develop and implement a master plan for the historic district.

WHAT TO EXPLORE WHILE IN TOWN: Visit the 1934 Preston County Courthouse and pick up a historic district walking tour brochure. For a taste of the world-famous buckwheat cakes and sausage any time of the year, visit the 1859 Preston County Inn or Mary's Restaurant in the 1888 Bishop Building. The West Virginia Northern Railroad near downtown provides an 11-mile trip through coal country.

GETTING THERE: Kingwood is located in northern central West Virginia, on West Virginia Route 7. It is equally accessible from Interstates 68 and 79, which are to the north and west, respectively.

FOR MORE INFORMATION: Main Street Kingwood, P.O. Box 357, Kingwood, WV 26537, 800/571-0912

MORGANTOWN, WEST VIRGINIA

West Virginia Birthday Party

For those who are rusty on U.S. history: West Virginia was formed when areas of Virginia loyal to the Union during the Civil War decided to break away from their neighbors of secessionist Virginia. Main Street Morgantown celebrates that event with its biggest festival of the year. It includes "A Taste of Morgantown," which provides samples from area restaurants, entertainment, children's games, and car and craft shows. Visitors celebrate with the locals by enjoying a piece of the huge birthday cake made each year, which feeds approximately 3,000 people and is served by local officials.

> ADMISSION: *None*
> DATE: *Third Saturday in June*

Kids' Day

On Kids' Day, High Street in Morgantown is blocked off to give kids of all ages their own day to enjoy laughter and games in an educational and entertaining format. Kids can participate in activities such as sidewalk chalk art, jewelry making, a petting zoo, and a popcorn hunt. Entertainment includes exotic animal displays, magicians, and ventriloquists. Local businesses sponsor the activities, and there is educational "fun" as well, such as the fire department showing off an antique fire engine while talking about fire safety and prevention. Give your kid (and yourself) the day off to enjoy a fun day together.

> ADMISSION: *None*
> DATE: *Second Saturday in July*

About Morgantown

MORGANTOWN WAS FIRST SETTLED in 1766 by Zackquill Morgan. As Morgan's Town grew in the 1800s, the name was simplified to Morgantown. The downtown quickly became a commercial district, much as it is today. Through the efforts of Main Street Morgantown, the downtown has preserved and restored its historic buildings, many of which are listed on the National Register of Historic Places. Some of the organization's more visual projects are the many renovated facades in the downtown area; they were completed through a low-interest loan pool of Main Street Morgantown. This organization is also responsible for the benches, planters, and banners downtown.

Kids of all ages have fun at Kids' Day.

WHAT TO EXPLORE WHILE IN TOWN: The Old Stone House on Chestnut Street, dating to 1795, is the oldest surviving stone house in Monongalia County. Morgantown is also home to West Virginia University and has a public transit system that links the campus to downtown. A walking tour brochure and other information on the downtown area is available at the Main Street office at 389 Spruce Street.

GETTING THERE: Morgantown is located in north central West Virginia, off Interstates 79 and 68.

FOR MORE INFORMATION: Main Street Morgantown, 389 Spruce Street, P.O. Box 90, Morgantown, WV 26507-0090, 304/292-0168

POINT PLEASANT, WEST VIRGINIA

Battle Days

During Battle Days, Point Pleasant steps back in history to the 1770s. Historical reenactors, settlers, and crafters don period clothing to take visitors back to the colonial era. Activities include a lantern tour, a colonial ball, a parade, and a juried art show. The Battle of Point Pleasant, a pre-Revolutionary War clash fought in 1774, is commemorated by a memorial service at the conclusion of the festival.

    ADMISSION: *Only to the colonial ball*
    DATE: *First Friday through Saturday in October*

About Point Pleasant

POINT PLEASANT WAS ESTABLISHED in 1794 and is said to be the site of the first battle of the American Revolution, fought on October 10, 1774, at the confluence of the Ohio and Kanawha Rivers. The Main Street Point Pleasant program has been working to revitalize the historic downtown area, assisting in the rehabilitation and construction of more than 40 buildings downtown and improvements to the street amenties.

WHAT TO EXPLORE WHILE IN TOWN: Battle Monument State Park is the site of the pre-Revolutionary War battle and is right on Main Street. The River Museum, dedicated to river lore, is at First and Main Streets. The Gallery, an unusual art gallery and restaurant combination, is located at 506 1/2 Main Street. Tourist information can be obtained at the Main Street Point Pleasant office at 305 Main Street.

GETTING THERE: Point Pleasant is located in western West Virginia, at the confluence of the Ohio and Kanawha Rivers. It is situated on West Virginia Route 62, but is near US-35, and about 25 miles west of Interstate 77.

FOR MORE INFORMATION: Main Street Point Pleasant, 305 Main Street, Point Pleasant, WV 25550, 304/675-3844

The Old Guard appears at Point Pleasant's Battle Days.

SOUTHERN
STATES

Alabama

Arkansas

Florida

Georgia

Kentucky

Louisiana

Mississippi

North Carolina

South Carolina

Tennessee

Alabama

---❖---

DOTHAN, ALABAMA

Kaleidoscope: Festival of the Arts

This free festival of the arts promotes all artistic disciplines—music, theater, dance, visual arts, and literature. Originally begun as a children's event providing fun and educational experiences in the arts, it has grown to include a highly respected arts show and sale. But because of its children's theater, hands-on art activities, storytelling, and dance performances, this is an event you'll want to bring the youngsters to. Bring your budding artist to the Discovery Zone, where kids can do everything from their own versions of Andy Warhol screen printing to sinking their fingers into Rodin's clay to building Monet's bridge. For more information, contact the Wiregrass Museum of Art at 334/794-3871.

ADMISSION: *Free*
DATE: *Last Saturday in April*

Kids at work in the discovery zone at Kaleidoscope.

The National Peanut Festival

As the producer of 70 percent of the nation's peanuts, the region around Dothan has reason to hail this nut as the savior of its economy and pay homage to the hard-working farmers of the "Wiregrass" area at the National Peanut Festival. Past festival traditions include the Miss and Little Miss National Peanut Pageant, the Goober Gamboleers square dance workshops, and the Saturday grand finale, "Peanuts on Parade," with more than 2 1/2 miles of peanut pageantry.

ADMISSION: *Parade is free; some events have entry fees*
DATE: *Last weekend in October to first weekend in November*

About Dothan

DOTHAN IS LOCATED in the Wiregrass region of Alabama. Its future was nearly wiped out when the infamous Mexican boll weevil ravaged the cotton plantations in the 1920s. When George Washington Carver discovered the many uses for the peanut, the area established this crop as a replacement for cotton and secured its future as the Peanut Capitol of the World. The Dothan Downtown Group has begun efforts to revitalize the downtown area, coordinating new sidewalks, streetlights, and benches. The murals downtown have also been developed by the Dothan Downtown Group.

WHAT TO EXPLORE WHILE IN TOWN: A must-see in Dothan is Porter Hardware on Main Street. Founded in 1891, Porter's is Alabama's oldest operating hardware store and still looks much the same as the day it opened. Other popular spots include the Wiregrass Museum of Art on Museum Street and various restaurants, including a microbrewery. Walking tour brochures are available at the Dothan Downtown Group office in the old jail building, next to the Opera House, at 111 North Saint Andrews Street.

GETTING THERE: Dothan is located in southeast Alabama at the intersection of State Highways 231, 431, and 84.

FOR MORE INFORMATION: The Dothan Downtown Group, P.O. Box 1005, Dothan, AL 36302, 334/793-3097

FLORENCE, ALABAMA

Tennessee River Fiddlers Convention

Bring your lawn chairs to hear a part of Florence's history at this celebration of "old-time" music. The sounds of dulcimers, mandolins, banjos, and, of course, fiddles, will guarantee you toe-tappin' fun. The competition includes bluegrass fiddling, clogging, and three categories of buck dancing (including No Holds Barred and Flat Foot Only). Crafts booths and refreshments fill out the event, held in McFarland Park.

ADMISSION: *Free*
DATE: *First weekend in May*

W. C. Handy Music Festival

This week-long jazz and blues festival celebrates Florence's most noted native son, William Christopher Handy, the world-renowned "Father of the Blues." With more than 150 events planned, restaurants, theaters, libraries, and even boats open their doors to musicians to become venues where visitors can get their fill of blues. This is a big event in Florence, so you'll want to book hotel reservations ahead of time. For more information on lodging and events, contact the Music Preservation Society at (800) 47BLUES.

The Handy Music Festival celebrates Florence's native son.

ADMISSION: *Most events free; a few have cover charges*
DATE: *First full week in August*

Festival of the Singing River

The festival with perhaps the prettiest name, this celebration of Native American heritage offers visitors a unique view of native culture through storytelling, arts and crafts, music and dance. The Indian Removal Act of 1830 authorized President Jackson to send west all tribes living east of the Mississippi on the great Trail of Tears. One of the three routes of the Trail of Tears followed the Tennessee River through the Shoals, and many local Native Americans departed from present-day McFarland Park in Florence. Every year representatives of a dozen tribes return to celebrate their way of life and the river they held sacred, which was said to "sing" at the shoals.

ADMISSION: *Free*
DATE: *Fourth weekend in September*

About Florence

FLORENCE, LOCATED ON THE TENNESSEE RIVER shoals and founded in 1813, was once part of the raw frontier of America. A series of booms and busts shaped its growth, along with the Civil War, during which the town changed sides several times. Henry Ford once had plans to build the "Detroit of the South" in Florence, but they never took shape. However, the plans of the Tennessee Valley Authority did, which has moderated the local economy. Today, Florence is the home of the University of North Alabama and a leader in arts and cultural events. With a strong volunteer base, the Main Street program manages the street banners and keeps the downtown area attractive. Behind the scenes, Main Street has encouraged building rehabilitations through its low-interest loan program and design assistance, as well as recruited new businesses.

WHAT TO EXPLORE WHILE IN TOWN: There's plenty to see in Florence, even if you're not passing through during one of its many events. A walking tour brochure and a shopping and restaurant guide are available at the Main Street office or at the chamber of commerce at the SunTrust Bank Building, 201 South Court Street. Of note to see, the W. C. Handy Home and Museum at 620 College Street preserves the log structure in which the blues founder was born and contains many of Handy's personal effects; the Indian Mound Museum at the end of South Court Street maintains the effects of earlier residents. If you're an architecture fan, swing by the Frank Lloyd Wright house at 601 Riverview Drive. Tired tourists can quench their thirst at Trowbridge's, at 316 North Court Street, which preserves much of the same soda shop atmosphere it had when it opened in 1918. Rogers Department Store, a Florence institution at 119 North Court Street, has been owned by the same family since 1894.

GETTING THERE: Florence is located in northwestern Alabama, at the intersection of State Highways 43 and 72, along the Tennessee River.

FOR MORE INFORMATION: Florence Main Street Program, 301 North Pine Street, Florence, AL 35630, 205/760-9648

MOBILE, ALABAMA

Bayfest

Mobile's Bayfest celebrates the city's musical heritage with a three-day extravaganza of blues, jazz, country, and rock and roll. For this event, set in downtown Mobile, streets are blocked off and mammoth stages are constructed to accommodate the thousands of visitors who come to see performers as diverse as

Little Richard, the Neville Brothers, Clay Walker, and Bela Fleck. Contact the Bayfest office at 334/434-7970 for this year's roster and current admission fees.

> ADMISSION: *A three-day pass is about $20; a one-day pass is about $15*
> DATE: *First full weekend in October*

First Night Mobile

First Night Mobile is a New Year's Eve celebration of the arts, with performance venues set up in buildings throughout the downtown. Artists of varying styles and repertoires take the stage in bank lobbies and other buildings, on street corners, in churches, and in parks to entertain thousands of revelers. Featuring local, regional, and national talent, First Night Mobile offers a variety of comedy, theater, music, fine art exhibits, dancing, and hands-on art experiences.

> ADMISSION: *Small fee provides First Night button, required for admission to all venues*
> DATE: *December 31*

About Mobile

ESTABLISHED IN 1702 as an outpost of the French Empire, Mobile has experienced its share of American history. At various times the city has been part of Britain, France, and Spain, and its colonial settlers as well as its African slaves have contributed to its distinct culture and architecture. But downtown was suffering from a lack of investment by the late 1980s, when the Main Street program began working with community partners to encourage reinvestment. The results have been a dramatic turnaround, with millions of dollars invested in buildings, businesses, and the city's downtown infrastructure.

WHAT TO EXPLORE WHILE IN TOWN: Dauphin Street has been the focus of Main Street Mobile's efforts. It boasts more than 40 building renovations, thanks to design assistance and grant programs, and now houses a variety of businesses. Dauphin Street is also home to two of Mobile's oldest confectionery shops: Three George's Candy, in business for 80 years, and the A & M Peanut Shop, celebrating 50 years in business. The Museum of Mobile and the Mobile Museum of Art, both located downtown, round out the visitor's experience. In addition, Mobile boasts a number of period house museums and offers a walking tour brochure to guide you to local sites of interest. More information is available at the Fort Conde Welcome Center.

GETTING THERE: Mobile is located at the intersection of Interstates 10 and 65 in southernmost Alabama on the Gulf of Mexico.

FOR MORE INFORMATION: Main Street Mobile, 205 Government Street, Mobile, AL 36644, 334/434-7540

Arkansas

HELENA, ARKANSAS

The King Biscuit Blues Festival

The King Biscuit Blues Festival is dedicated to the preservation of the heritage and culture of the Delta blues. In 1941, Sonny Boy Williamson began broadcasting King Biscuit Time, a daily live blues show on local radio, which is now the longest-running radio program of its kind. This nationally known festival celebrates King Biscuit Time and its founder by bringing together international, regional, and local blues artists and their fans. This four-day event is free to the public and includes four blues stages plus a gospel stage.

King Biscuit Blues Festival hosts an array of talent.

ADMISSION: *Free*
DATE: *The weekend preceeding Columbus Day in October*

About Helena

FOUNDED ON THE MISSISSIPPI RIVER as a bustling port in 1833, Helena reflects a diverse cultural and architectural history. African-American, Jewish, Italian, Chinese, and Swiss settlers have all left their marks on Helena. Many heritage bearers of these cultures can still be found, continuing a strong oral tradition that includes a history of the Civil War, the blues, agriculture, and river lore. Helena also has examples of a fair number of architectural styles. Row buildings along Cherry Street in the commercial district, feature Italianate and glazed brick. Also downtown are a 1908 Missouri Pacific train depot, the 1950s Malco Theater, and several Art Deco structures. The Crescent

Jewelry building at 413 Cherry Street was donated to Main Street Helena and completely renovated with proceeds from the King Biscuit Blues Festival. It now houses Main Street Helena and the Festival offices.

WHAT TO EXPLORE WHILE IN TOWN: The Delta Cultural Center, located at 95 Missouri Street in the former Missouri Pacific train depot, showcases a permanent exhibit of early life on the Mississippi River Delta. The King Biscuit Time radio show is also aired from here every weekday at 12:15 p.m. The Phillips County Museum, at 623 Pecan Street, offers a unique array of Phillips County memorabilia. St. Mary's Catholic Church, at 123 Columbia Street, was collectively designed by Charles Eames, Emil Frie, and Charles Quest. A walking tour brochure can be picked up at the Main Street Helena office at 413 Cherry Street.

GETTING THERE: Helena is located on the eastern border with Mississippi, on State Highway 243.

FOR MORE INFORMATION: Main Street Helena/King Biscuit Blues Festival, P.O. Box 247, Helena, AR 72342, 870/338-8798

NORTH LITTLE ROCK, ARKANSAS

Silver City Silly Shenanigans

Described as a family festival of community contests, competitions, cuisine, and craziness, this is an event for attendees and their dogs. Based on North Little Rock's history of silver mines and dogs (ask a local for the complete story), this event features contests such as Most Patriotic and Best Dog Trick categories for the dogs, and dog biscuit eating and barking contests for the owners. Also featured are the great hot dog cook-off (no relation to the canine contests) and a day of team competitions such as tug-of-war and soccer kick-off for both kids and adults. Held on July 4, the day ends with fireworks over the river.

ADMISSION: *None*
DATE: *July 4*

Arkansas River Blues Festival

A day-long event held on the banks of the Arkansas River, this blues festival highlights local blues artists. Hear the traditional stories of trouble and fortune in the music of this "blues for the people" event. Bring your blankets and lawn chairs to settle down to some B&B—blues and barbeque. The entrance fee covers a day of music.

ADMISSION: *$10*
DATE: *Second Saturday in September*

FORMERLY IN THE SHADOW of the larger Little Rock across the river, North Little Rock is experiencing growth and renewal, owing in part to the Main Street program that has initiated the renovation of the riverfront park, as well as physical improvements on Main Street. Its low-interest loan program has enabled downtown building owners to make facade renovations. The downtown area is a National Register Historic District.

WHAT TO EXPLORE WHILE IN TOWN: The Old Mill Park, a grist mill dating from 1828, had its 15 minutes of fame in the opening scenes of *Gone with the Wind*. A walking tour brochure can be obtained at the History House, 507 Main Street, in the downtown area.

GETTING THERE: North Little Rock, in central Arkansas and across the river from the state capital, is accessible by Interstates 40 and 30.

FOR MORE INFORMATION: Main Street Argenta, P.O. Box 9205, 502 North Main Street, North Little Rock, AR 72119, 501/375-6707

ROGERS, ARKANSAS

Frisco Festival

This two-day community event celebrates Rogers's beginning with the arrival of the Frisco Railroad in 1881. Featured activities include the Frisco Bed Race, with categories for students, adults, and a special "teachers challenge"; a chili cook-off, with prizes for taste and showmanship; and railroad spike driving and Moola Moola Hoola-Hoop contests for kids. Traditional regional music and storytellers entertain folks while the kids have fun at the Kritter Corner and the Dinosaur Dig.

ADMISSION: *None*
DATE: *Fourth weekend of August*

About Rogers

ROGERS WAS INCORPORATED in 1881, just two days after the first steam locomotive rolled into town. Named after C. W. Rogers, the general manager of the Frisco railroad, this small farming community is experiencing rapid growth. Through the Main Street program, Rogers has managed to maintain its historic commercial character in its downtown area, which comprises two National Register Historic Districts. Many buildings have been restored over the past 10 years with a private sector investment of more than $8 million.

WHAT TO EXPLORE WHILE IN TOWN: Rogers Historical Museum at 322 South Second Street gives an overview of Rogers's past, and a walking tour brochure available at the museum will guide you through the downtown's primarily Italianate architecture. Poor Richard's Confectionery, located in a restored 1905 drugstore, is worth a stop. There are plenty of eating spots downtown, along with cafes, bakeries, restaurants, and a variety of retail shops.

GETTING THERE: Rogers is located in northwestern Arkansas off State Highway 62/71 on Highway 12 east.

FOR MORE INFORMATION: Main Street Rogers, P.O. Box 935, Rogers, AR 72757-0935, 501/936-5487

Florida

MARIANNA, FLORIDA

St. Patrick's Day Downtown Celebration

Marianna celebrates the Day of the Green with a party that encompasses the entire downtown. Besides showcasing local musical talent and arts and crafts people, the celebration offers food and children's games. The highlight of the event is the Celebrity Slime Competition: four local celebrities work the crowd collecting money for the Main Street program, and the highest collector gets to "slime" the other three with green gooey stuff, à la Nickelodeon high jinks. Local charities, along with service and youth groups, raise money through food booths, and carnival-type entertainment is provided in the streets of downtown Marianna.

ADMISSION: *None*
DATE: *Saturday before St. Patrick's Day*

AutumnFest

This event celebrates the fall season with live music, a variety of food, and arts and crafts. At a special annual fund-raiser, fall leaves are sold to fund a specific landscaping project downtown, and cheerleaders and basketball players from the local college make an appearance to help kick off the basketball season. Be a part of Marianna's largest macarena or join in the pumpkin-carving contest at this hometown event.

ADMISSION: *None*
DATE: *First weekend in October*

About Marianna

FOUNDED IN 1827 by a Scottish immigrant who named the town after his wife, Marianna is the county seat and has enjoyed steady growth throughout its 150-year history. The Main Street Marianna program has been instrumental in the downtown's transformation to a vibrant retail, service, and professional district. It has brought attention to the long-ignored downtown area and put pride back into the hearts of Marianna residents.

WHAT TO EXPLORE WHILE IN TOWN: A downtown business guide and map of the area are available at the Main Street Marianna office. The Russ House, currently under renovation by the chamber of commerce, is located just outside downtown on Highway 90. The Florida Caverns are also in the area, and canoeing is available on the Chipola River.

GETTING THERE: Marianna is located in the Florida panhandle, 60 miles west of Tallahassee. It is accessible from Interstate 10 or US Highway 90.

FOR MORE INFORMATION: Main Street Marianna, 2880 Green Street, Marianna, FL 32446, 904/482-6046

MIAMI BEACH, FLORIDA

Art Deco Weekend

If you're any kind of architecture fan, you're going to love this weekend event, the largest devoted to the Art Deco era. Celebrating the astounding collection of Art Deco buildings constructed in South Miami Beach during the 1930s, as well as the glamour of that era, Art Deco Weekend is comprised of walking and bicycle tours, lectures, vintage film series, and expositions of Deco finery. Hosted by the Miami Design and Preservation League, this 20-year-old event has helped to garner support and change attitudes about saving the extremely significant 800-plus buildings in this original American style from the bulldozers of hotel and condominium developers. Attend the Moon over Miami Ball or just stroll down the streets, enjoying the Deco style.

ADMISSION: *Most events are free; ball requires tickets*
DATE: *Friday through Monday of the third weekend in January*

About Miami Beach

DURING THE GREAT DEPRESSION of the 1930s there was a building boom in southern Miami Beach. A small number of architects designed hundreds of Art Deco Style buildings that had a remarkably uniform appearance, and Miami Beach's tourism-driven economy experienced tremendous growth. In the 1960s this area began to decline as buildings aged and new development moved north on the coast. By the 1970s the area was on the brink of destruction to make way for new high-rise condominiums. The undaunted efforts of the Miami Design Preservation League, founded in 1976, began to turn the tide of opinion about these quaint but architecturally significant structures, sparking a new appreciation. The League gathered opposition to hotel demolition and appealed to city leaders, arguing that the district could become a tourist draw. The results are seen in the present square-mile historic district and the Art Deco Welcome Center. The transformation of this area—and its attitudes—has been hard won and has helped to "mainstream" historic preservation in American consciousness.

Art Deco Weekend is set among the buildings of South Miami Beach.

WHAT TO EXPLORE WHILE IN TOWN: Many printed brochures and guided tours of this fabulous, colorful area, are available, most of which can be obtained at the Art Deco Welcome Center as well as at area hotels. The buildings, which are mostly hotels, are too numerous to mention. The Miami Design Preservation League runs bus and bicycle tours weekly and walking tours daily. Or just get out of the car and walk through the district—you won't be disappointed.

GETTING THERE: Miami is one city you can't miss: located on the southeastern shore of Florida it's the southern terminus of Interstate 95. The Art Deco district is in the southern section of Miami Beach, from Nineteenth to Fourth Street, and from Michigan to Ocean Avenue. The Art Deco Welcome Center is located on Ocean Avenue at Tenth Street.

FOR MORE INFORMATION: Miami Beach Preservation League, P.O. Box 190180, Miami Beach, FL 33119, 305/672-2014

Georgia

AMERICUS, GEORGIA

Taste of Sumter

The Taste of Sumter is a panorama of cuisine offered in the Americus/Sumter County area. The variety of foods ranges from beef kabobs, stuffed potatoes, and roasted corn, to tea and scones. People gather here to get a taste of everything this area has to offer. Enjoy the late summer day in this charming Southern town.

ADMISSION: *None*
DATE: *Fourth Thursday in September*

First Night Americus!

This is a multicultural celebration of the visual performing arts, as well as a safe, educational, and alcohol-free way for families to celebrate the New Year. There is a Mardi Gras atmosphere, with a grand procession that includes Father Time and Baby New Year. Entertainment is provided all night long by native Georgia talent, ranging from musicians of all types to magicians, cloggers, actors, and storytellers. Downtown churches, plazas, storefronts, and the landmark Windsor Hotel are the venues for these events. And because this is Georgia, you'll watch a giant peach drop for the countdown to the new year.

ADMISSION: *$5*
DATE: *December 31*

About Americus

AMERICUS WAS FOUNDED IN 1832, and in its early days, cotton was king. During the War Between the States it served as the site of three Confederate hospitals. Characterized by its Victorian buildings and homes, the downtown is anchored by the Windsor Hotel, which has been restored to its former glory and again serves as a hotel through the work of the Americus Main Street program. Since its inception in 1984, the program has worked to revitalize the heart of the community and is currently engaged in the restoration of the Rylander Theater. It has also developed facade and sign grants for many of the businesses downtown, enabling owners to make improvements, and has coordinated many events, such as First Night and Taste of Sumter, to refocus downtown as the heart of the community.

WHAT TO EXPLORE WHILE IN TOWN: A downtown directory can be obtained at the Main Street office in the Municipal Building, 101 West Lamar Street, or better yet, at the restored Windsor Hotel at 104 Windsor Avenue. Civil War buffs can revisit the darker aspects of that conflict with a visit to the nearby Andersonville historic site and the National POW Museum. Habitat for Humanity headquarters are also in Americus, and the Jimmy Carter historic site is in nearby Plains.

GETTING THERE: Americus is located in southwestern Georgia, near the intersection of US Highways 19 and 280. It is west of Interstate 75 off exit 33 on US 280.

FOR MORE INFORMATION: Main Street Americus / D.D.A., P.O. Box M, Americus, GA 31709, 912/924-4411

DALTON, GEORGIA

The Kudzoo Cook-Off and Festival

This event celebrates that bane of Southern horticulture, kudzu. Kudzu experts from all over the state line the streets, displaying creative uses for this ubiquitous, pesky vine. Heralded as a "community unity" event, it's a full day of music, carnival rides, games, a petting zoo, and even a watermelon seed spitting contest. There's also a barbeque rib cook-off with $2,000 in prize money and title of Best Ribs in North Georgia at stake (judged by a panel who really know their ribs). Just follow the smell of barbeque off Interstate 75 right into historic downtown Dalton.

ADMISSION: *None*
DATE: *Last Saturday in April*

About Dalton

DALTON LIES IN THE BEAUTIFUL Appalachian foothills of northwest Georgia and is known for its enormous carpet and textile industries. Chartered in 1847, Dalton earned a place in Civil War history as a manufacturing town and the site of a Confederate hospital. Nearby locations of Civil War battles such as Dug Gap Battle Park are nearby, where breastworks used by Confederate soldiers are preserved. The Dalton Downtown Development Authority (DDDA) works to recruit new business to the downtown area and provides a financial incentive program for building owners to improve and rehabilitate their buildings.

WHAT TO EXPLORE WHILE IN TOWN: A walking tour guide booklet of historic downtown can be obtained at the DDDA offices located at 210 North Pentz Street. Close to downtown is the Crown Garden and Archives, the historic Hamilton House, the Crown Cotton Mill, and the Creative Arts Guild.

GETTING THERE: Located in northwestern Georgia off Interstate 75, Dalton is 30 miles south of Chattanooga, Tennessee, and 90 miles north of Atlanta.

FOR MORE INFORMATION: Dalton Downtown Development Authority, 210 North Pentz Street, Dalton, GA 30722, 706/278-3332

LAGRANGE, GEORGIA

Kaleidoscope, a Fair on the Square

Kaleidoscope, a Fair on the Square, is a juried fine arts festival sponsored by the Chat-

tahoochee Valley Arts Museum. In its 34th year, Kaleidoscope's purpose is to promote the visual arts, provide a venue for purchasing quality art, and offer hands-on activities in art for children. Categories include mixed media, sculpture, photography, printmaking, metal-work, jewelry, ceramics, and more. Along with art, visitors will find live entertainment, food, and fun, with something for everyone.

Kaleidoscope provides hands-on arts activities for children.

ADMISSION: *None*
DATE: *Third weekend in May*

About LaGrange

LAGRANGE IS A CITY FILLED with Antebellum, Victorian, Craftsman, and Art Deco architecture. Founded in 1828, it has the distinction of being the home of the only female militia unit during the Civil War; its members, called the "Nancy Harts," charged themselves with protecting the home. Today LaGrange is a vibrant community of 26,000, who are refocusing on their downtown as the heart of their community.

WHAT TO EXPLORE WHILE IN TOWN: The Chattahoochee Valley Art Museum (housed in a former jail building) is located just off the square. A local institution is Charlie Josephs, in business since 1920, which still serves little bottles of Coke as customers sit on old bar stools at the counter. There are several art galleries in the downtown, as well as a family-owned department store. Downtown maps and other visitor information can be obtained from the Main Street office at the chamber of commerce at 111 Bull Street, just off Lafayette Square.

GETTING THERE: LaGrange is located near the western border of Georgia, southwest of Atlanta off Interstate 85, at the intersection of US Highways 27 and 29.

Chattahoochee Valley Art Museum, 112 Hines Street, LaGrange, GA 30240, 706/882-3267

MILLEDGEVILLE, GEORGIA

The Festival of Ville

This three-day festival celebrates Milledgeville's heritage and optimism for the future of its community. Tours are available for some of the large collection of Federal Style structures that escaped General Sherman's path of destruction. Exhibitors and crafts, entertainment and performing and visual arts make up the agenda. Fun events for both kids and adults, such as a bicycle rodeo and storytelling, make for a memorable experience.

ADMISSION: *Tours are $5, the rest is free*
DATE: *Third weekend in May*

About Milledgeville

NAMED FOR A REVOLUTIONARY WAR VETERAN, Milledgeville was founded in 1803 and served as Georgia's antebellum capital city until 1868. Much of the city was built between 1803 and 1825, and it has been described as the only surviving example of a complete Federal period city. Union general William T. Sherman's march of destruction passed through Milledgeville, but spared its buildings. The city was originally laid out in a grid pattern of squares, which are still evident today; the old statehouse square serves as the campus of Georgia Military College, and others are occupied by the Georgia College and University and the historic Memory Hill Cemetery.

WHAT TO EXPLORE WHILE IN TOWN: A wealth of historic houses, churches, and commercial buildings in the Federal Style, as well as Greek Revival and Victorian, abound in Milledgeville. A tour of Milledgeville's National Register Historic District is available at the Convention and Visitor's Bureau on Hancock Street. A number of historic commercial buildings rehabilitated with the assistance of the Main Street program can be found on Hancock and Wayne Streets. The 1832 Masonic Hall on the corner, with its three-story unsupported staircase, is a gem.

GETTING THERE: Milledgeville is located in central Georgia, 90 minutes southeast of Atlanta. Take Interstate 20 to exit 51 at Madison and follow US-441 south, or take Interstate 75 to exit 2, then State Highway 49 north.

FOR MORE INFORMATION: Milledgeville MainStreet/Downtown Development Authority, P.O. Box 1900, Milledgeville, GA 31061, 800/653-1804

NEWNAN, GEORGIA

The Magnolia Blossom Arts and Crafts Festival

The Magnolia Blossom Festival, sponsored by Main Street Newnan, began with a few local craftsmen set up around the courthouse lawn. Today the festival has grown to include more than 100 artists and craftsmen from across the state, plus food, children's activities, and entertainment near the courthouse square. Magnolia trees on the courthouse square and throughout Newnan are usually in beautiful full blossom for this one-day event, held rain or shine.

ADMISSION: *None*
DATE: *First weekend in June*

About Newnan

NEWNAN, FOUNDED IN 1828 and the county seat of Coweta County, was named in honor of General Daniel Newnan of Georgia. Fortunate to be spared the ravages of  the Civil War, its quiet, tree-lined streets boast a large number of Victorian and Classical Revival homes. Newnan has five National Register Historic Districts, including the downtown area. Since its inception, the local Main Street program has assisted commercial building owners in rehabilitation efforts and has recruited new businesses and promoted downtown with several events throughout the year.

WHAT TO EXPLORE WHILE IN TOWN: Of note are the former opera house building that now houses the Bank of Coweta, and the old Carnegie Library, which was rehabilitated into courtrooms and offices for Main Street Newnan. The Lee-King Pharmacy on the square still has an old-fashioned soda fountain and counter food service. Downtown maps, driving tour maps, restaurant and business guides, and other travel information are all available at the Main Street office in the Carnegie building, the Coweta County Welcome Center, and area restaurants and businesses. Newnan is also part of the Chattahoochee-Flint Heritage Scenic Highway.

GETTING THERE: Newnan is located southwest of Atlanta, off Interstate 85 at exit 9 on State Highway 34. For a scenic route take exit 10 to US Highway 29, proceeding nine miles to Newnan.

FOR MORE INFORMATION: Main Street Newnan, P.O. Box 294, Carnegie Building, 1 LaGrange Street, Newnan, GA 30264, 770/254-3703

THOMASVILLE, GEORGIA

Thomasville Rose Show and Festival

Thomasville is a city that can actually "promise you a rose garden"—and much more—at this event dating from 1922. At the center of the festival is a rose show with floral entries of all types, but it also includes the Rose Festival Parade, a Confederate reenactment, and a Jump for the Roses Charity Horse Show. Capturing the "oohs" and "aaws" for cuteness is the Children's Rosebud Parade, which is made up entirely of children dressed as roses, buds, flowers, and even caterpillars. Other fun for kids is the Bark in the Park Fun Dog Show, where canines are judged on best trick, fastest wagging, and best costume.

ADMISSION: *Some events require tickets, but most are free*
DATE: *Events held throughout the month of April; call for details*

Victorian Christmas

Relive a nostalgic Christmas past with this noncommercial event, held in a downtown with authentic Victorian architecture. Thomasville turns back the clock to the late 1800s and rolls out the welcome mat as local residents and shopkeepers dress in Victorian finery and greet you on Broad Street. The sounds of carolers and jingle bells on horse-driven carriages will put you in the Christmas spirit, and puppet shows, jugglers, and other street theater will entertain the kids. Hot wassail and Christmas delicacies are offered, and a live Nativity scene will remind you of what Christmas is all about.

Victorian carolers entertain downtown.

ADMISSION: *None*
DATE: *Second Thursday and Friday in December*

About Thomasville

MORE THAN A CENTURY AGO Thomasville was celebrated as one of the most fashionable places in the world to visit. Settled in the 1820s, Thomasville was an agricultural center with many large plantations, but following the Civil War it became a playground for the many wealthy northerners and others who used it as a winter resort. Remnants of Thomasville's past mark the city's determination to hold onto its history. Its Main Street program, begun in 1982, is one of the oldest and most successful in the country. Well over 100 building rehabilitation projects and compatible new development projects have occurred downtown, creating a thriving shopping district that offers a variety of specialty shops, restaurants, and antique stores.

WHAT TO EXPLORE WHILE IN TOWN: Izzo's Pharmacy at North Broad Street is a favorite stopping place for visitors and locals alike, with an old-fashioned soda fountain that serves cherry Cokes, milkshakes, and sodas. Farther down Broad Street is Joe's Billiard Parlor, where the line forms daily at the take-out window for the "world's best chili dog." The Welcome Center, located in the newly restored Old Post Office building (135 North Broad Street, basement level), offers maps, shopping guides, and information on area plantation tours, walking tours of Thomasville's seven historic districts, and historic bed and breakfasts.

GETTING THERE: Thomasville is located in southwest Georgia, 35 miles north of Tallahassee, Florida. It is accessible from both Interstate 10, via US Highway 19 or 319 north, and Interstate 75 from US Highway 84 west.

FOR MORE INFORMATION: Thomasville Main Street, 135 North Broad Street, Second Floor, Thomasville, GA 31792, 912/225-3920

TOCCOA, GEORGIA

Taste of Toccoa

This food festival allows local restaurants to set up for "tastes" of the best of their cuisine. Visitors purchase 50¢ tokens, which are used to redeem food. In addition to the wide assortment of foods served, entertainment is offered, including square dancing, children's games, Maypole dances, and music.

> ADMISSION: *None*
> DATE: *Last Thursday in April*

Toccoa Harvest Festival

The Harvest Festival has been an annual event in Toccoa for 20 years, celebrating autumn and the brilliant colors of the hills of north Georgia. It brings in hundreds of juried crafters and food vendors from the region who are allowed to sell only home-produced foods and crafts. Performances of clog dancing and bluegrass music provide a real flavor of the local culture.

> ADMISSION: *None*
> DATE: *First weekend in November*

**Artisans and crafters demonstrate
their skills at Toccoa Harvest Festival.**

TOCCOA IS THE SEAT of Stephens County in the northeast corner of Georgia, adjacent to the South Carolina border. The region was inhabited first by the Catawba Indians, and later by the Cherokee, who named a nearby waterfall Toccoa, which is Cherokee for "beautiful." Originally a frontier town, Toccoa began to develop in 1873 with the coming of the railroad. By the early 1900s it was considered the second largest manufacturer of furniture in the United States. The town is still situated in forested land, surrounded by the Chattahoochee National Forest. The Main Street program has been in existence since 1990 and continues to recruit new businesses downtown, improve the downtown's appearance with the addition of flower beds, trees, and landscaping, and encourage building owners to rehabilitate their buildings with facade improvement grants.

WHAT TO EXPLORE WHILE IN TOWN: A walking tour guide booklet is available at the Main Street office at City Hall, 203 North Alexander Street and at the Welcome Center at 907 East Currahee Street. The Stephens County courthouse and the historical museum on Pond Street are both local sites of interest. Situated in the vicinity of the woodlands of the Chattahoochee National Forest are several natural sites to visit: Toccoa Falls, Tallulah Gorge, and Traveler's Rest State Historic Site—all located outside the town. Scenic drives are abundant in this northern part of Georgia.

GETTING THERE: Toccoa is in the northeastern corner of Georgia, adjacent to the South Carolina border on US-123. It is accessible by Interstate 85 by taking either exit 57 or 58 and following State Road 106 or 17 north, respectively.

FOR MORE INFORMATION: Toccoa Main Street Program, City of Toccoa, P.O. Box 579, Toccoa, GA 30577, 706/282-3269

VIDALIA, GEORGIA

The Vidalia Onion Festival

As Vidalia celebrates the spring harvest of its world-famous sweet Vidalia onions, the landscape is said to release its aroma and the warm breezes carry the sweet perfume of Georgia's state vegetable. If you're not convinced, a trip to Vidalia during this festival is worthwhile to find out. You'll find plenty of onions: onion-eating contests, onion cooking school, an onion cook-off, and other good things not onion related. The Festival also offers the Little Miss Vidalia Onion Pageant, an onion rodeo, a 10k onion run, and an air show.

ADMISSION: *None*
DATE: *Last weekend in April*

About Vidalia

 KNOWN AS THE "SWEET ONION CITY," Vidalia was founded in 1892 after the railroad was built in 1890. A daughter of the president of the railroad named the town that has since become famous for its sweet onions. Vidalia's Main Street program, the Downtown Vidalia Association, is a vital part of the growing community of the historic downtown area. Named as a National Register Historic District, the downtown has been experiencing rebirth with new businesses, downtown upper-floor housing, and special events designed to keep people focused on the downtown as the heart of the community.

WHAT TO EXPLORE WHILE IN TOWN: A tour guide in the form of a game called "Doors to Downtown" can be picked up at the Main Street office located in Vidalia City Hall, 114 Jackson Street. Also downtown is the Ladson Geneological Library, with more than 30,000 volumes on regional and East Coast family and state history. Exhibits by the Ohoopee Regional Council for the Arts are also displayed downtown.

GETTING THERE: Vidalia is located in southeastern Georgia, situated between Macon and Savannah. It is accessible by Interstate 16; take exit 21 to US Highway 1 south for 15 miles.

FOR MORE INFORMATION: Downtown Vidalia Association, P.O. Box 1605, Vidalia, GA 30475, 912/537-8033

Kentucky

ASHLAND, KENTUCKY

Summer Motion

Summer Motion is a five-day long series of activities and entertainment over the Fourth of July holiday that includes musical performances by top names in country, rock, and Motown. There are also arts and crafts, sports tournaments, a car show, and a petting zoo and pony rides for the kids. Events are held on the banks of the Ohio River and at Ashland's Central Park.

ADMISSION: *None*
DATE: *July 1-5*

Poage Landing Days Festival

This family-oriented event, held on the banks of the Ohio River, harkens back to the first days of Ashland's settlement by the Poage family. It's a down-home celebration, with activities such as a lumberjack show, the Great Bed Race, and an antique car show, and a whole city block of children's activities. There are also musical performances by notable national and local country and gospel musicians.

ADMISSION: *All events free except river concert admission, which is $5*
DATE: *Third weekend in September*

About Ashland

ALTHOUGH THE CITY was originally settled in 1786 by the Poage family, it wasn't until 1854 that Ashland was laid out and named in honor of Kentucky statesman Henry Clay's home. Ashland's strategic location on the Ohio River and the region's wealth of timber, clay, coal, and iron ore led to its development as the major center in eastern Kentucky for shipping and industrial expansion. During the 1970s and early 1980s, industrial downsizing and corporate office relocations contributed to the decline of downtown Ashland. Ashland Main Street was formed in 1989 and has been instrumental in the rebirth of the city's downtown. Reinvestment has been spurred by financial assistance made possible by Ashland Main Street, such as facade improvement matching grants, low-interest loans, and free facade design advice. With commitment and vigilance, Ashland has reemerged with a vital, healthy downtown, a center for culture, commerce, and tourism.

WHAT TO EXPLORE WHILE IN TOWN: The Paramount Arts Center at 1300 Winchester Avenue, is a restored Art Deco theater, now a performing arts center that showcases local and national talent. The Kentucky Highlands Museum at 1620 Winchester Avenue houses exhibitions on heritage, history, and country music. Ashland's US-23 is known as the "Country Music Highway" because of the large number of country music notables that were born and raised along that route. Information on walking tours, other attractions, accommodations, and more can be obtained at the Convention and Visitors Bureau at 728 Greenup Avenue.

GETTING THERE: Ashland is located on the Ohio River in northeastern Kentucky where its neighbors, Ohio and West Virginia, meet. Situated on US-23, the city is minutes from Interstate 64, to the south.

FOR MORE INFORMATION: Ashland Main Street, P.O. Box 830, 1733 Winchester Avenue, Ashland, KY 41105, 606/325-7692

DANVILLE, KENTUCKY

Great American Brass Band Festival

The most likely place to see 76 trombones is at the Great American Brass Band Festival. In the tradition of the town bands that entertained at the turn of the century, this event brings world-class brass bands together for an unprecedented weekend of free music with lots of oompah-ing.

Bring your lawn chairs and picnic baskets to Centre College, where there will be plenty of uniforms and music ranging from Civil War era tunes to bugle calls, circus music, waltzes, and, of course, marches. The weekend is kicked off with an old-fashioned parade when the bands march into town.

Center stage at the Brass Band Festival.

ADMISSION: *None*
DATE: *Mid-June*

Historic Constitution Square Festival

This is a living-history type of event, with reenactors and craftspersons demonstrating their skills. Set in the 1780s, it allows visitors to sample life as it was 200 years ago when the first European settlers arrived in Kentucky. Daily activities common to the region's pioneers, including chores, celebrations, dancing, storytelling, and games, are included in the event. You'll hear the sounds of dulcimers and other traditional instruments, with live entertainment all day long. There is a large exhibition of juried artisans and crafters, including such traditional crafts as broom making, tin smithing, and basket weaving, as well as contemporary forms like stained glass, wood crafts, and ceramics.

ADMISSION: *None*
DATE: *Third weekend in September*

About Danville

DANVILLE WAS THE SITE of Kentucky's first government, organized as European settlers began reaching the area. It was the home of the first post office west of the Alleghenies, and nearby Perryville was the site of one of the fiercest battles of the Civil War. The Main Street program, with a million dollar loan pool for improvements, has worked hard since its inception in 1986 to guide historic preservation and encourage rehabilitation. It has also facilitated more than $36 million in reinvestment in downtown and 150 new businesses since it started.

WHAT TO EXPLORE WHILE IN TOWN: A walking tour brochure and other site and travel information are available at the McClure-Barbee House and at Constitution Square State Museum Park. The town's courthouse, built in 1860, once housed Civil War wounded as a Union hospital after the Battle of Perryville in 1862. Trinity Church on Main Street is one of the area's oldest churches, built in 1830. Centre College is a large part of Danville, and its campus makes a nice stroll. Burke's Bakery, a local institution, is well known for its bread and rolls. A drive in the countryside can take you to Penn's store, billed as the oldest country store in America.

GETTING THERE: Danville is located in the heart of Kentucky, at the junction of US Routes 127 and 150 south of Lexington.

FOR MORE INFORMATION: Heart of Danville, 304 South Fourth Street, Danville, KY 40422, 606/236-1909

ELIZABETHTOWN, KENTUCKY

Court Day

On Court Day, downtown Elizabethtown relives the days when people came to do business at this county seat on Saturday mornings. Features include antiques, arts and crafts, a farmers market, and food. Activities include a pet contest, a car show, a cake walk, and childrens' activities, concluding with a duck race. All proceeds from this event benefit the preservation of downtown Elizabethtown.

ADMISSION: *None*
DATE: *First Saturday in May*

About Elizabethtown

HARDIN COUNTY WAS FORMED IN 1792 and, not long after, streets were laid out and plots sold for a town. In 1795 a log courthouse was built, and other structures soon sprang up around the public square. By the 1820s, the town was equipped with its own bank, post office, and newspaper. Elizabethtown's newly formed Heritage Council, charged with preserving this historic character and promoting the revitalization of the area, is currently working on the rehabilitation of a theater downtown, which will become a live performing arts venue.

WHAT TO EXPLORE WHILE IN TOWN: Elizabethtown offers interactive walking tours, complete with living-history characters, on Thursdays at 7:00 P.M. in the summer months. The Heritage Council Office, at 177 West Dixie, can also provide a walking tour brochure and other information.

GETTING THERE: Elizabethtown is located just south of Louisville in central Kentucky, at the junction of Interstate 65 and the Bluegrass Parkway, and is also accessible by US-31 and US-62.

FOR MORE INFORMATION: Elizabethtown-Hardin County Heritage Council, 117 West Dixie, Elizabethtown, KY 42701, 502/737-4126

HARLAN, KENTUCKY

The Poke Sallet Festival

This three-day festival celebrates an indigenous mountain green called Poke Sallet, which has a long and honorable history dating back to the original Native American inhabitants of this area. This event is more than 40 years old with plenty of traditions. Visitors can attend an old-fashioned lawn party or an ice cream social, see the crowning of Miss Harlan County, walk into the past at a classic car show, ride the "Hillbilly Choo-Choo," and attend a concert with star performers. There are also handmade crafts, local music, and games for kids. And, of course, while you're there, don't forget to eat your fill of Poke Sallet, served with buttermilk and cornbread.

ADMISSION: *None*
DATE: *Thursday through Saturday of the first full weekend in June*

About Harlan

HARLAN COUNTY WAS FOUNDED IN 1819, but it wasn't until 1884 that the county seat of Mount Pleasant was established here. In 1911 the railroad finally reached the county, which was an event of tremendous importance to the economy. Mines opened in every valley, populations doubled and tripled, and an era of prosperity began in which Harlan was the coal capital of Kentucky. In 1912, Mount Pleasant changed its name to Harlan. Harlan has had some "firsts": the first radio station in any small town in the United States, the first Boy Scout troop south of the Ohio River, and the first and only FM broadcast over a television network. After the coal industry's recent decline, the town has stayed active through the efforts of local leaders and the Main Street program. Downtown Harlan remains a hub of activity and the heart of the community.

WHAT TO EXPLORE WHILE IN TOWN: Drop by the chamber of commerce and pick up a map of the downtown historic walking tour which will lead you to the most interesting sites in downtown Harlan. Near the courthouse, you can visit a memorial to coal miners and mining. Drop by the Creech Drug Store and have a fountain soda, check out the daily special at the Main Street Cafe located in the historic Newberry's

Building, or try Jay's Restaurant for some real home cookin'.

GETTING THERE: Harlan is located in extreme southeastern Kentucky, near the border with Virginia. The nearest Interstate is I-75, west, or the Daniel Boone Parkway to the north. Harlan is on US Highway 421, but also near US-119.

FOR MORE INFORMATION: Harlan Revitalization Association, P.O. Drawer 1709, Harlan, KY 40831, 606/573-7698

HARRODSBURG, KENTUCKY

Pioneer Days Festival

This event, held in the heart of downtown, commemorates the founding of Harrodsburg. Highlights include original Kentucky arts and crafts, the Pioneer Pig-Out Supper, a pipe-smoking contest, fiddling contests, gospel singing, a flintlock long rifle championship shoot, clogging, and more. It's a three-day-long history lesson that both adults and kids will love.

ADMISSION: *None*

DATE: *Third Friday through Sunday in August*

The friendly folks at Pioneer Days.

About Harrodsburg

ESTABLISHED IN 1774, Harrodsburg was Kentucky's first settlement. Daniel Boone's major role in the founding of Harrodsburg is recognized today at Old Fort Harrod State Park, a living-history museum located in the heart of the downtown historic district. Harrodsburg First, the Main Street program, was established in 1987 in an effort to reverse the trend of downtown business closings and building deterioration. Since its inception the program has been instrumental in the reinvestment of more than $4 million in the downtown for historic preservation, restoration, and business recruitment.

WHAT TO EXPLORE WHILE IN TOWN: The Mansion Museum, located on the grounds of Old Fort Harrod State Park, houses extensive Lincoln and Native American artifact collections. During the summer, mid-June through August, an outdoor drama, *The Legend of Daniel Boone*, is performed six nights a week in the amphitheater on the grounds of the fort. The Beaumont Inn, located downtown, is run by fourth-generation owners. The Old Happy Days Diner, at 122 West Lexington, is a local barbeque favorite. Outside town lies Shaker Village of Pleasant Hill, a living-history museum reflecting the Shaker community that once lived in Harrodsburg.

GETTING THERE: Harrodsburg is located in central Kentucky, southwest of Lexington, at the intersection of US Routes 127 and 150. It is accessible by either Interstate 75 or 64.

FOR MORE INFORMATION: Harrodsburg First, Inc., 122 South Main, Harrodsburg, KY 40330, 606/734-6811

HENDERSON, KENTUCKY

W.C. Handy Blues and Barbecue Festival

Honoring the "Father of the Blues," who lived for a decade in Henderson, the Handy Blues and Barbecue Festival has grown by leaps and bounds over the years, providing visitors with good blues and good barbecue. One of Handy's first musical gigs in Henderson was to play at a barbecue, so organizers found it appropriate to make this a hotly contested cook-off competition. Categories include the official, traditional pork competition and backyard barbecue events for "anything but pork." The music is just as hot, with national and local performers setting the tone with all styles: zydeco, Dixieland, and, of course, blues. With this festival's location on the beautiful riverfront area, its good barbecue, and its good music, it's a *good* time.

Discussing the finer points of barbecue.

ADMISSION: *None*
DATE: *Week preceding Father's Day, usually second full week in June*

Bluegrass in the Park

This event provides a venue for western Kentucky's musical gift to the world—bluegrass. It features local, regional, and national talent performing under the tall shade trees of Transylvania Park and in the local fine arts center. Bluegrass reflects the cultural roots of the people of western Kentucky, many of whom overcame tremendous hardships to survive. The outdoor performances are free, and are guaranteed to be a toe-tapping, family-oriented good time.

ADMISSION: *Most performances free*
DATE: *First full weekend in August*

About Henderson

HENDERSON, LOCATED ON THE OHIO RIVER, was founded in 1797 with an agreement from Native Americans and mapped with the guidance of Daniel Boone. It was once the tobacco capital of the United States, with its river providing transportation of this product to the world. This made it one of the richest towns per capita in the United States at one time. Home to four past Kentucky governors, Henderson harbors the architectural legacy of its nineteenth-century wealth. The Downtown Henderson Project was initiated to protect and preserve that legacy, and to keep downtown as the heart of the community. It has created a low-interest loan pool, which has encouraged building owners to rehabilitate many downtown buildings. It has also provided the banners that are hung downtown and, through technical assistance and seminars, has helped downtown businesses to compete in the changing retail economy.

WHAT TO EXPLORE WHILE IN TOWN: Downtown Henderson Project has walking tour brochures available at its office at 201A North Main Street. The Delta Steamboat company's flagships, *The Delta Queen* and *Mississippi Queen,* frequently make stops in Henderson, and Audubon State Park Museum and Nature Center is nearby on US Highway 41 north.

GETTING THERE: Henderson is located in western Kentucky, along the Ohio River. It is accessible by the Pennyrile Parkway, US-41, the Audubon Parkway, and US Highway 60.

FOR MORE INFORMATION: Downtown Henderson Project, 201A North Main Street, Henderson, KY 42420, 502/827-0016

HOPKINSVILLE, KENTUCKY

Jazz & Blues Festival

The annual Jazz & Blues Festival is an opportunity to hear some great music in a wonderful downtown setting. Regional and national acts appear at this event, which also features crafts exhibitions and children's activities. Visitors can enjoy a homemade ice cream competition, with teams vying to create the best hand-powered ice cream on-site. Watch them hand-crank their concoctions, then chill out with samples of their products while enjoying some great sounds.

ADMISSION: *None*
DATE: *Last weekend in June*

BBQ Festival

Barbeque is a favorite pastime in Hopkinsville, and the town is proud to hold the Barbeque Festival to showcase local talent and attract regional teams. Sanctioned by the Kansas City Barbeque Society and authorized by a proclamation of the governor of Kentucky, the festival promises

OF HOPKINSVILLE

good food and good times. It also offers children's games and activities, as well as music and other fun.

ADMISSION: *None*
DATE: *First weekend in September*

About Hopkinsville

HOPKINSVILLE WAS NAMED after a man who never lived here. In the late 1700s, Revolutionary War veterans were honored by having towns in the new frontier named for them. General Samuel Hopkins, for whom Hopkinsville was named, was a resident of the distant town of Henderson. The pennyroyal is a rare regional wildflower, and over the years its name was colloquialized to "pennyrile." The area of 35 counties in central and western Kentucky has come to be known as the Pennyrile Region. The Main Street program, Heart of Hopkinsville, has worked to revitalize the downtown. It restored the historic town clock, recruited new businesses, and assists in organizing special events downtown to bring people back to the heart of the community.

WHAT TO EXPLORE WHILE IN TOWN: The Pennyroyal Area Museum, at 217 East Ninth, gives visitors a glimpse of local history. The First Presbyterian Church was used as a hospital during the War Between the States, and the Jefferson Davis Monument Historic Site remembers the first and only president of the Confederacy. The Trail of Tears Commemorative Park is the location of an important campground used during the oppressive forced march of the Cherokee Indians to Oklahoma. A walking tour brochure is available at the library, the museum or the Heart of Hopkinsville office.

GETTING THERE: Located in western Kentucky, Hopkinsville is at the southern terminus of the Pennyrile Parkway (US-41), and is also accessible by Interstate 24 and the Western Kentucky Parkway. It is located at the junction of US Routes 41 and 68.

FOR MORE INFORMATION: Heart of Hopkinsville, P.O. Box 305 , Hopkinsville, KY 42241-0305, 502/887-4015

LEBANON, KENTUCKY

Country Ham Days

The Country Ham Days celebration was started in 1969 with six hams and a few dozen eggs, served early in the morning to entice folks to come downtown, eat, and shop. Now the event includes 600 hams and uncountable eggs, attracting more than 50,000 to this small community of 5,600. Country Ham Days features pig pen relays, a pig pusher race, and the ever-popular hog slopping contest. There are also horseshoe pitchin', hay bale tossin', nail drivin', hog callin', and pipe smokin' contests, not to mention the PIGasus Parade, sack races, and the Little Miss Ham Days pageant.

ADMISSION: *None*
DATE: *Last full weekend in September*

About Lebanon

LEBANON WAS INCORPORATED in 1815, and at one time the style, beauty, and elegance of its homes and flourishing businesses made it a contender for the site of the state capital. During the Civil War, General John Hunt Morgan and his raiders descended on Lebanon to seek retribution for the death of John's brother. Even though most of the town's buildings were destroyed, Lebanon recovered, and more recently the downtown historic district was placed on the National Register of Historic Places. As part of the revitalization process, new lampposts, traffic lights, and sidewalks have been added, and Lebanon's Main Street, US Highway 68, is a designated Scenic Highway.

WHAT TO EXPLORE WHILE IN TOWN: The Marion County Public Library has extensive geneology records, with microfiche equipment and facilities frequently used by family researchers. At the town's southern limits is the National Cemetery, where Union soldiers fallen at the 1862 Battle of Perrysville are laid to rest. Many homes and buildings downtown have a connection to the Civil War. Brochures on walking tours of these sites and other information are available at the Lebanon-Marion County Chamber of Commerce at 21 Court Square.

GETTING THERE: Located in central Kentucky, Lebanon is southwest of Lexington. It is accessible by the Blue Grass Parkway on US Route 68. Take exit 55 heading south on US-150, then go south on State Highway 55.

FOR MORE INFORMATION: Lebanon-Marion County Chamber of Commerce, 21 Court Square, Lebanon, KY 40033, 502/692-9594

MOUNT STERLING, KENTUCKY

October Court Days

Dating back 200 years, Mount Sterling Court Days is a tradition that stems from the days when county residents came from the hinterlands to buy, sell, and trade livestock, produce, and goods. What began as the last county trading day in the area has become a huge event for Mount Sterling, drawing thousands to the downtown. Good nature and friendly hospitality abound as locals look forward to this event to see old friends and family. You'll find handmade crafts, antiques, autumn produce, and plenty of country ham and biscuits.

ADMISSION: *None*

DATE: *Third Saturday through Monday in October*

About Mount Sterling

FIRST KNOWN AS LITTLE MOUNTAIN TOWN, Mount Sterling has a 200-year history, as reflected in its architecture and and traditions. The town is working to use its past to build its economic future with the Main Street program. This program has helped to revitalize the downtown with a number of projects. It redeveloped the oldest section of downtown, finding a number of businesses to fill vacancies and rehabilitate buildings. In a lot where a building burned, the program created a park, complete with a gazebo; it also coordinated the installation of the banners downtown.

October Court Days around the courthouse.

WHAT TO EXPLORE WHILE IN TOWN: Mount Sterling is very walkable. Begin your walk with a visit to the historic Bell House, circa 1815, at 51 North Maysville Street, which houses the county historical society and the Main Street program. Here you'll be able to obtain information, including walking tour guides, maps, and brochures on what to see in the area. There are many antique stores, shops, and restaurants located downtown; on West Main is a sweet tooth's haven, the Ruth Hunt Candy Co., in business and tempting the palate for more than 60 years.

GETTING THERE: Mount Sterling is located in eastern central Kentucky, approximately 30 miles east of Lexington. It is on US Route 60, also just off Interstate 64 at exit 113.

FOR MORE INFORMATION: Main Street Program, 51 North Maysville Street, Mount Sterling, KY 40353, 606/498-5343

PAINTSVILLE, KENTUCKY

The Kentucky Apple Festival

The Kentucky Apple Festival features everything *apple:* apple butter making on the street, apple pies and cakes, an apple auction, and even an apple run. It's an autumn festival that lets visitors soak up the local culture with a country music show, clogging, the "Terrapin Trot" (you'll have to ask), gospel music, and square dancing.

ADMISSION: *None*
DATE: *First Friday and Saturday in October*

About Paintsville

PAINTSVILLE, THE SEAT OF JOHNSON COUNTY, was established in 1790 but not incorporated until 1872. The Paintsville Main Street program has worked diligently to build a positive image of the downtown and ensure that it remains the region's economic center. Projects include the development of Paint Creek Park, restoring a historic bell originally from a steamship but now located downtown, the placement of directional signs downtown, assisting in business advertising, and coordinating special events such as the Apple Festival.

WHAT TO EXPLORE WHILE IN TOWN: Local spots of interest in the area include the Mountain Homeplace, a recreated 1800s working farm; the Van Lear Coal Camps, relics of the days when coal mines boomed; Loretta Lynn's home place; and the Stafford House, the oldest house in Paintsville. Walking tour guides and information about these sites are available at the Main Street office, located in the Citizens Bank on Main Street, or at the tourism office, also on Main.

**Making apple butter
at the Kentucky
Apple Festival.**

GETTING THERE: Paintsville is located in central eastern Kentucky on US-23, which is accessible by taking exit 191 off Interstate 64 for 50 miles. Or take the Combs Mountain Parkway to its terminus at US-460, then drive 13 miles to Paintsville.

FOR MORE INFORMATION: Paintsville Main Street, 340 Main Street, Paintsville, KY 41240, 606/789-6487

SOMERSET, KENTUCKY

Somerfest Arts and Heritage

Somerfest is an annual downtown street fair with the primary goals of providing entertainment and fun, fostering pride in the community while focusing on the downtown area, and celebrating the arts. Each year it celebrates a different aspect of the community's heritage. Last year's activities reflected the rural economy, saluting the region's farmland with pig racing, a mother/daughter look-alike contest, a kids' pedal-powered tractor pull, a petting zoo, gospel music, and storytelling by nationally recognized storytellers. The event also offers an opportunity for local artists to showcase their talents in exhibitions.

ADMISSION: *None*
DATE: *Third weekend in September*

About Somerset

SOMERSET WAS LAID OUT from a 40-acre tract of land in 1801, incorporated in 1810, and grew rapidly when the railroad arrived. This is a town rich in agricultural heritage. Many of the existing downtown buildings date from the early twentieth century. Between the 1950s and the 1970s, during a period of modernization so common among downtowns at the time, many building facades were covered over with false, "modern" aluminum facades. By 1980 preservationists, businesses, and government began to work together to reclaim the heritage of downtown. This work continues today with the Downtown Somerset Development Corporation, which has developed a matching grant program to encourage facade improvements, including the removal of those false facades of the 1970s. It has also provided trees, flower baskets, and benches to encourage people to use the downtown and retain it as a community gathering place.

WHAT TO EXPLORE WHILE IN TOWN: The homes of the historic Harvey's Hill area predate 1920 and constitute the largest concentration of historic architecture in Somerset. Civil War buffs may be interested in the house at 109 North Main, which was once a sanctuary for a wounded Confederate soldier fleeing Union troops—his bloodstains are still evident in an upstairs closet where he hid. Other points of interest are the RiverStone Art Gallery, upstairs at 209 East Market Street, which has a display of photos depicting the town's history. A walking tour guide, *Steps into the Past*, is available at the Downtown Somerset Development Office at 209 East Mount Vernon Street.

GETTING THERE: Somerset is in southern Kentucky, about 80 miles south of Lexington. It is located at the intersection of the eastern terminus of the Cumberland Parkway and US-27.

FOR MORE INFORMATION: Somerfest, P.O. Box 683, Somerset, KY 42502, 606/679-8376

WINCHESTER, KENTUCKY

Daniel Boone Pioneer Festival

This annual festival, held during Labor Day weekend, honors Daniel Boone and the area's history of early settlement with events on the Courthouse Square and Main

Street. Festivities include a juried arts and crafts show, a talent contest, and the Pioneer Classic Stage bicycle races. On Sunday evening there are fireworks and a free concert, with nationally known entertainers, at a local park. A Labor Day Parade marches down Main Street on Monday.

ADMISSION: *None*
DATE: *Labor Day weekend*

About Winchester

ESTABLISHED IN 1783, Winchester is positioned where the Appalachian Mountains, Daniel Boone's Fort Boonesborough, and the marvelous bluegrass horse country con-

Pioneer Festival parade.

verse. The downtown is rich in an original blend of cultural and historic character. Its elevated grandstand sidewalks once allowed seating for those who attended the horse racing down Main Street. Winchester First, the local Main Street program, has facilitated building rehabilitations, improved street amenities, and Winchester's economic rebound. Most important, it has returned a "sense of place" to downtown.

WHAT TO EXPLORE WHILE IN TOWN: Architectural must-see sites in Winchester include the restored Art Deco Leeds Theater, the Historic Clark Mansion, and the Carnegie Library. Local fun can be found at Jazzman's Cafe, with its live music and good food; visit the Cafe Collage for the ultimate in desserts and the Corner Drug for an old-fashioned "soda fountain" lunch. Just outside town is Fort Boonesborough State Park, and Natural Bridge State Park and Red River Gorge are nearby. Tourist information can be obtained at the Tourist Information Center on the corner of Maple and Broadway.

GETTING THERE: Winchester is located in central Kentucky, 16 miles east of Lexington. It is accessible from Interstate 64 by taking exit 96 to Highway 627 south, or from Interstate 75 by taking exit 95 to Highway 627 north.

FOR MORE INFORMATION: Winchester First, P.O. Box 935, Winchester, KY 40392-0935, 606/737-0923

Louisiana

ABBEVILLE, LOUISIANA

Vermilion Carousel of Arts

This is a parishwide 10-day festival celebrating the visual and performing arts and artists of the area. There are vocal performances ranging from classical to cajun, piano concerts, jazz and concert band performances, student art exhibits, community theater performances, and the all-important gumbo cook-off. Most events take place under century-old oak trees in Magdalen Square in the heart of Abbeville.

> ADMISSION: *None*
> DATE: *Second full week in April*

Louisiana Cattle Festival

This event pays tribute to the Vermilion Parish cattle industry, the leading cattle producer in the state of Louisiana. There's a livestock show, a Fais-Do-Do (street dance), a parade, the Cattle Festival Queen Pageant, and a baby contest.

> ADMISSION: *None*
> DATE: *First weekend in October*

Giant Omelette Celebration

If you've got a little *envie* (that's French for "longing") for Cajun culture, come to Abbeville to see these folks scramble about 5,000 eggs and "pass a good time." The history of the giant omelette is a long story dating to the time of Napoleon Bonaparte. For this two-day celebration of cultural exchange and camraderie, visitors from fellow *confrèries* in France and Canada come for the cooking of a giant omelette over an open wood fire in a skillet that measures 12 feet in diameter. The giant omelette is the culmination of a festival that includes a Visite des Maisons (tour of homes), arts and crafts booths, and heritage craft demonstrations such as decoy carving, lace making, tatting, and whip making, to name a few.

> ADMISSION: *None, except for tour of homes*
> DATE: *First full weekend of November*

About Abbeville

LOCATED IN THE HEART OF CAJUN COUNTRY, Abbeville was founded in 1843 by a Catholic priest, who established a church along the Vermilion Bayou and then proceeded to lay out a French-style village surrounding the church. The three squares he

The cooking of the giant omelette.

laid out are still prominent gathering places. Abbeville boasts 110 properties listed on the National Register. Abbeville MainStreet has been assisting building owners with improvements to their structures through the development of a grant program. It also holds events downtown, including the Sac à Papier Déjeuner (brown bag lunches), and a farmers market. Abbeville's economy is based on food production and agriculture, with rice processing, Cajun spice manufacturing, and syrup milling industries nearby.

WHAT TO EXPLORE WHILE IN TOWN: The beautiful St. Mary Magdalen Catholic Church with its amber-hued stained-glass windows, is where most people begin their visit to Abbeville. The town's three squares make for leisurely walks and good opportunities for people watching. There's a wide variety of dining options, based on the local seafood and food-processing economy. Walking tour brochures are always available at the Main Street office, and volunteer guides can provide a colorful tour if you contact the Main Street office in advance. If you want to venture farther afield, there are area museums, alligator and crawfish farms, and bird-watching opportunities along the Jean Lafitte Scenic Byway.

GETTING THERE: Abbeville is in the heart of Cajun country in southern Louisiana. Located at the junction of US-167 and State Road 14, it is also accessible by Interstate 10 at exit 103.

FOR MORE INFORMATION: Abbeville MainStreet, P.O. Box 1170, Abbeville, LA 70511, 318/898-4110

COVINGTON, LOUISIANA

Mardi Gras in Covington

This one-day festival is held on "Fat Tuesday" every year. The parade begins at 11:00 A.M. and is followed by a free Mardi Gras Fest in the Bogue Falaya Park. Refreshments and entertainment are provided. Children and adults of all ages compete for trophies and prizes in the costume contest.

> ADMISSION: *None*
> DATE: *Fat Tuesday, the day before Ash Wednesday*

Art in the Park

A fun-filled one-day children's art festival, held on the banks of the Bogue Falaya River, highlights the unique role of arts and crafts in the community. Children are provided with creative opportunities such as model boat building, tie-dyeing, frame and photo design, and bug box construction. Local artists display and sell their works, and children's theater and musical productions provide entertainment.

> ADMISSION: *None*
> DATE: *First Saturday in April*

Louisiana Bluesberry Festival

This is a one-day event celebrating the locally grown blueberry and blues music. Blueberry beignets, blueberry lemonade, blueberry cobbler, and a blueberry cook-off are all featured as part of this event. Local musicians sing the blues, area growers sell the real thing, and you can eat your fill of blueberry pie.

> ADMISSION: *$5.00*
> DATE: *Third Saturday in June*

Covington Three Rivers Art Festival

This is a two-day fine arts and crafts juried show in the streets of historic downtown Covington, showcasing artists in the Gulf-South region. It features 50 local exhibitors, a children's tent and performance area, local music, and a food court. The festival exhibits, for show and sale, the highest quality artwork and craftsmanship available.

An artist's demonstration at the Three Rivers Art Festival.

> ADMISSION: *None*
> DATE: *First Saturday and Sunday in November*

About Covington

IN 1813, JOHN WHARTON COLLINS, a New Orleans merchant, founded the city that became Covington on the edge of a parcel of land he owned between the Bogue Falaya and Tchefuncte Rivers. Collins laid out an unusual system of streets and squares, with central lots and alleys that are popularly known as "ox lots." Today, quiet Victorian homes and turn-of-the-century storefronts house art galleries, restaurants, and businesses. The historic Patecek Building at 301 Columbia Street and the Covington Bank and Trust Building at 236 Columbia are excellent examples of renovation projects sponsored by Covington Downtown Development Corporation (CDDC), the Main Street initiative in Covington, and have been rehabilitated for office and residential use. The Columbia Street Landing was recently reclaimed by CDDC and is now the location of many festivals and free concerts.

WHAT TO EXPLORE WHILE IN TOWN: There is a large artist contingent in Covington, and you'll have no trouble finding art galleries and fun eating spots to explore. Pick up the *Visitors Guide* brochure, which combines a walking tour with a directory of local establishments, at any restaurant or shop downtown. Visitors will enjoy H.J. Smith's Son Hardware Store and Museum at 308 North Columbia, the oldest hardware and general store in the parish.

GETTING THERE: Located north of New Orleans across Lake Pontchartrain, Covington is accessible by a number of routes. The city is on US-90, just off Interstate 12 and a stone's throw from the Lake Pontchartrain Causeway.

FOR MORE INFORMATION: Covington Downtown Development, P.O. Box 778, Covington, LA 70434, 504/892-1873

DENHAM SPRINGS, LOUISIANA

Springfest

When Springfest highlights the downtown Denham Springs Historic District, the street is closed to vehicular traffic and the area becomes a festival with an open marketplace atmosphere. Visitors can buy crafts, ranging from handmade clothing to wood carvings, from the dozens of booths that fill the street. Throughout the day live entertainment is provided by bands, choirs, dancers, and solo performers. A children's village offers activities and entertainment for kids. Food includes everything from hamburgers to boiled crawfish to funnel cakes. This is a day of entertainment for the entire family.

ADMISSION: *None*
DATE: *Third Saturday in April*

Olde Downtown Antique Festival

This event focuses on the unique Antique Village in downtown Denham Springs. The street is closed for the day, and antique stores offer furniture, jewelry, baseball cards, Civil War items, books, and other collectibles. New items are also showcased. Live entertainment and an antique auction provide day-long activity, and visitors can refresh their shopping strength at the local gourmet coffee shop.

ADMISSION: *None*
DATE: *First Saturday in April*

About Denham Springs

DENHAM SPRINGS WAS INCORPORATED in 1903 and became the shipping hub of a large truck-crop region. The railroad and new highways provided access, and it has become the hometown of many Baton Rouge workers. Main Street Denham Springs is focusing its efforts on bringing entertainment and the arts into the historic district and is currently working on the refurbishment of the Old City Hall building to create a visitors center and offices.

WHAT TO EXPLORE WHILE IN TOWN: The Whistle Stop Coffee Shop, across from the train station park at Railroad and Range Avenues, is open all night. The Old City Hall, built in 1940 as a WPA project, is listed on the National Register of Historic Places, and is currently undergoing restoration.

GETTING THERE: Denham Springs is located on Interstate 12, about 5 miles east of Baton Rouge. It is also easily accessible from Interstate 55, which is 25 miles east.

FOR MORE INFORMATION: Main Street Denham Springs, P.O. Box 1629, Denham Springs, LA 70727-1629, 504/665-8121

MORGAN CITY, LOUISIANA

Shrimp and Petroleum Festival

Yes, you read correctly. This event combines, with gusto, the two economic bases that are Morgan City's lifeblood: shrimp and petroleum. Dating from 1936, one of this festival's highlights is the historic blessing of the fleet and a water parade featuring elaborately decorated shrimp trawlers. There's also the Shrimp Cook-Off, with tons of food to sample, Cajun and zydeco music, a massive arts and crafts show, and a children's village to keep the little ones happy.

ADMISSION: *None*
DATE: *Thursday through Monday night on Labor Day weekend*

About Morgan City

MORGAN CITY, LOCATED ON THE BANKS of the Atchafalaya River, was originally incorporated in 1860 when the local sugar plantation owner divided his lot to
form a town. Originally named Brashear, Morgan City was renamed in 1876 in tribute to rail and steamship magnate Charles Morgan, who first
dredged the Atchafalaya Bay Ship Channel to accommodate ocean-
going vessels, thus launching the river communities as port cities.
Still a center of commerce and industry, and home to numerous
festivals and celebrations, the town has just launched a Main Street
program that hopes to use these assets, along with its multitude of
historic buildings, to return vitality to the downtown area.

WHAT TO EXPLORE WHILE IN TOWN: A walking tour guide booklet for the historic
district, as well as other materials, are available at the Tourist Center, City Hall, and
Front Street Pleasure Dock. You can walk aboard an authentic offshore drilling rig at
the Rig Museum, and a wonderful view can be had of the Atchafalaya, at no charge,
atop the 20-foot floodwall along the river. Other sites of interest are the Carillon Bell
Tower, the Swamp Gardens, and a Civil War Museum.

GETTING THERE: Morgan City is located in southern Louisiana on US-90. It is accessible from Interstate 10 by taking US-90 south from exit 103 at Lafayette, then driving south 100 miles.

FOR MORE INFORMATION: Shrimp and Petroleum Festival Office, 710 Third Street,
P.O. Box 103, Morgan City, LA 70381, 504/385-0703

NATCHITOCHES, LOUISIANA

Jazz Fest

The annual Jazz Fest is held on the banks of Cane River Lake the Saturday prior to St.
Patrick's Day each spring. Such famous performers as Irma Thomas have provided entertainment in the past. Local jazz and rhythm and blues bands also entertain the hundreds
that line the riverbank. Family fun with food and good music is the order of the day.

> ADMISSION: *None*
> DATE: *Saturday prior to St. Patrick's Day*

About Natchitoches

NATCHITOCHES (pronounced Nach-a-tish) is a mecca for historic preservationists,
not only because it is the oldest permanent settlement in Louisiana, but also because

so many of its late eighteenth-century buildings still stand, in good repair. It has a 33-block National Register Historic District, and for good reason: here you can find architecture of many styles, at a high level of quality, ranging from Creole bungalows to Queen Anne houses. Natchitoches, originally part of French Louisiana, has an interesting history. Several overland highways met here, including the Natchez Trace from the east and El Camino Real from Mexico. Combined with river trade, these routes created a bustling community. Over the years the wealth of trade provided an abundance of buildings created in the high style of their period. During the past two decades, Nachitoches has embraced historic preservation, engaging in efforts to stabilize these treasures. The city has recently organized a Main Street program, which will no doubt be capitalizing on these assets even further.

WHAT TO EXPLORE WHILE IN TOWN: Natchitoches has the largest assortment of Creole structures in the Mississippi Valley, and the tourism information office on the banks of Cane River Lake can provide you with a walking tour brochure of the historic district and other information on area history and attractions. They can also suggest tour guides who can provide a personal touring experience by boat, trolley, or on foot. Creole food abounds, including the locally famous Natchitoches meat pie, and the friendly locals can also direct you to their favorite dining spots.

GETTING THERE: Natchitoches is located in northwestern Louisiana, about 60 miles south of Shreveport. It is just off Interstate 49 at the Highway 6 exit.

FOR MORE INFORMATION: Natchitoches Main Street Project, 716 Second Street, Natchitoches, LA 71458, 318/357-3837

RUSTON, LOUISIANA

Louisiana Peach Fest

This festival was created in 1950 by area peach growers to celebrate their crop and the town made famous by it. Today it is a community-wide spectacular encompassing a week of activities, including one of the area's largest arts and crafts shows, the Queen Dixie Gem and Princess Peach pageants, a rodeo, a parade, and a peach cookery contest for the tastiest peach creation. Kids will love the pet show, where locals bring their pets to compete in "best dressed" and other categories.

ADMISSION: *None*
DATE: *First week in June*

Ruston is wild about peaches.

About Ruston

FOUNDED IN THE 1870s, Ruston is known for its good economy and untypical Louisiana terrain of rolling hills and pine trees. Restoring and maintaining the downtown comes naturally to its citizens, and the Main Street program has coordinated the refurbishment of an 18-block district while recruiting new stores, specialty shops, businesses, and residents. One of the successes of the program is that downtown currently has a zero percent vacancy rate, with 100-year-old businesses continuing to thrive next to recently established ones.

WHAT TO EXPLORE WHILE IN TOWN: There is much to interest visitors among the many shops and businesses. Park Avenue is home to one of the oldest clothing stores in Louisiana, Lewis and Company. The Lincoln Parish Museum is a house museum that reflects local parish history. The Ruston/Lincoln Convention and Visitors Bureau, located at 900 North Trenton, can provide brochures, hotel/restaurant guides, and maps of the area.

GETTING THERE: Ruston is located in northern Louisiana, off Interstate 20 on US-167.

FOR MORE INFORMATION: Louisiana Peach Festival, 900 North Trenton, Ruston, LA 71270, 318/255-2031

ST. FRANCISVILLE, LOUISIANA

Audubon Pilgrimage

To honor wildlife illustrator John James Audubon who spent time in West Feliciana Parish as a tutor and artist, St. Francisville holds the annual Audubon Pilgrimage. During three days in March, private antebellum plantation and town homes are opened to the public for tours. Local children sing and dance to period tunes of the 1820s, and there are evening musical performances at area churches.

> ADMISSION: *$15*
> DATE: *Third weekend in March*

The Festival of St. Francis

In honor of the patron saint of the town, this festival celebrates his feast day in October with a family-oriented event that offers children's activities, a Blessing of the Animals, entertainment by performers of various types, and an artists' and craftsmen's sale. Not to be missed is the Rib Shoot-Out, a barbecue cook-off that's sure to please the palette.

> ADMISSION: *None*
> DATE: *The Saturday prior to October 2*

Christmas in the Country

Christmas in the Country is an open-house event held downtown at night. Merchants and shops offer refreshments, church choirs are a-caroling, and a live Nativity scene enhances the downtown, where the historic old buildings are all outlined in tiny white lights.

ADMISSION: *None*
DATE: *The first full weekend in December*

About St. Francisville

ST. FRANCISVILLE IS SITUATED in the magnificent Tunica Hills of West Feliciana Parish, Louisiana. In the heart of the state's plantation country, it has an exceptional collection of ante- and post-bellum architecture. The National Register Historic District boasts more than 140 structures. Founded in 1730 by Spanish Capuchin monks seeking a burial place safe above the Mississippi's floods, the town has benefited from the rich Louisiana history reflected in its structures. Since the Main Street program has been active in St. Francisville, 27 facade renovations have been completed. The cooperative spirit of downtown building owners is evident in the beautifully rehabilitated structures of this district.

WHAT TO EXPLORE WHILE IN TOWN: Most of the area's antebellum plantation and town homes are open daily for tours. Visitors can enjoy a button museum at Grandmother's Buttons, the St. Francisville Railroad Park, and the Riverbend Energy Center, with its hands-on exhibits for kids of all ages. The West Feliciana Historical Society Museum on Ferdinand Street can provide walking tour brochures and information on the history of the area.

GETTING THERE: St. Francisville is located near the Mississippi River north of Baton Rouge. It is on US-61, and accessible via Interstate 10 by taking US-61 north at Baton Rouge.

FOR MORE INFORMATION: St. Francisville Main Street, P.O. Drawer 400, St. Francisville, LA 70775, 504/635-3873

VIVIAN, LOUISIANA

Redbud Festival

This event is Vivian's way of celebrating the coming of spring. The beautiful redbud trees are usually in bloom all over town. The varied activities, ranging from rodeos to pancake breakfasts, attract some 50,000 spectators to the downtown on festival day. Food, crafts booths, and entertainment provide something for everyone, all dished up with Southern hospitality.

ADMISSION: *None*
DATE: *Third Saturday in March*

About Vivian

HISTORICALLY, VIVIAN AND NORTHERN LOUISIANA had a stronger tie to Texas than to French culture and today it still has a "cowboy" feel. Originally in an area of dispute between the United States and Spanish Texas, this was a no-man's-land until the Caddo Indian Treaty of 1835. When the railroad came through in 1898, linking Texarkana to Shreveport, the town of Vivian was formed and named for a railroad official's daughter. At the turn of the century it was a thriving farming and lumber community, but by 1911 oil and gas had become, as they are today, the most important economic products. The Vivian Main Street program has recently been organized and has seen early successes in recruiting businesses and working with building owners in improving their facades.

The Shriners do their thing at the Redbud Festival.

WHAT TO EXPLORE WHILE IN TOWN: The North Caddo Drug Store has the only existing original soda fountain in the area. Visit the Redbud Museum at the old railroad depot or the Vivian Main Street Office, at 121 East Louisiana Avenue, to obtain visitor information.

GETTING THERE: Vivian, in extreme northwestern Louisiana, is on the border with Texas. Located on State Highway 1, it is very near US-71 and Interstate 20.

FOR MORE INFORMATION: Vivian Main Street, 121 East Louisiana Avenue, Vivian, LA 71082, 318/375-3470

Mississippi

ABERDEEN, MISSISSIPPI

Blue Bluff River Festival

This festival celebrates Aberdeen's heritage as a river town. Held on the banks of the Tennessee-Tombigbee waterway, its visitors may arrive by car or boat. The three-day event offers continuous music, arts and crafts, great Southern food, and children's activities. It features a firemen's rodeo and the reenactment of a Civil War skirmish. Transportation is provided for special shopping trips into downtown Aberdeen.

ADMISSION: *None*
DATE: *Second weekend in October*

About Aberdeen

ABERDEEN WAS FOUNDED IN 1835 by a Scotsman, who recognized the value of the site next to the Tombigbee River. During the 1840s it became the largest port on the river, exporting the cotton crops that were flourishing nearby.  Wealthy landowners and merchants competed in the building of stately homes, many with furnishings purchased in Europe and shipped up the river via steamboat. The benefits of that home-building spree are being reaped today in Aberdeen, where homes are being preserved and are contributing so much to the community's character. Many commercial storefronts are being renovated through the efforts of Aberdeen Main Street, which has set up a low interest loan pool for downtown building owners. In addition to finding new owners for several buildings, Main Street has recruited new businesses and maintains the flower planters along the sidewalks.

WHAT TO EXPLORE WHILE IN TOWN: Aberdeen offers a "Search for the Gold" architectural tour, showcasing its magnficent homes and buildings. A booklet about the town is available at the Main Street office in City Hall and from local merchants. The Old Aberdeen Cemetery has a brochure for a self-guided tour, outlining interesting and unusual headstones. A popular spot downtown is Tony's Café, the second oldest restaurant in Mississippi.

GETTING THERE: Located in northeastern Mississippi, Aberdeen is on US-45, about 40 miles south of Tupelo.

FOR MORE INFORMATION: Aberdeen Main Street, 125 West Commerce Street, Aberdeen, MS 39730, 601/369-4864

CANTON, MISSISSIPPI

Canton Flea Market Arts and Crafts Show

For this event, Canton opens its doors to thousands of artists and craftsmen from Mississippi and across the nation who converge on this historic city. It proudly exhibits the best in handcrafted toys, pottery, homespun fabrics, art, quilts, carvings, baskets, antiques, and other unique regional items. More than 1,000 exhibitors display their work on the turn-of-the-century square and grounds of the historic Madison County courthouse—one of the oldest pre-Civil War structures in Mississippi.

ADMISSION: *None*
DATE: *Second Thursday in May and October*

Safe Halloween Children's Festival

On the Saturday before Halloween, Canton becomes a haven for little ghosts and goblins with this event. The historic courthouse square is decorated with hay bales, spider webs, and pumpkins, and costumed helpers provide games and goodies for area children. Appearances are made by Woodsy the Owl, McGruff the Crime Dog, and other characters. A creative costume contest is held, with three different age groups competing for prizes. There are games, such as a pumpkin toss, and candy is given away by merchants. The police and fire departments are on hand to show kids their vehicles and teach them about safety.

ADMISSION: *None*
DATE: *Saturday before Halloween*

Canton's Victorian Christmas Festival

Avoid the mall mobs and start the Christmas season in a truly festive way with a visit to downtown Canton the weekend after Thanksgiving. The historic downtown is decorated with thousands of white lights outlining its turn-of-the-century architecture. There are horse and buggy rides and a carousel set up on the courthouse lawn. Children from area schools decorate the community Christmas tree with their own handmade ornaments, and area merchants stay open late, serving refreshments.

ADMISSION: *None*
DATE: *Weekend after Thanksgiving*

About Canton

CANTON WAS INCORPORATED IN 1836, and in its early days its economy was based on farming and cotton growing. Many of its affluent residents of this era built beautiful antebellum homes. Later the town became a railroad, lumber, and saloon center. Battered by two Union invasions during the Civil War and challenged by the financial and political chaos of Reconstruction, it recovered only to be rocked economically by the collapse of the lumber and sawmill market during the Depression. Torn by racial strife in the 1960s, Canton has survived to remain a friendly and progressive community. Ten years ago it was a scene of deteriorating buildings and sparse commercial development. These days the town square and downtown thrive again, thanks to the Canton Main Street program, the Canton Redevelopment Authority, and public and private investors.

WHAT TO EXPLORE WHILE IN TOWN: Canton's Greek Revival courthouse and downtown area are on the National Register of Historic Places, as are the many antebellum homes near the square. The Allison's Wells School of Arts and Crafts is also located downtown, providing instruction and business incubation for the arts. Housed in the recently restored Trolio Hotel, it also has an Elderhostel program. The Old Jail Museum, built in 1870 and used for 90 years, is now the  historical society headquarters. Walking tour guides and other information can be found at the Chamber of Commerce/Main Street office in City Hall, 226 East Peace Street. Canton is also 18 miles from the historic Natchez Trace Parkway.

GETTING THERE: Canton is located in central Mississippi, just north of Jackson. Situated on US-51, it is accessible via Interstate 55 by taking the exit for Route 16 east.

FOR MORE INFORMATION: Canton Chamber of Commerce/Main Street Association, 226 East Peace Street, P.O. Box 74, Canton, MS 39046, 601/859-5816

CLEVELAND, MISSISSIPPI

Crosstie Arts Festival

The aim of this longtime arts festival is to make the arts accessible to the people of Cleveland and the Delta, in an educational and entertaining format. Held under the courthouse oaks, this juried fine arts show features more than 100 artists from across the Southeast, exhibiting paintings, sculpture, pottery, fabric and paper designs, handmade furniture and jewelry. At the Children's Area, kids can be involved in hands-on activities all day. Live entertainment is featured throughout the day, and local school, church, and civic groups offer a variety of foods.

ADMISSION: *None*
DATE: *Fourth Saturday in April*

Art is fun for kids too at the Crosstie Arts Festival.

Octoberfest

Octoberfest is Cleveland's big fall bash with a barbecue contest, arts and crafts exhibitions, children's activities, a car show, and live entertainment, all held on the Greenstrip in downtown Cleveland. You won't want to miss the hog-calling contest and the Kissing of the Pig. And don't forget to sample the barbecue winners in the whole-hog, shoulder, ribs, and patio porker categories.

ADMISSION: *None*
DATE: *Second weekend in October*

About Cleveland

NAMED FOR PRESIDENT GROVER CLEVELAND in 1886, the town was established as an important railroad post connecting Vicksburg and Memphis. Home to Delta State University, it has a fast growing student population. Through the efforts of Team Cleveland, the local Main Street program, many old downtown buildings have been saved. Occupancy downtown is at 90 percent, and now many specialty stores offering a wide range of merchandise are near downtown. Team Cleveland has also funded the banners hanging downtown and is in the process of designating a Historic District in Cleveland, which will include the downtown.

WHAT TO EXPLORE WHILE IN TOWN: Visitors can explore Cleveland using the walking tour brochure provided at the Cleveland/Bolivar County Chamber of Commerce, 600 Third Street off US-61. Cleveland is home to K.C.'s Restaurant on Highway 61, listed as the only four-star restaurant in the state.

GETTING THERE: Cleveland is located in the northwestern section of the state, on US-61, 95 miles south of Memphis.

FOR MORE INFORMATION: Cleveland/Bolivar Chamber of Commerce, 600 Third Street, P.O. Box 490, Cleveland, MS 38732, 601/843-2712

CORINTH, MISSISSIPPI

Slugburger Festival

You haven't lived until you've had a Corinth Slugburger: a meat and soybean burger, deep fried and served on a bun with pickles, onions, and mustard. The festival pays tribute to this local treat, but, of course, attendees can enjoy other food, along with carnival rides and day-long entertainment culminating with a local headliner act each night.

ADMISSION: *$5*
DATE: *Second weekend in July*

About Corinth

ESTABLISHED IN 1854, Corinth was the crossing point of the Memphis & Charleston and the Mobile & Ohio railroads. The town was the site of one of the bloodiest engagements of the Civil War, as approximately 300,000 Union and Confederate troops came through the area and clashed in battle. Many of the surviviors of the war were so enamored with Corinth that they returned to settle here, building many of the historic homes seen in the town today. The local Main Street program, the Downtown Corinth Association, has worked to preserve the buildings of downtown Corinth with low-interest loan pools and tax abatement programs. It has purchaed banners, landscaped sidewalk and parking lot areas, and recruited new businesses to available properties downtown.

WHAT TO EXPLORE WHILE IN TOWN: A stop at the Civil War Visitors Center, at 705 Jackson Street, will put you on the right track to see all the local war sites and memorabilia, such as the Corinth National Cemetery and the Curlee House, which at different times served as headquarters for both Union and Confederate forces. Also check out the Coliseum Theater, built in 1923, and Waits Jewelry, founded in 1865, with its ornate pressed tin ceiling and hand-painted panels. Borrum's Drug Store, in continuous operation since 1869, still has its authentic soda fountain. Other visitor information can be obtained at the Downtown Corinth office at 406 Taylor Street.

GETTING THERE: Located in the northeastern corner of Mississippi, Corinth is situated on US-45. It is also near US-72 and about 30 miles west of the Natchez Trace Parkway.

FOR MORE INFORMATION: Downtown Corinth Association, 406 Taylor Street, P.O. Box 393, Corinth, MS 38835-0393, 601/287-1550

GREENWOOD, MISSISSIPPI

Cotton Row on Parade Day

First held to commemorate the locally significant Cotton Row buildings' entry to the National Register of Historic Places, this celebration continues as a community event to honor its heritage as Mississippi's foremost cotton market. It includes live musical entertainment on three stages, children's activities, crafts booths, food vendors, and tours of Cotton Row buildings. The events all take place in the downtown area and usually draw between 10,000 and 20,000 attendees for this one-day occasion.

ADMISSION: *None*
DATE: *First Saturday in August*

Delta Band Festival

Start your holiday season with this festival of marching bands and music. Established in 1935 by a local high school band director, this Greenwood tradition features marching bands from local high schools, academies, colleges, and universities. A parade of bands downtown also includes floats, celebrities, horses, clowns, beauties in convertibles, mascots, and marching units, all followed by Santa Claus. The event is concluded with a gigantic fireworks display.

ADMISSION: *None*
DATE: *First Friday in December*

About Greenwood

GREENWOOD BEGAN AS A SMALL SETTLEMENT, incorporated in 1844, and was named for Greenwood Leflore, the last Choctaw chief east of the Mississippi.

MAIN STREET GREENWOOD, INC.
*intersecting
past & future...*

After the Civil War the federal levee system opened up hundreds of thousands of acres to cotton production in the Delta. Following the Civil War came the cotton boom, and by 1900, Greenwood was the location of the state's major cotton market. The six historic districts in Greenwood contain Mississippi's most significant collection of buildings associated with the marketing of cotton. Main Street Greenwood is promoting the unique commercial district and has provided tax incentives for the rehabilitation of riverfront cotton district property. It has also provided signs, designating the historic district area, and landscaping projects around the levee.

WHAT TO EXPLORE WHILE IN TOWN: The best way to enter Greenwood is by driving down Grand Boulevard, with its majestic oaks lining the street. The downtown Leflore County Courthouse was once the site of Choctaw rites of trial and execution. Explore the many historic districts, including Cotton Row and the Railroad District, which offer shopping, dining, and a look at some interesting architecture. Information can be obtained at the Greenwood Chamber of Commerce at Sycamore Street and Highway 82.

GETTING THERE: Greenwood is located in eastern Mississippi, between Memphis and Jackson. It's situated on US-82, about 25 miles west of Interstate 55 at exit 185.

FOR MORE INFORMATION: Main Street Greenwood, 218 West Washington, Greenwood, MS 38935, 601/453-8098

GumTree Festival

The GumTree Festival promotes the arts in the Tupelo community and its schools. The annual spring outdoor fine arts show is held on the lawn of the Lee County Courthouse in downtown Tupelo. Juried craftsmen and artists from 14 states are selected to participate and sell their art, as well as compete for cash prizes. There are also creative writing contests and musical competitions for adults and children. Activities for children include hands-on art fun, storytelling, and performances by a local children's theater group. Musical performances by the Tupelo Community Theater and food are included in this weekend event.

ADMISSION: *None*
DATE: *Mother's Day weekend*

Oleput

Oleput (Tupelo spelled backwards) is the city's biggest party weekend, with music, food, and fun in downtown Tupelo. Concerts are given on Thursday, Friday, and Saturday evenings, and have featured such notables as B.B. King and Roddie Romero and the Rockin Cajuns. Special events include a hot air balloon competition, barbeque cooking, a Mardi Gras-style parade, and a gigantic fireworks display each evening. Music is nonstop on multiple stages, with everything from brass bands to zydeco.

ADMISSION: *Varied fees for events; three-day passes are available*
DATE: *First full weekend in June; events begin the preceding Thursday*

About Tupelo

SET AMID THE GENTLE ROLLING HILLS of northeast Mississippi, Tupelo was established when key railroads converged here. Located on the historic Natchez Trace, Tupelo is headquarters for the Natchez Trace Corridor National Park stretching from Nashville, Tennessee, to Natchez, Mississippi. Visitors here can learn the history of the Chickasaw Indians and see the birthplace of Elvis Presley. Recognizing that downtown represents the heart of the community, the city and the Downtown Tupelo/Main Street partnership have joined together in planning for development of the downtown and the improvement of its image.

WHAT TO EXPLORE WHILE IN TOWN: Visit the Natchez Trace Visitors Center for information on area history and the parkway. A visit to the Elvis Presley Birthplace and Museum is, for many, the only reason to come to Tupelo. There are also artists galleries, restaurants, and many shops to entertain. Maps, guides, and information can be obtained at the Tupelo Visitors Center on the corner of Franklin and Main.

GETTING THERE: Tupelo is located in northeastern Mississippi at the junction of US Routes 78 and 45.

FOR MORE INFORMATION: Downtown Tupelo/Main Street Partnership, P.O. Box 1485, Tupelo, MS 38802, 601/841-6431

VICKSBURG, MISSISSIPPI

Riverfest

Each April, the people of Vicksburg celebrate the arrival of spring with Riverfest. Held in downtown with the mighty Mississippi providing the backdrop, this three day festival offers a wide array of family fun and entertainment. A giant block party, the music ranges from jazz to country, and the food from boiled crawfish to shish kebobs. Children's activities include pig races, a petting zoo, clowns, and a miniature train.

ADMISSION: *Approximately $6*
DATE: *Third weekend in April*

About Vicksburg

VICKSBURG, THE "RED CARPET OF THE SOUTH," was founded in 1811 on a plantation, and by 1825 was a thriving frontier settlement. The city grew and prospered until the start of the Civil War era in 1861. Vicksburg's role during the war is historic: the Confederates, surrounded and with few supplies, no ammunition, and no hope for reinforcements, were starved out by General Grant and forced to surrender the city on July 4, 1863. Reconstruction was a trying period for Vicksburg, as it was for the South in general. Civic progress was slow, but the packet boat and Vicksburg's location on the river made it a center for steamboat trade. It slowly developed through the next hundred years to become a sleepy, but close-knit, community. Turning to its history and its historic downtown buildings, the Main Street program has worked to enhance the downtown's economy and appearance by promoting historic preservation. It has developed a review board to monitor proposed construction, demolition, signs, and landscaping to ensure a quality environment. It has also improved the downtown's appearance with new benches, lights, and landscaping.

WHAT TO EXPLORE WHILE IN TOWN: The Old Court House Museum, at 1008 Cherry Street, is Vicksburg's most historic building. Constructed with slave labor, it has hosted such notable figures as Jefferson Davis, Teddy Roosevelt, Booker T. Washington, and U.S. Grant. The Biedenharn Candy Company at 1107 Washington Street, is the site of the first Coca-Cola bottling in 1894. The Gray and Blue Naval Museum, also on Washington Street, features the world's largest collection of Civil War gunboat models. The Vanishing Glory Museum, on Clay Street, offers a 30-minute presentation on the historical campaign and siege of Vicksburg, and nearby is Vicksburg National Military Park. Tourism information is available at the Visitors Bureau at the corner of Washington and Clay Streets.

GETTING THERE: Vicksburg is located in western Mississippi, along the Mississippi River, about 45 miles west of Jackson. It is just off Interstate 20 at exit 1c.

FOR MORE INFORMATION: Vicksburg Main Street Program, 1415 Washington Street, Vicksburg, MS 39181, 601/634-4527

WEST POINT, MISSISSIPPI

Prairie Arts Festival

This greatly anticipated local event displays works of more than 600 artists and craftsmen in a relaxed outdoor setting. The day begins with a 5k run, as crowds start to gather for a day of browsing and visiting with friends. With a variety of Southern home cooking and four stages of live entertainment, visitors often stay all day. A special section, Kidsville, is the highlight of the festival for little ones; they also like riding the Prairie Arts Express. The day ends with a free concert and street dance in the city park.

ADMISSION: *None*
DATE: *Last Saturday in August*

About West Point

WEST POINT RECEIVED ITS MUNICIPAL CHARTER in 1855 after the coming of the Mobile and Ohio Railroad. It is easy to see why West Point has been included in two editions of Norman Crampton's *100 Best Small Towns in America*. West Point is a clean and quiet town, with a downtown second to none. Parks are everywhere, and the old buildings are neat, well kept and restored, thanks to the Main Street program that started here in 1987. West Point is a town where citizens work together for the betterment of the community, and its warm and friendly people are proud of their accomplishments.

WHAT TO EXPLORE WHILE IN TOWN: The Waverly Mansion, an antebellum home just outside town, is famous for its Southern elegance. Built in 1852, the mansion is known for its striking octagonal cupola and self-supporting curved stairways. The recently built Old Waverly Golf Club, located in West Point, is a nationally recognized championship course.

GETTING THERE: West Point, in northeastern Mississippi, is located off Highways 45 and 50 and is less than 3 hours from Jackson, Memphis, and Birmingham.

FOR MORE INFORMATION: West Point Main Street, P.O. Box 177, West Point, MS 39773, 601/494-5121, e-mail: ccedc@bizci.west-point.ms.us, http://llbiz.ci.west-point.ms.us

North Carolina

ALBEMARLE, NORTH CAROLINA

Stanly County International Festival

This is a one-day event showcasing all the nationalities and cultures within the community of Albemarle. From chitterlings and collards to eggrolls and tacos, a wide variety of ethnic food is available for attendees. Multicultural entertainment is provided as well, with various types of music, song, and dance on stages set up in the downtown area. International and cultural exhibits are displayed, promoting racial harmony and a greater awareness of the heritage of the community.

ADMISSION: *None*
DATE: *First or second weekend in April*

About Albemarle

ALBEMARLE WAS ESTABLISHED in 1857 and became an agricultural community. At the turn of the century, the textile industry and the railroad provided economic growth, employing any who wanted to work. Following the decline of the textile industry throughout the nation, this community has striven to overcome the loss of jobs and the erosion of its tax base. Through the efforts of the Main Street program, seasonal street banners color the downtown and new trees line the streets. It has also developed a facade grant program and encouraged the rehabilitation of many downtown buildings.

WHAT TO EXPLORE WHILE IN TOWN: The Visitors Center can provide tours, as well as walking tour brochures and information about the area. The Marks and Snuggs

Houses are two National Register-listed buildings in the downtown that feature original and period furniture.

GETTING THERE: Albemarle is lcoated in southern North Carolina, 40 miles east of Charlotte. It is situated on North Carolina Route 24/27 and is also accessible from Interstate 85 from US-52 south at Salisbury.

FOR MORE INFORMATION: Albemarle Downtown Development Corporation, 157 North Second Street, P.O. Box 190, Albemarle, NC 28002, 704/982-0131

BOONE, NORTH CAROLINA

Olde Boone Streetfest

The annual Olde Boone Streetfest marks the coming of fall to the North Carolina mountains. This old-fashioned country fair downtown celebrates the mountain tradition of art, crafts, music, and delicious foods. Music is an integral part of the festival, ranging from the latest rock by a university student band to folk ballads played on dulcimer and other instruments. Quilters, weavers, and potters demonstrate their skills during the day. Highlights of the event include competitions for the biggest pumpkins, the tastiest pickles, and jams and jellies produced in the Boone community.

ADMISSION: *None*
DATE: *Fourth Saturday in September*

About Boone

FROM ITS EARLIEST DAYS as a bustling frontier trading post and favorite hunting ground of Daniel Boone to its present-day status as a regional center for education, culture, and business, Boone has always been a community with strong roots in its past.

Historic downtown Boone, a North Carolina Main Street community since 1993, is a thriving business district surrounded by the campus of Appalachian State University.

WHAT TO EXPLORE WHILE IN TOWN: Unusual businesses in the town include traditional mountain crafts and contemporary pottery, jewelry, and fine art galleries such as Hands, one of the region's oldest craft cooperatives. Wilcox Ware-

A proud owner of some of the biggest pumpkins in Boone, North Carolina.

house Emporium is a fine old warehouse which now houses an array of shops. A walking tour guide of the downtown area is available free at the Jones House Community Center on King Street and at the chamber of commerce at 208 Howard Street.

GETTING THERE: Boone is located in the Appalachians of western North Carolina. Situated on US-421, it is adjacent to the Pisgah National Forest and 7 miles from the Blue Ridge Parkway. It is also accessible by Interstates 81 and 40, which run to the north and south, respectively, of Boone.

FOR MORE INFORMATION: Downtown Boone Development Association, 736 West King Street, P.O. Box 362, Boone, NC 28607, 704/262-4532

BREVARD, NORTH CAROLINA

Fourth of July Celebration

Experience the heart of Brevard and catch some hometown spirit at this Fourth of July Celebration. There's lots of old-fashioned fun, with a pet show, an antique car show, a bicycle parade, food, crafts, and youth activities. This is truly a family event, culminating with a traditional fireworks display on the campus of Brevard College.

ADMISSION: *None*
DATE: *July 4*

Twlight Tour and Christmas Parade

The heart of Brevard opens its Christmas season with thousands of twinkling lights and this festive event. Twilight Tour celebrates the holidays in an old-fashioned way, with horse-drawn carriages, musicians, carolers, and activities for everyone. Warm drinks and goodies are sold by community groups, and merchants open their doors for refreshments and a first peek at their Christmas offerings.

ADMISSION: *None*
DATE: *First Saturday in December*

About Brevard

THIS COMMUNITY, FOUNDED IN 1861, is nestled in the Blue Ridge Mountains of Transylvania County, North Carolina, and the Pisgah National Forest. The area prides itself on having more deciduous tree species and more varieties of birds and flowers than are found anywhere else in the country. It is also home to Brevard College and Brevard Music Center, which provide artists and musicians of the finest caliber to the area. The Main Street program, the Heart of Brevard, has worked on many fronts to improve the vitality of the downtown area. It offers matching grants for reha-bilitation of buildings and is responsible for the many rehabilitated storefronts down-town. It also offers a loan pool to help businesses with major renovation work. The program has planted trees, provided planters, widened the sidewalks, and overseen the variety of shops and restaurants moving into downtown.

WHAT TO EXPLORE WHILE IN TOWN: The heart of Brevard offers a dining, shopping, and services guide at its office at 62 West Main Street. While in Brevard, visit the Jim Bob Tinsley Museum, which reflects the heritage of mountain culture in song and art, at 20 West Jordan Street. Rocky's Soda Shop, at 36 South Broad Street, has a 1950s soda fountain that serves the best burgers and shakes in town. The town landmark is the county courthouse at the square, built in 1874. In nearby Pisgah National Forest, there are miles of trails and waterfalls to explore.

GETTING THERE: Brevard is located in extreme western North Carolina, just north of the South Carolina/Georgia border and south of Asheville. It is situated on US-64, 25 miles west of Interstate 26 at exit 18.

FOR MORE INFORMATION: Heart of Brevard, 62 West Main Street, Brevard, NC 28712, 704/884-3278

BURLINGTON, NORTH CAROLINA

Easter Eggstravaganza

The Easter Eggstravaganza is an arts and activity day for children in downtown Burlington. Well-known local artists lead children's activities in art, and a local children's theater group puts on several performances throughout the day. The day includes face painting, magic shows, bal-loon critters, giveaways from downtown merchants, and an appearance by the Easter Bunny.

ADMISSION: *None*
DATE: *Saturday before Easter*

Meeting the Big Bunny at the Easter Eggstravaganza.

Halloween Happenings

Historic downtown Burlington hosts a full day of activities on Halloween for the ghosts and goblins in all of us. The day begins with a Halloween Costume Parade of all downtown workers, followed by a costume contest and a lunchtime concert. Later, there's a pumpkin carving contest and trick-or-treating for kids at downtown businesses. The day is capped off with a fireworks show at the city park at 8:00 P.M.

ADMISSION: *None*
DATE: *October 31*

Dickens of a Christmas

Dickens of a Christmas is an annual event when historic downtown Burlington is transformed into an old English village of the 1800s. Victorian costumed characters roam the streets as carriage rides take passengers on sightseeing tours. Old-fashioned Santas tell stories on street corners, and all businesses are open late, offering refreshments. Brass bands play, strolling carolers sing, and the sounds of bell choirs put visitors in the holiday spirit.

ADMISSION: *None*
DATE: *First Friday evening in December*

About Burlington

ORIGINALLY KNOWN AS "COMPANY SHOPS," Burlington grew up around the railroad industry. It was the center of the rail line, and a roundhouse was built here for train repair. The city was incorporated in 1866, but by 1886 the railroad announced that it was moving shop operations. With the railroad gone, the people of the town felt the name was no longer appropriate, and the town was renamed Burlington. Today one section of the original "Company Shops" roundhouse still exists, and many of the old buildings have been renovated. In 1919 much of the downtown burned, but the spirit of the people survived and the city was rebuilt. In the last 30 years, as with many downtowns, there was a period when businesses migrated to the outlying areas; recently, however, with city redevelopment funds and the diligent eye of Downtown Burlington Corporation and its supporters, downtown Burlington has undergone a face-lift and is once again a bustling commercial center.

WHAT TO EXPLORE WHILE IN TOWN: The historic depot, located at the end of South Main Street, has been totally renovated and features a mural of the history of Burlington. It also houses the offices of Burlington Downtown Corporation, where you can pick up brochures and a map of the area. Every Thursday from June to September, the historic depot is the location of the Burlington Farmers Market. More than 20 local farmers sell produce, and other goodies—pies, bread, plants, herbs, and crafts—are available.

GETTING THERE: Burlington is located in central North Carolina, situated on US-70. It's also just off Interstate 40/85; take exit 143, Alamance Road north. Turn right at Church Street, and veer right on Main Street, which will take you to downtown.

FOR MORE INFORMATION: Burlington Downtown Corporation, P.O. Box 761,

200 South Main Street, Burlington, NC 27216, 910/222-5002, e-mail: downtown@netpath.net

CONCORD, NORTH CAROLINA

Share Cabarrus Festival

This family-oriented festival invites everyone to share in Cabarrus County—with lots of events to appeal to kids of all ages. The fun includes panning for real gold and gold panning competitions, car shows, and a race/walk. Entertainment is provided from two stages, featuring local musicians, cloggers, and dancers. For kids, there is a petting zoo, as well as a magic show, crafts, and rides. Foods include ostrich burgers, barbecue, lemonade, and ice cream. It all adds up to big fun in downtown Concord for the approximately 25,000 visitors attending.

> ADMISSION: *None*
> DATE: *Third Saturday in April*

Fallfest

Fallfest is held each year in downtown Concord, for families to come enjoy fun-filled activities. Kids can dress up in their Halloween best and trick-or-treat at downtown merchants' establishments. This event features storytellers, children's games, sidewalk art contests, food, music, and dancing—all to celebrate autumn and its colorful foliage.

> ADMISSION: *None*
> DATE: *The Saturday before or of Halloween*

A Dickens Christmas

Concord's downtown steps back into the Victorian era for the day, at A Dickens Christmas. The streets come alive as strolling Dickens characters greet visitors. A local actor appears as Ebeneezer Scrooge, performing a one-man show of *A Christmas Carol*. Hammered dulcimer and Celtic lap harp musicians fill the air with original music. Carriage rides offer a tour of the downtown's sights, and downtown businesses are decorated and open for the first days of holiday shopping. Local residents sponsor a "Tidings of Joy" candlelight tour of historic homes and buildings.

> ADMISSION: *None; carriage rides and tours of homes are $10*
> DATE: *First Sunday of December*

About Concord

IN 1793, CONCORD WAS SETTLED by German and Scotch-Irish immigrants, who, after many arguments about the county seat's location, named it Concord, meaning "harmony," and situated it in the middle of the county. Concord continues to be a city where people and organizations come together. The downtown experienced a particularly difficult time in the 1970s and 1980s, with businesses leaving for outlying areas. With the support of the Main Street program, downtown has developed a diverse retail mix and has held on to its position as the governmental and banking center of the county. Many downtown buildings have been rehabilitated through the efforts of the Main Street program and property owners, and there is a wide range of retail shops and restaurants to entertain any visitor.

WHAT TO EXPLORE WHILE IN TOWN: The Cabarrus County Courthouse, constructed in 1876, now serves as a Revolutionary War museum and exhibition area. A walking-tour brochure is available at the courthouse, as well as downtown shopping guides.

GETTING THERE: Concord is located in southern North Carolina, north of Charlotte. It is situated on US-29, just off Interstate 85 at exit 55. It is also accessible via US-601, and by NC-73 and NC-136.

FOR MORE INFORMATION: Concord Downtown Development Corporation, 65 Union Street South, P.O. Box 62, Concord, NC 28026, 704/784-4208

LEXINGTON, NORTH CAROLINA

The Barbecue Festival

Lexington claims to be the Barbecue Capital of the World, and its Carolina-style barbecue is legendary. The Barbecue Festival is definitely the "piggest" thing going in October in Lexington. It celebrates the rich barbecue heritage of Lexington, with some 20,000 barbecue sandwiches, using 10,000 pounds of barbecue, served to more than 100,000 visitors. While barbecue is the star of the festival, there are special attractions offering something for everyone through-

Thousands come to Lexington for Carolina-style barbecue.

out the day. Don't miss the Parade of Pigs, in which local bands, businesses, and organizations dress for the pork-themed march, with entries ranging from Harley Hogs to Pig Buses. Four hundred juried artisans, featuring handcrafted goods from the eastern region of North Carolina line the streets. The Piglet Land and Carnival provides rides and games for children, and entertainment is featured on five stages.

ADMISSION: *None*
DATE: *Last Saturday in October*

About Lexington

LEXINGTON WAS SETTLED IN 1775 and named in honor of Lexington, Massachusetts. It is best known for the furniture that is produced by a number of area manufacturers and its Lexington style pork barbecue, which is smoked over a pit of hickory logs and served with a tomato-based sauce. Lexington has more barbecue restaurants per capita than any other city in the nation. Through the Main Street program, efforts to spur investment in the uptown area through streetscape and building improvements have resulted in the relocation of businesses uptown and a renewed sense of pride in the heart of the city.

WHAT TO EXPLORE WHILE IN TOWN: The dominant Davidson County Courthouse on the square, circa 1856, serves as the focal point of uptown Lexington and houses the Davidson County Historical Museum. It is also where a walking tour brochure and other area information are available. The Davidson County Museum of Art is located in the former post office building. There are plenty of unique and interesting shops in the uptown area, including Conrad & Hinkle, an old-fashioned grocery and produce market, and The Whirling Dervish, a coffee shop and local gathering place.

GETTING THERE: Lexington is located in central North Carolina, south of Winston-Salem on US-29/70. It is off Interstate 85, and is accessible by US-52 and Interstate 40.

FOR MORE INFORMATION: Lexington Barbecue Festival, P.O. Box 1642, Lexington, NC 27293-1642, 910/956-2952

NEWTON, NORTH CAROLINA

Newtonfest

A one-day festival celebrating the community, Newtonfest is a hometown event, showcasing local entertainment from the schools along with regionally known groups. It's a day for folks to gather under the massive oak trees around the courthouse for lively entertainment, good food, and beautiful weather. Arts and crafts vendors display handmade works, while church and civic groups sell food and other items as fund-raisers. There are hands-on activities for kids, as well as a magician and a balloon artist.

ADMISSION: *None*
DATE: *Fourth Saturday in April*

About Newton

NEWTON, THE COUNTY SEAT of Catawba County, was established in 1842. The square surrounding the 1924 courthouse is often a gathering place for festivals and celebrations in the community. With the encouragement of the Main Street program, more than 40 facades on downtown buildings have been improved, entire buildings have been rehabilitated, new street lights have been added downtown, and businesses are prospering. Newton's motto is "Where the Heart Is," and Newton Downtown Revitalization has worked to keep downtown Newton the heart of the community.

WHAT TO EXPLORE WHILE IN TOWN: The 1924 courthouse is home to the Catawba County Museum of History, with displays on local history dating back to the Revolutionary War. The North Main Avenue Historic District adjacent to the downtown contains the vast majority of Newton's significant residential architecture. Two of Newton's churches, with splendid stained-glass windows, date from the 1880s. Within a short drive of Newton is the Bunker Hill Covered Bridge and Murray's Mill, both recently restored.

GETTING THERE: Newton is located in western North Carolina, northwest of Charlotte. Situated at the junction of US-321, NC-16 and NC-10, it is just off Interstate 40 at exit 131.

FOR MORE INFORMATION: Newton Downtown Revitalization, P.O. Box 550, Newton, NC 28658, 704/465-7425

REIDSVILLE, NORTH CAROLINA

Antique Alley Street Festival

Originating from the large number of antique stores in Reidsville, this event focuses on the past and attracts many "antiquers" who come just for the 70+ dealers who exhibit at the festival. But there is much more for the visitor, especially the demonstrations of heritage skills such as making molasses, cider milling, chair caning, wool spinning, peanut roasting, and quilting—all to educate and entertain. Good foods, including samples of those just made in the demonstrations, as well as children's games and musical entertainment round out the activities of this family-oriented event.

ADMISSION: *None*
DATE: *Second Saturday in October*

About Reidsville

REIDSVILLE'S HISTORY is primarily that of a post–Civil War, New South tobacco town. Although David Settle Reid established a post office in 1829, it was the Piedmont Railroad, built to transport supplies and reinforcements during the Civil War, that proved to be the key to growth. During the 1860s to the 1870s, Reidsville developed rapidly as a tobacco town. In 1984, with the downtown area in a state of physical and economic decline, Reidsville joined the North Carolina Main Street Program. Through Main Street Approach, Reidsville Downtown Corporation has been successful not only in attracting new businesses downtown, but in drawing industries to the area as well. The Main Street program found a developer for the Belvedere Hotel, who rehabilitated this condemned building into apartments. It also lobbied the city council to rehabilitate a 1928 municipal building for the local police department instead of building a new facility. This organization's facade grant program has assisted many business and property owners in improving their buildings.

WHAT TO EXPLORE WHILE IN TOWN: You can pick up a walking tour brochure, as well as maps of the Antique Alley District, at the Reidsville Downtown Corporation offices in City Hall, at 230 W. Morehead, or at the chamber of commerce in the historic Governor Reid House on Southeast Market Street. Korner Hardware on Settle Street is a beautiful rehabilitation of the 1908 Pettigrew Clothing and Dry Goods Store. Outside town is the Chinqua-Penn Plantation on Wentworth Street, a whimsical piece of architecure built by a world-explorer couple in the 1920s.

GETTING THERE: Reidsville is located in northern North Carolina, 25 miles north of Greensboro. Situated at the junction of US-158 and NC-87, it is just off US-29.

FOR MORE INFORMATION: Reidsville Downtown Corporation, 230 West Morehead Street, Reidsville, NC 27320, 910/349-1045

WAYNESVILLE, NORTH CAROLINA

Folkmoot USA

An annual two-week festival now in its 15th year, Folkmoot is patterned after classic European festivals. More than 300 musicians and dancers from around the globe visit Waynesville each year, sharing their cultural heritage through folk dance, music, and colorful native costumes. Events include an opening parade down Main Street; International Festival Day, which turns Main Street into a bazaar of crafts, dance, and food; a Children's Fest; and performances throughout the two-week period.

Folkmoot features more than 300 musicians and dancers from around the world.

ADMISSION: *None for parade and festival day; fees for scheduled performances*
DATE: *Second through third weekend in July*

Church Street Art and Craft Show

This annual festival, held when autumn colors are at their peak in the Great Smoky Mountains, attracts more than 100 artists, crafters, musicians, and dancers from across the Southeast. What began as a small gathering of artisans has evolved into a high-quality, well-balanced juried show, now widely known as the finest in the region. Waynesville's picturesque Main Street is closed to vehicular traffic the day of the show, transforming it into a marketplace.

ADMISSION: *None*

DATE: *Second Saturday in October*

About Waynesville

WAYNESVILLE WAS ESTABLISHED IN 1808 as the seat of Haywood County. It is located in the Southern Appalachian Mountains, surrounded by the Great Smoky Mountain National Park and the Shining Rock Wilderness area of Pisgah National Forest. By the late 1890s, Waynesville had become one of the leading resorts of the Southeast, attracting tourists to take advantage of the nearby mineral springs and mountain climate. Timber, furniture making, and agriculture were the basis of the economy. With the introduction of the Main Street program in 1986, Waynesville has experienced a second renaissance; there have been major investments in the downtown area, including building restorations and streetscape improvements.

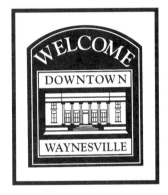

WHAT TO EXPLORE WHILE IN TOWN: The historic Shelton House is home to the Museum of North Carolina Handicrafts. Visit the Mast General Store, see craft demonstrations, and pick up a walking tour brochure of downtown Waynesville. During the summer, visitors can attend the Friday Night Street Dances featuring traditional mountain music and dance.

GETTING THERE: Waynesville is located in western North Carolina, 25 miles west of Asheville, on US Highway 23/74. Waynesville is accessible by Interstate 40, situated 10 miles north.

FOR MORE INFORMATION: Downtown Waynesville Association, 19 South Main Street, P.O. Box 1409, Waynesville, NC 28786, 704/456-3517

South Carolina

McCORMICK, SOUTH CAROLINA

Gold Rush Days

This event celebrates McCormick's heritage as a former gold mine area. A full day of festivities is planned, with gold panning, a parade, arts and crafts, food, entertainment, and an evening "Beach Blast" in the park.

ADMISSION: *$1 donation*
DATE: *Last Saturday in June*

Folks try a little panning.

About McCormick

INCORPORATED IN 1882, but settled earlier as gold was discovered and mined here, McCormick is named for Cyrus McCormick, inventor of the reaper, who donated land for the town, school, and churches. This community of 1,600 has bounced back from "ghost town" status with its revitalization efforts. As you walk down Main Street, built over mining tunnels dating from the mid-1800s, you'll notice that most of the buildings have been rehabilitated in the three-block business district. Of note is the county's first service station, circa 1920, that was restored by the town and now houses the McCormick Visitors Center.

WHAT TO EXPLORE WHILE IN TOWN: Fountain cokes, ice cream, and shakes are still available at Strom's Drug Store. The McCormick Arts Council offers exhibits and a gallery shop, housed in the historic Hotel Keturah, circa 1911. Spend the night at Fannie Kate's Inn, a restored hotel, circa 1884—its porch rockers make for great people and train watching. Walking guides and brochures are available at the Visitors Center at 100 South Main Street at US-378.

GETTING THERE: McCormick is located in the western part of South Carolina, nestled in Sumter National Forest. It is situated at the intersection of US-378 and US-221 which is the Savannah River Scenic Highway. The nearest Interstates are 20 and 85.

FOR MORE INFORMATION: McCormick County Chamber of Commerce, 100 South Main Street, McCormick, SC 29835, 864/465-2835

Tennessee

COOKEVILLE, TENNESSEE

Fall Funfest

This one-day event is a community-wide celebration of Cookeville's heritage and pride in its
community. Previous celebrations have included
a wide variety of entertainment, a juried craft
exhibition and art show, children's activities, an
antique car show, and lots of wonderful food.
The event is focused on the diversity of the
community and offers something for everyone.

ADMISSION: *None*
DATE: *Last Saturday in September*

**Fall Funfest celebrates
Cookeville's heritage.**

About Cookeville

COOKEVILLE WAS ESTABLISHED in 1854 as the seat of Putnam County. The
growth of the town was rapid and continuous, stimulated by the development of the
local railroad. The town now flourishes as a vibrant community of 26,000. Cityscape,
the local Main Street organization, works with merchants and business owners to promote the downtown as a place to shop and assists building owners by bringing in
new businesses. It also coordinates special events in the downtown area and acts as liai-
son with the city regarding issues that affect downtown.

WHAT TO EXPLORE WHILE IN TOWN: A walking tour brochure of the downtown
area is available at the chamber of commerce at 302 South Jefferson Avenue. The
historic structures downtown include the 1909 Cookeville Depot museum and
the courthouse located on the square. There are numerous renovated buildings in
the downtown area that now house strong businesses such as retail shops, restaurants, antique stores, and coffee houses. Sightseers can take in the beauty of nearby
Burgess Falls, and Tennessee Tech University, with a picturesque campus, is also
located in Cookeville.

GETTING THERE: Cookeville is located in eastern Tennessee, 80 miles east of Nashville.
It is situated on Tennessee Route 42, which is just off Interstate 40.

FOR MORE INFORMATION: CityScape, Arcade Building, Box 14, 9 South Jefferson
Avenue, Cookeville, TN 38501

FAYETTEVILLE, TENNESSEE

Fayetteville . . . Host of Christmas Past

This annual Christmas festival is an opportunity for downtown Fayetteville to host an open house for merchants. Past events have included the appearance of the great-great-grandson of Charles Dickens, a high tea, and storytelling. Merchants offer refreshments and a peek at their Christmas offerings. Other activities include magic shows, a costume contest, band performances, and a candlelight walking tour.

ADMISSION: *None*
DATE: *Second weekend in November*

About Fayetteville

FAYETTEVILLE, FIRST SETTLED IN 1809, was named for Fayetteville, North Carolina, from which many of its new settlers came. It has had a number of notable visitors, including Andrew Jackson, Daniel Boone, David Crockett, and Sam Houston. With strong pride in its history, a group of community leaders saw the need for Fayetteville to become a Main Street community. Today it boasts a healthy downtown with a mix of retail, offices, and restaurants employing 585 full-time workers. Rehabilitations of buildings continue to improve the image and appeal of the downtown area.

WHAT TO EXPLORE WHILE IN TOWN: Visit the Lincoln County Museum, housed in the old Borden Milk Plant that was once a mainstay of the area's economy and is listed on the National Register. Have lunch or dinner in the slammer at Cahoots, located in a former jail (built in 1867) and reused as restaurant space in 1987. Enjoy a movie at the Lincoln Theater, whose facade and lobby have remained unchanged since 1951. Main Street Fayetteville has developed a walking tour brochure, available at most businesses.

GETTING THERE: Fayetteville is located in southern central Tennessee, at the junction of US Routes 64 and 231. It is about 20 miles east of Interstate 65 at exit 14.

FOR MORE INFORMATION: Fayetteville Main Street, P.O. Box 162, Fayetteville, TN 37334, 615/433-9543

FRANKLIN, TENNESSEE

Main Street Festival

This annual festival features more than 250 of the South's leading craftsmen in a very competitive juried arts and crafts show, drawing people from 24 states. A big fund-raiser for the Main Street organization, it features music on two stages, with everything from rock to country, big band, and jazz. The event ends with Dancin' in the Street, where the whole town comes together for a bash. There's a food alley offering ethnic and traditional carnival food, and a kids' street with rides and games.

ADMISSION: *None*
DATE: *Last full weekend in April*

The Franklin Jazz Festival

Held in August, the Franklin Jazz Festival enlivens the elegantly restored town square in the heart of downtown Franklin. Celebrating the indigenous American art form, national and local groups perform all day. The continuous jazz includes styles ranging from Dixieland to blues to progressive and often highlights famous musicians from nearby Nashville. The sampling of Southern foods offered always includes a taste of Cajun spice.

ADMISSION: *None*
DATE: *First full weekend in August*

Dickens of a Christmas

This event takes you back to Dickens' time—downtown Franklin is alive with carolers in Victorian costumes, strolling minstrels, street vendors, hot wassail, and horse-drawn carriages. Historic characters demonstrate arts and crafts, and downtown restaurants feature nineteenth-century dishes and tea time treats.

ADMISSION: *None*
DATE: *Second weekend in December*

About Franklin

FRANKLIN, FOUNDED IN 1799, is listed in the National Register of Historic Places, including the entire 15-block downtown area and Main Street shopping district. It's been billed as "15 miles and a hundred years down the road from Nashville." Franklin's successful Main Street program has spurred more than $50 million in reinvestment in buildings and the downtown, with 250 rehabilitation projects, 1,500 new jobs, and 165 new businesses. The program fought and successfully won the battle to keep its post office downtown, which was threatening to move to the outskirts of town.

WHAT TO EXPLORE WHILE IN TOWN: This town was the site of the bloody Civil War Battle of Franklin, and it still bears the scars of that encounter. Both Carter House National Monument, built in 1830, and Carnton Plantation, built in 1826, figured heavily in the battle. Several generals were laid out on the porch of Carnton, and adjacent to it is the nation's only private Civil War cemetery, the resting place of 1,481 soldiers. The Masonic Hall in Franklin was the first three-story building in Tennessee, and St. Paul's Episcopal Church has a striking Tiffany window. A walking tour brochure, available from the Visitor Information Center at 209 East Main Street, lists more than 44 notable sites in the downtown.

GETTING THERE: Franklin is located just south of Nashville in central Tennessee, at the junction of US-31, US-431, and TN 96. It is just off Interstate 65 at exit 65.

FOR MORE INFORMATION: Downtown Franklin Association, P.O. Box 807, Franklin, TN 37065-0807, 615/791-9924

MURFREESBORO, TENNESSEE

Main Street JazzFest

The Main Street JazzFest brings great jazz music to the historic Murfreesboro public square and provides family entertainment in a restored downtown. The JazzFest is kicked off with a New Orleans-style parade and provides continuous entertainment from noon until 10:00 P.M. Featured are nationally renowned jazz artists, along with regional and local talent. Food and drink are available, so bring your lawn chairs and settle down for a relaxing day of music in historic, beautiful Murfreesboro.

ADMISSION: *None*
DATE: *First Saturday in May*

About Murfreesboro

LOCATED APPROXIMATELY 30 MILES southeast of Nashville, Murfreesboro was planned as a town in 1812. It functioned as the state capital from 1818 to 1826. At the center of town is the Rutherford County Courthouse, built in 1859, one of only six pre-Civil War courthouses still in use today. Murfreesboro is a renowed Civil War site, the location of the Battle of Stones River, as well as the location of Fortress Rosecrans, the largest earthen fort of the war. The Main Street program has brought cosmetic improvements, such as new sidewalks, landscaping, benches, and banners that line the street. But it has also brought deeper change with a low-interest loan program that has encouraged 131 rehabilitations and the recruitment of 83 businesses to the downtown.

WHAT TO EXPLORE WHILE IN TOWN: Visit the 90-year-old City Cafe for some good pie and a chat with the locals. Kids will like the Children's Discovery House, a hands-on children's museum located four blocks north of the public square on Maple Street. A walking tour brochure and additional information are available at the Main Street office, and at the chamber of commerce, the public library, and City Hall.

GETTING THERE: Murfreesboro is located in central Tennessee at the junction of US-41, US-70 and TN-96. It is also 25 miles east of Interstate 65 at exit 65.

FOR MORE INFORMATION: Main Street: Murfreesboro/Rutherford Co., Inc., P.O. Box 5075, 120 East Main Street, 2nd floor, Murfreesboro, TN 37133, 615/895-1887

MIDWESTERN
STATES

Illinois

Indiana

Iowa

Michigan

Missouri

Wisconsin

Illinois

AVA, ILLINOIS

Ava Emu and Craft Festival

"Emus. Crafts. Together at last!" announces the brochure for this one-of-a-kind event. The "Emu Capitol of Illinois" has partnered a local livestock economy with the local craft

Seniors cooking apple butter at the Ava Emu and Craft Festival.

festival. The Emu and Craft Festival has quite an agenda of events planned combining the two. Get ready for emu cook-off contests with emu kabobs, emu burgers and emu barbeque. There's also an emu-lation contest (best impression), as well as live appearances of this big bird. Other events not centered on emus include a crafts exhibition, horseshoe tournaments, square dancing, and a pies, pickles, and jams contest.

ADMISSION: *None*

DATE: *First weekend in October*

About Ava

THIS CENTURY-OLD TOWN OF 800 is located in the rolling farm fields of southwestern Illinois, near the Mississippi River bottoms. Named for its first postmaster's baby daughter, it sits on the northwest edge of the Shawnee National Forest, 5 miles north of the attractive Lake Kincaid area. Ava's Main Street organization, All for Ava, begun in 1996, has taken the first steps to address the challenges of its town's economic, design, and public activity issues. It has provided a matching grant program for downtown business owners and developed reguarly scheduled downtown cleanup days.

WHAT TO EXPLORE WHILE IN TOWN: Nearby this tiny town are the mighty Mississippi and the Shawnee National Forest. Outside town are emu ranches, which offer tours, and nearby Kinkaid Lake. Visitors can enjoy scenic drives along the Great River Road that follows the Mississippi.

GETTING THERE: Located in southwestern Illinois, Ava is accessible by Interstates 64 and 57. From I-64, take exit 50 south on Illinois Route 127, which becomes 13/127, to Illinois 4 west 11 miles. From I-57, take exit 54 to Illinois 13 west to Illinois 4 west 11 miles. From Illinois Route 3, take Illinois 151 north 9 miles.

FOR MORE INFORMATION: All for Ava, Main Street, Ava, IL 62907, 618/426-3871

GALESBURG, ILLINOIS

Railroad Days

If you or someone you know has always been interested in trains, then this event's for you. Railroads have long contributed to Galesburg's economic base and Railroad Days celebrates theis heritage. You can find many displays of railroad cars and equipment, featuring both historic rail lines and the Burlington Northern and Santa Fe companies that still operate in and out of Galesburg. There are also model railroad exhibitions, a car show, a street fair, kids' activities, square dancing, musical events, and more.

ADMISSION: *None*
DATE: *Fourth full weekend in June*

About Galesburg

IN 1834, George Washington Gale, a Presbyterian minister from western New York, came to this area to establish a college. Through his planning efforts grew Knox College, site of a famous Abraham Lincoln - Stephen Douglas debate in 1858. Some of the original college buildings and colonists' homes remain as significant structures in the community. The railroad industry arrived in Galesburg in the mid-1850s and forever changed the direction of the economic and political bases of the city. In 1977, Galesburg was chosen to be one of the first three National Main Street Center pilot communities, and the Galesburg Downtown Council is still charged with keeping the downtown a viable part of the com-  munity. It has coordinated the street banners and flower boxes and, behind the scenes, has developed a low-interest loan program to assist building and business owners with improving their facades, signs, and other property improvements to keep the downtown looking its best.

WHAT TO EXPLORE WHILE IN TOWN: The unique collection of buildings in Galesburg includes Victorian, French Second Empire, Georgian, Queen Anne, Italianate, Prairie, and Art Deco styles. The most striking building on Main Street is the Odd Fellows Building, built in 1895, with decorative terra-cotta panels and brick craftsmanship. A walking tour guide, restaurant maps, and city directory are available from the Chamber of Commerce, 292 East Simmons Street. Local gathering places include the cafes and brew pub of the Cherry Street area.

GETTING THERE: Galesburg is located directly off Interstate 74 in northwestern Illinois.

FOR MORE INFORMATION: Galesburg Convention and Visitors Bureau, 292 East Simmons Street, P.O. Box 749, Galesburg, IL 61402-0709, 309/343-1194

GOLCONDA, ILLINOIS

River to River Relay

The River to River Relay brings thousands of runners and spectators into Golconda just in time to enjoy the beautiful spring blossoms. Starting at the Mississippi River, more than 2,000 runners on eight-person relay teams begin the race to Golconda. Early in the afternoon the runners begin to arrive at the finish, where the atmosphere is that of a fair, with music, crafts, and lots of food.

ADMISSION: *None*
DATE: *Third Saturday in April*

Trail of Tears Commemorative Event

In 1838 thousands of Cherokee passed through Golconda on the historic Trail of Tears march to Oklahoma. At this event that remembers their passage, members of the Cherokee Nation of Talequah, Oklahoma, are on hand to offer insight into the Cherokee heritage. Stomp dances, blowgun demonstrations, corn stalk shooting, Cherokee language seminars, and native arts and craft demonstrations take place on the courthouse lawn.

ADMISSION: *None*
DATE: *Last weekend in September*

Halloween Festival

Spooks, goblins, and ghosts invade the downtown area each year on Halloween night to enjoy a fun-filled evening. A blazing bonfire, haunted hayrides, costume judging, jack-o'-lantern contests, and a street dance delight children and grown-ups alike. Chili, hot dogs, hot chocolate, and toasted marshmallows ward off hunger for the ghouls.

ADMISSION: *None*
DATE: *October 31*

Deer Festival

Long regarded as the "Deer Capital" of Illinois, Pope County has always attracted thousands of hunters hoping to "bag the big one." Hunters gather here, too, at the huge exhibition tent on the town's courtyard during this event. Nightly entertainment includes traditional events, such as the crowning of the Deer Queen and performances by musical groups. Saturday afternoon finds thousands lined along Main Street for the colorful Deer Festival Parade. Come hungry for its world-famous barbecue, cooked on the spot.

ADMISSION: *None*
DATE: *Thursday through Saturday before Thanksgiving*

About Golconda

GOLCONDA IS LOCATED along the beautiful Ohio River in southeastern Illinois, in the heart of the Shawnee National Forest. Its settlement began with a ferry house, constructed from keel boat timbers. The Cherokee crossed the Ohio on that ferry at Golconda on the Trail of Tears, their forced march to Oklahoma. A number of local institutions date from this early settlement: the First Presbyterian church, which is the oldest in Illinois, and the *Golconda Herald*, the weekly newspaper, which has been published continuously since 1858. This is a wonderful, sleepy river town, with great buildings, 823 residents, and no stop light.

WHAT TO EXPLORE WHILE IN TOWN: There's much to be seen that reflects Golconda's early settlement and history as a river town. The Buel House, once a cabin whose residents witnessed the Trail of Tears march, is on the National Cherokee Trail of Tears Register. It is located on the south end of Columbus Street. A walking tour guide and other information may be obtained at the chamber of commerce, located in the Not-So-New Variety shop on Main Street. The Main Street program has initiated a bustling farmers market, which is open Saturday mornings, May through September, on the courthouse lawn.

GETTING THERE: Golconda is located 25 miles east of Interstate 24. Take exit 16 (Vienna/Golconda). Go east on State Highway 146, and after a short, scenic drive, you'll arrive on Main Street at a four-way stop sign in Golconda. (There are no stop lights in Pope County.)

FOR MORE INFORMATION: Main Street Golconda, P.O. Box 482, Golconda, IL 62938, 618/683-6246

MACOMB, ILLINOIS

Macomb Heritage Days

Since 1982, Macomb has been celebrating the many aspects of its community heritage with this event. Given a different theme each year, the festival always has its traditions: an airplane fly-in and show, a cow chip slinging competition, the crowning of Little Miss Heritage Days, a parade, and its world-famous butterfly pork chop sandwiches.

A pipe and drum band appearing at Macomb Heritage Days.

Sources say the warm weather always is a constant, but there are plenty of ways to keep cool, such as enjoying a snow cone.

ADMISSION: *None*
DATE: *Last weekend in June*

Dickens Christmas on the Square

A family event held just after Thanksgiving, Dickens Christmas is the perfect alternative to those mall Santas: Bring your tyke downtown to see Santa arrive in a horse-drawn carriage. As he greets children (young and old), he heads toward the courthouse, and kids stream after him as though he were the Pied Piper. While the little ones put in their requests, you can enjoy the atmosphere—greenery decorating the historic courthouse, the twinkling lights, the carolers and musicians—and even speak with Queen Victoria and Prince Albert. Chandler Park is lighted during a ceremony officially opening the holiday season in this community, and hot drinks are available at several establishments.

ADMISSION: *None*
DATE: *The Saturday after Thanksgiving*

About Macomb

FOUNDED IN 1831 by a group of settlers who were looking for a new home, Macomb now boasts a population of 20,000. The focal point of the community is the McDonough County Courthouse, which has been renovated. The courthouse square and the surrounding business district consists of more than 100 establishments. Macomb Downtown Development Corporation (MDDC) oversees the revitalization of this area and has seen more than $4 million reinvested in this area over the last four years.

WHAT TO EXPLORE WHILE IN TOWN: There's a lot to browse in the courthouse square area. On the northwest corner is a pharmacy with a busy lunch counter, and across the street you can sit at the counter of an original Maidrite sandwich shop. The Bailey House, a restored Victorian mansion, located a block from the square, is open to visitors. The Amtrak rail station has been rehabilitated and contributes to the vitality of the community. A shoppers and travelers guide, maps, and other information are available from the MDDC office at 232 East Jackson and at downtown businesses.

GETTING THERE: Macomb is in western Illinois, near the Iowa and Missouri borders. Located on US Highway 136, it is accessible by many of the U.S. and state highways and interstates crossing Illinois in this area.

FOR MORE INFORMATION: Macomb Downtown Develoment Authority, 232 East Jackson, Macomb, IL 61455, 309/833-1827

Bagelfest

This is a festival that partners the community with the local Lender's Bagel plant. Initially begun as a free breakfast to the community by Lender's, it has become a multiday affair. On the agenda are a Miss Bagelfest pageant, the Beautiful Baby Bagel contest, and the Bagelfest parade. The centerpiece of this event is the World's Biggest Bagel Breakfast Procession led by the World's Largest Bagel, weighing in at more than 550 pounds. The festival culminates in the World's Biggest Bagel Breakfast, held at a table three blocks long.

Measuring the World's Largest Bagel.

ADMISSION: *None*
DATE: *Last week in July, beginning Tuesday night*

About Mattoon

MATTOON WAS ORGANIZED as a town in 1854 at the junction of the new Illinois Central Railroad Line and the Terre Haute and Alton line. The town grew and developed with the railroads and has continued to prosper despite the railroads' decline. Through the efforts of the Midtown Mattoon organization, the traditional downtown area is being preserved and retained as the center of the community.

WHAT TO EXPLORE WHILE IN TOWN: The original Illinois Central depot, built in 1916, is still in use today by Amtrak as a stopping point for passenger lines running from Chicago to New Orleans, and another depot still stands behind the Illinois Central depot. Other buildings rich in local history have been preserved along Broadway Avenue in midtown Mattoon.

GETTING THERE: Mattoon is located on Interstate 57, about 180 miles south of Chicago and 50 miles south of Champaign/Urbana. Or take the Amtrak passenger line that stops at the historic Illinois Central depot right in the heart of Mattoon.

FOR MORE INFORMATION: Midtown Mattoon, 1701 Wabash Avenue, Mattoon, IL 61938, 217/234-3087

MORRISON, ILLINOIS

Paint the Town

This one-day event celebrates the creativeness in all of us; everyone is given an opportunity to contribute to a three-block art gallery on the very asphalt of Main Street in downtown Morrison. Three blocks of Main and Market Streets are cordoned off and divided into 3- by 4-foot rectangles. Given a rectangle number, children often partner with friends to create their masterpieces. Various music groups entertain during the day and into the evening, when the street becomes venue to a party. Kids can also participate in a Walk of Art Scavenger Hunt, in which they must visit downtown businesses and locate each item of art in the store. These activities coincide with other events downtown: the Hammer Jammer three-on-three basketball tournament and the Harvest Hammer long-distance run.

ADMISSION: *$6 registration fee to paint a square; other events free*
DATE: *Third Saturday in September*

About Morrison

A RAILROAD TOWN that was incorporated in 1856, Morrison prides itself on its tradition of growth and prosperity through community involvement. In 1996 residents sensed an urgency to save their downtown and reclaim it as the center of the community, and the town joined the Illinois Main Street program. The program's purpose is to coordinate the downtown's revitalization through historic preservation, economic development and promotion of the area. Projects so far include developing a low-interest loan pool to encourage building renovations in downtown Morrison and working with the chamber of commerce to provide banners for the downtown area.

WHAT TO EXPLORE WHILE IN TOWN: Situated near the Mississippi on the western border of Illinois, Morrison is near several historical and natural attractions. Scenic drives include the Lincoln Highway for its architecture, and the Great River Road, which runs along the Mississippi, for its views. Morrison is near lock and dam No. 13 on the Mississippi, part of a series of dams that make up the Great River Road Corridor. Also of interest are the Albany Indian Burial Grounds, and visitors may enjoy antiquing in the county. Information on attractions, lodging, and restaurants is available from the chamber of commerce at 200 West Main Street.

GETTING THERE: Morrison is located in northwestern Illinois, near the Iowa border. It's accessible by the many interstates crossing northern Illinois. The closest is I-88; take exit 36 and head west on US Highway 30.

FOR MORE INFORMATION: Morrison Main Street, 200 West Main Street, Morrison, IL 61270, 815/772-2078

PONTIAC, ILLINOIS

Hang Loose, Let the Good Times Roll

Hang Loose celebrates the 1950s–1960s era with an antique and classic car show, a craft show, games and activities for children, and the Mighty Vermilion Duck Race. See the classy chassies buzz the square at this event, always held on Father's Day.

ADMISSION: *None*
DATE: *Father's Day, third Sunday in June*

Heritage Day Riverfest

Step back in time with a celebration on the courthouse square in downtown Pontiac. All the characters in Pontiac's history will be returning: Native Americans, European settlers, even Abraham Lincoln. Native Americans perform traditional dances, reenactors portray the settlers and demonstrate pioneer crafts and skills, and Honest Abe greets his constituency. In addition, there are antique tractor displays, a historic tram ride, buggy rides, canoe races, and a homemade pie baking contest.

ADMISSION: *None*
DATE: *First Saturday of August*

First Night

First Night is a family-oriented New Year's Eve celebration. A non-alcoholic event, it offers entertainment in 10 different locations in the downtown area. Entertainment includes barbershop harmony groups, rock, jazz, gospel, and bluegrass. Included are an ice sculpture demonstration, a local variety show, storytellers' groups, comedians, food, and fun for everyone. The evening is topped off with fireworks at a local park.

ADMISSION: *$8; $6 in advance*
DATE: *December 31*

About Pontiac

PONTIAC, NAMED FOR THE legendary Indian chief, was plotted in 1837 and became the center of growth and county seat for the area. The Main Street organization, PROUD (Pontiac Redeveloping Our United Downtown), was organized when a group of citizens combined to battle the effects of the giant discounters and strip shopping centers surrounding the area. Where once 20 percent of the downtown buildings were vacant, PROUD has worked to recruit and improve businesses, as well as stimulate public and private reinvestment in downtown buildings, and, through promotional events, reestablish downtown as the center of activity for the community.

WHAT TO EXPLORE WHILE IN TOWN: A downtown retail shops guide and a visitors guide are available at the chamber of commerce and at the PROUD office. The old City

Hall complex was restored through the efforts of PROUD volunteers and converted to a small business incubator. The complex was built in 1900 and is on the National Register of Historic Places, along with the courthouse. Humiston Riverside Park is on the south edge of the downtown square, and visitors can feed the ducks along the Vermilion River and take a look at one of Pontiac's unique swinging bridges located there.

GETTING THERE: Pontiac, located 100 miles southwest of Chicago, is just off Interstate 55 on Illinois Highway 166 west.

FOR MORE INFORMATION: PROUD, P.O. Box 622, Pontiac, IL 61764, 815/844-6692

RUSHVILLE, ILLINOIS

Rushville Goes Chocolate

If you're a chocoholic, here it is: an event devoted entirely to chocolate. Held in conjunction with American Chocolate Week, it features opportunities to satisfy the urge. The event includes a chocolate scavenger hunt, a bake sale featuring chocolate goodies, candy making classes, and chocolate sampling in area businesses. On the nonchocolate side, there's also an art show and tours of historic sites and a pancake breakfast.

ADMISSION: *Most events are free*
DATE: *Third weekend in March*

An All American Arts Fair

On the second weekend in June, Rushville's Central Park becomes a small town art festival with paintings, music, crafts, and food for all. The Schuyler Arts Council awards prizes to the best painters, sculptors, and photographers. Visitors can also enjoy a community band concert and an old-fashioned ice cream social under the shade trees at the courthouse square.

ADMISSION: *None*
DATE: *Second weekend in June*

Smiles Day Weekend

The community began Smiles Day in 1919 to welcome home World War I soldiers. The first was so successful that the event became an annual celebration of homecoming and community spirit. Still billed as "A Day to Remember," it traditionally has a smile contest, a firemen's pancake breakfast, a homecoming football game, a street dance, and a parade.

ADMISSION: *A smile*
DATE: *Late September during homecoming*

About Rushville

FOUNDED BY THE SCRIPPS FAMILY of newspaper fame, Rushville has a long history as a farming and trade center. The quaintness of Rushville with what some have called the prettiest town square in Illinois, is enhanced by its bandstand and brick streets. Although it has never suffered with the problem of decline and empty storefronts, Rushville has benefitted enormously from its involvement in the Main Street program through downtown rehabilitation and the revitalization of community pride and spirit.

WHAT TO EXPLORE WHILE IN TOWN: The Schuyler County Jail Museum and Historical/Geneological Center, two blocks south of the square, is a treasure house of frontier memorabilia as well as family and social history. The Schuyler County Courthouse, the restored 1882 seat of local government, anchors the southwest corner of the district. After 75 years of neglect and a 1995 fire, the Phoenix Opera House again occupies the south side of the square. Renovation of the Princess Theater, a movie house, has brought acclaim to the community's volunteer spirit.

GETTING THERE: Rushville is located at the junction of US Routes 67 and 24 in west central Illinois.

FOR MORE INFORMATION: Rushville Main Street, P.O. Box 111, 117 South Congress, Rushville, IL 62681, 217/322-6277

SALEM, ILLINOIS

Days Fest and Fanfare

Not many small towns get to bring Hollywood home, but that's just what the Days Fest and Fanfare allows Salem, Illinois. The town pretends for the weekend to be the real "Salem" of the popular daytime drama, *Days of Our Lives*. This interactive event brings in stars and lots of star-studded activities, such as trivia contests, star interviews, lookalike contests, makeup demonstrations, and autograph sessions. Days Fest promotes lots of fun as Salem attracts fans, as well as the simply curious, from across the country.

ADMISSION: *None*
DATE: *Third weekend in September*

About Salem

SALEM'S FIRST EUROPEAN SETTLER came to this area after the great New Madrid earthquake of 1811. He settled in what is now the courthouse area, which evolved into a stagecoach stop on the Vincennes Trail from Vincennes, Indiana, to St. Louis. As the Conestogas rolled through town with the western migration of land-hungry settlers, Salem snoozed, but it was eventually incorporated in 1855. The arrival of three railroads produced Salem's first boom, as they led to the development of the region's agricultural wealth. The discovery of oil in the early 1900s brought another boom; with the nation's second largest oil field by 1939, Salem was hard pressed to accommodate the influx of speculators. Salem is proud to be the birthplace of William Jennings Bryan, and the G.I. Bill of Rights was composed in its local Legion Post in 1944. An aggressive spirit pervades this little community, especially evident in its volunteer support of architectural and historic preservation. An active Main Street program has rapidly become the driving force enabling the community to transform its ideas and dreams into reality.

WHAT TO EXPLORE WHILE IN TOWN: There are lots of interesting historical sites in Salem that give a flavor of the town's past: the William Jennings Bryan birthplace and museum on South Broadway; Boone Street, allegedly part of Daniel Boone's trail; the Halfway Tavern, east of town, a stagecoach stop on the Vincennes Trail; the fire bells, on display in front of the Fire Station, one of which was in service to call firemen between 1892 and 1957; and a one-room schoolhouse on the Salem High School campus. A walking tour brochure and other information are available at City Hall and at the Main Street office at 101 South Broadway.

GETTING THERE: Salem is located in south central Illinois, just off Interstate 57. It is also accessible by US-50.

FOR MORE INFORMATION: Main Street Salem, 101 South Broadway, Salem, IL 62881, 618/548-5000

SAVANNA, ILLINOIS

Fly away Home—Celebrating International Migratory Bird Day

Savanna's celebration of International Migratory Bird Day is a partnership between the Savanna Main Street Association, the U.S. Fish and Wildlife Service, the Savanna Army Depot, and the Illinois Department of Natural Resources. This coalition seeks to educate and report on the local habitats of migratory birds that come through Savanna. Guided tours identify local habitats and the measures being implemented to conserve and protect migratory birds in the area. The local elementary school is the setting for a seminar and exhibition of birds of prey, such as eagles, hawks, and owls. For kids, the movie *Fly away Home* is shown free.

ADMISSION: *None*
DATE: *Second Saturday in May*

NESTLED ON LIMESTONE BLUFFS along the Mississippi River, Savanna lies amid thousands of acres of preserved natural wilderness. Settled in 1828, packet boats traveling the river soon made Savanna a trading community. In 1862 the railroad reached Savanna benefitting its trading-center status more; by the turn of the century it was a "boom town" based on the railroad and, later, an army ordinance depot. However, by the late 1970s, Savanna felt the impact of having a one-industry economy, and as the railroad industry began to slump, so did the community. With the imminent closure of the army depot, Savanna is now at a crossroads, and its people and leaders are pursuing a realistic plan to achieve a healthy economic base with long-term stability. That plan's focus has the downtown serving as the center of the community, capitalizing on its traditional storefronts and low vacancy rate. Savanna Main Street has already documented significant successes since its beginning a short time ago in 1996, including $1.8 million spent in new construction, $200,000 spent on public improvements downtown, and over 1,000 volunteer hours logged–it looks forward to creating more change in the years to come.

WHAT TO EXPLORE WHILE IN TOWN: The Railroad Car Museum gives tribute to the days when the Milwaukee and the Burlington Northern railroads brought new life to the area's economy. The Pulford Opera House, an early center of Savanna culture, is now open as an antique mall. Campers, hikers, and picnickers can enjoy the Mississippi Palisades Park; visitors may also bring their boat and enjoy a weekend on the river.

GETTING THERE: Savanna is located in northwestern Illinois, north of Interstate 80. At I-80 just outside Moline, take exit 1 onto scenic Illinois Highway 84, and head north for 60 miles.

FOR MORE INFORMATION: Savanna Main Street Association, Main and Washington Streets, Savanna, IL 61074, 815/273-3754

TUSCOLA, ILLINOIS

Flower Fairie Festival

Held to observe May Day, the Flower Fairie Festival is a celebration of spring and the rebirth of nature. It kicks off with a Maypole ceremony in the center of downtown, when little girls dressed as flower fairies distribute packets of "fairy dust." Other activities in this spring-oriented event include master gardener presentations, garden teas, nature walks, and a marketplace selling arts, crafts, and plants for the new season.

ADMISSION: *None*
DATE: *First Saturday in May*

Fourth of July

The Fourth of July celebration in Tuscola promises to be a traditional hometown experience. There are loads of activities sure to please kids and parents alike, including contests of every kind: back seat driver, pet parade, horseshoe pitching, bicycle decorating, cakewalks, and mud volleyball. Other events include pony cart rides, cow pattie bingo, remote control car races, and hot air balloon rides. The day of family fun is capped off with fireworks.

Get the traditional hometown experience at the Tuscola Fourth of July celebration.

ADMISSION: *None*
DATE: *July 4*

Tuscola Harvest Homecoming

The Tuscola Harvest Homecoming is held to celebrate the coming of autumn, with activities for people of all ages. It features pumpkin decorating contests, pie eating contests, scarecrow decorating, food, entertainment, and a 1950s car show and cruise.

ADMISSION: *None*
DATE: *Last weekend in September*

Christmastown and Dickens Walk

Come home for the holidays to Tuscola's community-wide celebration. It begins with a Santa Parade, a Christmas craft fair, and a quilt raffle. A community choral concert is followed by a Dickens Walk, when Dickensian carolers and bell ringers stroll through the streets serenading visitors. Jugglers and magicians entertain, the shops have open house with refreshments, and free carriage rides are offered.

ADMISSION: *None*
DATE: *First weekend in December*

About Tuscola

TUSCOLA, WHOSE NAME comes from an Indian word meaning "level plain," was laid out in 1857 after the Illinois Central Railroad was completed in 1855. Quickly developing into a thriving community, it won a contest to become the county seat in 1859. The name of the county was embroiled in controversy until a compromise was reached to name it after Illinois senator Stephen A. Douglas. In an area that was once wild prairie, farmers have continued to prosper since their settlement here because of the soil, often called the richest in the world. After a long, painful decline of the downtown area, the citizens of Tuscola have recently organized a Main Street program and are spearheading initiatives to rehabilitate downtown buildings, improve the downtown's image as a place to shop and work, and restore its place as the heart of the community.

WHAT TO EXPLORE WHILE IN TOWN: Tuscola's legendary Candy Kitchen is being restored to its nineteenth-century facade. The stone-faced Carnegie Library and the Civil War exhibit at the courthouse are both points of local interest. The Douglas County Museum mounts regular and special exhibits and offers visitors an interpretation of local history.

GETTING THERE: Located in eastern central Illinois, Tuscola is just off Interstate 57 at exit 212. It is also accessible by US-36.

FOR MORE INFORMATION: Main Street Tuscola, 103 North Main, Tuscola, IL 61953, 217/253-3141

Indiana

EVANSVILLE, INDIANA

Evansville Riverfest

This is a four-day family event that includes four stages of local and regional entertainment, plus kids' activities, more than 30 food booths, contests, raffles, rides, and games. More than 80 teams from local businesses compete in the wacky Office Olympics, where visitors witness the classic Office Chair Roll-Off and the Post-It Note Stick competitions. Held in downtown Evansville along the riverfront, this event includes an amateur talent show, music concerts of all types, and an antique and classic car show.

ADMISSION: *Most events are free*
DATE: *Last week of July*

About Evansville

THE CITY OF EVANSVILLE, located at the bend of the Ohio River in southwest Indiana, was founded in 1812 and soon prospered from commerce along the river. By

1900, Evansville was home to more than 300 iron, steel, and woodworking companies and had become a world center for furniture manufacturing. During World War II many factories were converted to build aircraft. Today, Evansville's economy is still based in manufacturing, including pharmaceutical, aluminum, food, and home appliance production. Evansville's revitalization efforts have led to the renovation of a historic theater as a performance venue, established collaboration with merchants to produce promotional events, and recruited new businesses to the area.

WHAT TO EXPLORE WHILE IN TOWN: Walking tour guides of the downtown's historic district are available at Center City's offices at 209 Main Street and at the convention and visitors bureau at the pagoda on the riverfront. The Museum of Arts and Science, performances by the Evansville Philharmonic at the Vanderburgh, shops, restaurants, and historic homes are all downtown to explore.

GETTING THERE: Evansville, located in southwestern Indiana along the Ohio River, is accessible by taking Interstate 64 to the 164 spur.

FOR MORE INFORMATION: Center City Corporation, 209 Main Street, Evansville, IN 47708, 812/424-2986

FRANKFORT, INDIANA

The Hot Dog Festival

The puns never end at this festival that relishes its high school mascots, the Fighting Hot Dogs. The Hot Dog Festival has events for adults, kids, and, of course, dogs. For Fido and the kids, there are the Puppy Park of kids' activities, the Parade of Pooches, the Dog Haven obstacle course, and displays by Whitney, the Wonder Frisbee Dog. For the adult crowd, there are a four-mile Bun Run, a three-on-three Wiener Classic basketball tournament, the Every Dog Has a Flea Market, the Mixed Mutts Tennis Tournament, and Dog Days of Summer Sales. Music and hot dogs, certainly, are always available. Previous events have featured appearances by the Oscar Meyer Wienermobile. Have a wienerful time at this very original event.

ADMISSION: *None*
DATE: *Last Saturday in July (National Hot Dog Month)*

About Frankfort

FRANKFORT, LOCATED NEAR INDIANAPOLIS, has always benefited from its proximity to the railroads radiating outward from that city. After the railroad industry declined, Frankfort was fortunate to be near a major interstate and many state roads. However, the roads took their toll on the retail climate of Frankfort. As roads improved, people took to them to venture to larger retail areas to do their shopping; consequently, the downtown declined in importance as a traditional shopping area. Since the start of the Main Street program, however, downtown has made great strides, encouraging more than $18 million in reinvestment in the downtown by private and public sources. Besides encouraging investment, the Main Street program has assisted building owners with facade renovations, worked with the city to reuse "Old Stoney"—the former high school building—for city offices, and organized promotional events to make downtown Frankfort once again the true center of the community.

WHAT TO EXPLORE WHILE IN TOWN: There are a lot of great buildings being put to new use in Frankfort. Old Stoney, a former high school building, now houses city offices; a Carnegie Library has had a recent addition of gallery space and a theater on West Clinton Street; and the old post office building has been rehabilitated into the city police station. There's a cigar factory on North Main Street that has been producing cigars since 1917.

GETTING THERE: Frankfort is located 50 miles northwest of Indianapolis in central Indiana. It is accessible by Interstate 65 off exit 158; take State Highway 28 east.

FOR MORE INFORMATION: Frankfort Main Street, 301 East Clinton Street, Frankfort, IN 46041, 765/654-4081

GREENCASTLE, INDIANA

Heritage Fest

The Heritage Fest is a two-day celebration of National Historic Preservation Week. It includes living history events and opportunities for discovery of this community's rich history via covered bridge tours and walking tours. Each year the highlight of the festival is the fiddle and banjo contest, which takes place Saturday afternoon. The courthouse square is alive with ongoing entertainment and plenty of food, crafts, and fun for the whole family. This event won the Indiana Main Street Outstanding Special Event award in 1992.

ADMISSION: *None*
DATE: *Third weekend in May*

About Greencastle

GREENCASTLE BEGAN as a pioneer village but had the advantage of opportunities associated with being the county seat. In 1837, the Methodist Church selected Greencastle to be the site of what is now DePauw University. The courthouse square has always been the hub of political and commercial activity; it was on the square that Eli Lilly opened his first drug store, and John Dillinger made his biggest haul here. Fertile lands, successful industries, and a university of great repute all serve to make Greencastle an attractive and prosperous community. Since 1983, Main Street Greencastle has given the city a facelift with new sidewalks, trees, and street lights. It has also restored the Granada Opera House and continues to provide design assistance to many building owners in their facade renovations.

WHAT TO EXPLORE WHILE IN TOWN: Greencastle has some interesting local history, and walking tour guides are available at the Main Street Greencastle office in the Partnership Center at 2 South Jackson Street. The south side of the square, at Washington and Indiana, is where Eli Lilly operated his first drug store and where Lincoln's law partner compiled *Herndon's Life of Lincoln* (in the Dogwood Lane Antiques building). The restored Opera House on the west side of the square is where the famous William F. "Buffalo Bill" Cody made an appearance in 1879. The site of the old Central National Bank (southeast corner of Washington and Jackson) is where John Dillinger and his gang made the largest single haul of his infamous career: $75,000.

GETTING THERE: Greencastle is in western central Indiana, southwest of Indianapolis. It is located on US Highway 231, and is also accessible by US-40, Interstate 70, and Interstate 74.

FOR MORE INFORMATION: Main Street Greencastle, Partnership Center, 2 Jackson Street, Greencastle, IN 46135, 765/653-4517

MADISON, INDIANA

Madison in Bloom

Madison greets spring among green hills dotted with pink and white dogwood and redbud trees. Here the historic district showcases its intimate gardens with tulips, daffodils, hyacinths, and other minions of spring. The Jefferson County Historical Society hosts a tour of the private gardens and courtyards of eight historic homes. These sites vary from formal recreations of English gardens to delightful small terraces and courtyards.

ADMISSION: *$9 at event; $7 in advance*
DATE: *Last weekend in April and first weekend in May*

The Madison Regatta

Watch the world's fastest speed boats (Unlimited Hydroplanes) compete at speeds in excess of 200 miles per hour on a 2 1/2-mile oval race course at this regatta held on the banks of the Ohio. A week of festivities leads up to the race, with hot air balloons, a Miss Madison Regatta pageant, a parade, musical entertainment, and fireworks. A food court and race pit tours are available on race weekend, so bring your lawn chairs and picnic basket to one of the best viewing areas of the whole racing circuit.

ADMISSION: *$20 at door; $15 in advance*
DATE: *July 4 and 5*

Madison Chautauqua

Come to the banks of the Ohio River for the Madison Chautauqua "Festival of Art." A jury has chosen more than 250 artists and craftsmen from all over the country, whose exhibits of painting, sculpture, stained glass, textiles, folk art, and more are to be offered for sale. A riverfront food fest offers a wide variety of treats, and there is free musical entertainment throughout the weekend. Kids can stop by the children's activity tent to experience hands-on art activities and to view examples of local talent.

ADMISSION: *None*
DATE: *Fourth weekend in September*

About Madison

FOUNDED IN 1809, Madison was a very important port on the Ohio River. A planned community with wide boulevards, it contains a grand collection of Federal, Greek Revival, and Italianate architecture, built during the height of its prosperity. As traffic on the river gave way to the not-so-bustling commerce of the local railroad in the 1870s, Madison became a sleepy, but beautiful river town. During the 1960s, Madison, like so many other towns, was faced with deterioration, and its citizens realized that action had to be taken. By 1973 the entire downtown area, including more than 133 blocks, was placed on the National Register of Historic Places—one of the earliest districts to be protected. In 1977, Madison became one of the first three pilot communities for the Main Street Program of the National Trust. Today it still participates in the National Main Street Program and remains an active and effective force in the revitalization of its commercial district.

WHAT TO EXPLORE WHILE IN TOWN: Madison, as a riverfront town is steeped in river history. You may catch a glimpse of the *Delta Queen* or the *Mississippi Queen*, which frequently make stops at Madison, on their way down the Ohio. The Jefferson County Historical Museum at the Madison Railroad depot, a local history museum with exhibitions on steamboating, the Civil War, and other events, is located at 615 West First Street in an unusual octagonal rail station. The Shrewsbury-Windle House Museum and Decorative Arts Museum, at 301 West First Street, is a National Historic Landmark (constructed 1846-1849) and noted for its free-standing spiral staircase. The J.F.D. Lanier State Historic Site and Gardens at 511 West First Street, also a Landmark designee, recalls principal characters of Indiana history. Other great buildings include: the Masonic Schofield House at 217 West Second Street, the first two-story tavern house in Madison, and the Jeremiah Sullivan House Museum at 304 West Second Street. The historic Broadway fountain, at North Broadway and Main Streets, was originally cast in iron and exhibited at the Centennial Exposition in Philadelphia in 1876. A walking tour brochure is available at the Visitors Center at 301 East Main Street.

GETTING THERE: Madison is located in southeastern Indiana, along the Ohio River. It is accessible via two interstates: I-65, by taking exit 33 and then State Highway 256 east for approximately 20 miles; and I-71 in Kentucky, by taking exit 34 and State Highway 421 north approximately 20 miles, then crossing the Ohio River into Madison.

FOR MORE INFORMATION: Madison Main Street Program, 312 Jefferson Street, Madison, IN 47250, 812/265-3270

SOUTH BEND, INDIANA

Ethnic Festival

This three-day event celebrates the wealth of cultural diversity in the South Bend community, offering ethnic foods, crafts, music, and dance. Held in an urban setting, the area includes four blocks of downtown and features more than 150 food, craft, and display booths and continuous ethnic entertainment.

ADMISSION: *None*
DATE: *Third weekend in June*

About South Bend

THE EARLIEST EXPLORERS came to where the St. Joseph River bends in north central Indiana. Marquette and Jolliet are believed to have traveled here while exploring the Mississippi Valley in the 1670s; French explorers came later and negotiated peace treaties with the local Miami and Illinois tribes. The first European settler arrived in 1802, an agent for a fur trading company that established trade in the area, which became known as South Hold. The name was changed to South Bend in 1830, and a long era of industrial enterprise began when two brothers, Henry and Clement Studebaker, started a wagon business. South Bend mixes the past and present in a dynamic blend of activities and attractions. The University of Notre Dame was founded here, and visitors will find the newly opened College Football Hall of Fame. South Bend is also the home of the first man-made white-water course, which is used for several world-class kayak races every year.

WHAT TO EXPLORE WHILE IN TOWN: Besides the College Football Hall of Fame, visit the Studebaker National Museum, a treasure chest full of South Bend's history. Catch minor league baseball at Stanley Coveleski Stadium. Visit Potowatomi Zoo, Indiana's oldest zoo, and the historic State Theater, newly renovated through the efforts of Center City Associates, the Main Street program in South Bend. Visitors here on the first Saturday in June can catch the World's Largest Garage Sale, when a municipal garage becomes six floors full of bargains.

GETTING THERE: Located east of the sprawling metropolis of Chicago, South Bend is accessible by the east/west Interstate 80/90 toll road, as well as by north/south-running US-31 and other highways crisscrossing the area.

FOR MORE INFORMATION: Park and Recreation Department, City of South Bend, County-City Office Building, South Bend, IN 46601, 219/235-9952

Iowa

BURLINGTON, IOWA

Snake Alley Criterium

Olympic-style bicycle racing convenes in Burlington on Memorial Day weekend with the Snake Alley Criterium. Join the locals as they watch top cyclists from all over the world race up Snake Alley from the river, said to be the "crookedest" street in the world. Other road races are held as well, and a mountain biking event, the Cobble Climb, challenges riders to compete for the fastest time in climbing a cobblestone alley. There's even a race for the kids on Big Wheels. This two-day event is a great way to spend Memorial Day with the whole family.

Cyclists wind up the "crookedest" street in the world.

ADMISSION: *None*
DATE: *Memorial Day weekend*

Burlington Steamboat Days—American Music Festival

Steamboat Days is a music festival held on the banks of the Mississippi in Burlington. It features national headlining acts in rock, pop, country, rhythm and blues, jazz, and big band, performing on outdoor stages. Other entertainment and events are held in the refurbished Port of Burlington building. Fireworks, a parade, a talent show, bingo, and lots of food round out the festivities.

ADMISSION: *Week-long pass is $18 in advance, $23 at the gate*
DATE: *Third week in June*

The Sight of Music

This is an annual drum and bugle corps competition that will appeal to seasoned music lovers and neophytes alike. It includes competition by top world-ranked groups in a night of pageantry, power, and musical excellence. The young adults who play in these corps devote their entire summers to touring the country and playing, traveling in austere conditions. Proceeds from the event go in part to local band programs.

ADMISSION: *$10 in advance, $12 at the gate*
DATE: *Fourth week in July*

About Burlington

BURLINGTON IS A CITY RICH in history and unique beauty, with roots dating back to 1805. Located on scenic bluffs overlooking the mighty Mississippi, Burlington has come a long way. Fifteen years ago it experienced disinvestment, a downtown vacancy rate hovering around 50 percent, and a feeling of hopelessness.

The Main Street program, started by concerned citizens, has turned Burlington back into a vital community, and pride has been restored. The program was active in renovating the Port of Burlington Building, combining efforts with the city to turn it into a welcome center. It has also been working to redevelop the riverfront area, as well as encouraging the rehabilitation of buildings and helping local businesses to prosper in their downtown locations.

The Sight of Music brings musicians from all over the country.

WHAT TO EXPLORE WHILE IN TOWN: Burlington is a historic community featuring the Heritage Hill National Historic District and several Des Moines County Historical Society Museums. The city is also home to the reportedly "crookedest street in the world," Snake Alley, and its riverfront offers many activities. Information on local recreation and a walking tour guide can be obtained from the Welcome Center located in the Port of Burlington Building along the waterfront.

GETTING THERE: Burlington is situated on the southeastern border of Iowa, along the Mississippi River. It is located on US Highway 34 and is also accessible by the many interstates that go through the region. The nearest interstates are I-80, to the north—take US Highway 218 south to US Highway 34 east to Burlington; and I-74 in Illinois—take US Highway 34 west at Galesburg.

FOR MORE INFORMATION: Downtown Partners, Inc., 214 North Fourth Street, Suite 3C, Burlington, IA 52601, 319/752-0015

CONRAD, IOWA

Black Dirt Days

This festival is uniquely named to boast of the rich, fertile land around Conrad. Events here are based on the agricultural economy and will definitely give visitors a taste of Iowa. You'll find plowing matches, quilting exhibitions, even the "Farmer Olympics." There are also pony rides, pie eating contests, slow-pitch softball, fireworks, and, certainly, good food. Make sure to sample Conrad's famous Black Dirt Cake, an original recipe. And, of course, you haven't lived until you've witnessed cow patty bingo.

ADMISSION: *None*
DATE: *First Friday and Saturday in August*

About Conrad

FOUNDED IN 1880, when the railroad arrived, this tiny town of 964 suffered when the farm crisis of the late 1980s brought economic problems that shook its very foundations. Initiating a Main Street program in 1989, Conrad has worked through its problems to become once again a vital, thriving, little community. It has experienced a net gain of 21 new businesses and 34 new housing units in an area that was once losing people. The Main Street facade grant program has been a catalyst in improving buildings in Conrad, and the self-determined efforts show in the new pride of its people.

WHAT TO EXPLORE WHILE IN TOWN: The General Store, 103 years old and going strong, is a step back in time with its authentic interior fixtures. Adults may want to visit the Heritage Hall Museum at 204 East Center Street, which features local history, and kids of all ages enjoy Dreamland, a gigantic wooden playground constructed entirely with volunteer labor. Conrad also has a family aquatic center, complete with water slide, which is good for hours of kid fun, located in Reunion Park at the north edge of town.

GETTING THERE: You may have a hard time finding this tiny town of 964 on your map, but it's located southwest of Waterloo, just north of Marshalltown and northeast of Des Moines. One can take many of the angular, gridlike state and county highways to get there. Interstate 80 is the closest; take exit 159 to State Highway 6 east, which intersects State Highway 14. Follow 14 north to Conrad, approximately 30 miles.

FOR MORE INFORMATION: Conrad Main Street, P.O. Box 414, Conrad, IA 50621, 515/366-2108

CORNING, IOWA

Le Festival de l'Heritage

Le Festival de l'Heritage is a celebration of the culture and contributions of the Icarians who settled in Adams County. These were French democratic socialists, who initiated an experiment in communal living by establishing their own estate on 3,000 acres of rolling prairie east of Corning in 1852. The Icarians were skilled musicians, artists, and craftsmen and were quite hospitable to their frontier neighbors. This festival, held in that tradition of hospitality, features strolling musicians and artists, quilt and flower shows, a French market, folk dancers, heritage skill demonstrations, and a parade. Kids will like the puppetry performances and workshops and the poodle contest. Guided tours of the original Icarian area are also available.

ADMISSION: *General admission is $5; other events require additional admission fees*
DATE: *First Saturday in June*

About Corning

CORNING, WITH A CURRENT POPULATION of 1,806, was founded in 1857. When the railroad came through, the town grew, serving a wide trade area in the territory. The community became known as the most progressive town in southwestern Iowa, the first to install water and electrical systems. Faced with the same problems experienced by other farm-based communities, Corning has used the Main Street program to bring together elements of the community, now working for its survival and restoring a sense of pride. This spirit is reflected in Main Street Corning's volunteer corps, whose members range from elementary school kids to senior citizens. They do everything from running special events, to conducting demographic research, to acting as community ambassadors. With rehabilitated buildings, new businesses, and events happening downtown, Corning's sense of community commitment is hard to miss.

Le Festival de l'Heritage remembers a group of French democratic socialists who established a commune in Adams County in 1852.

WHAT TO EXPLORE WHILE IN TOWN: Take a stroll around this small town using the walking tour brochure available at the Main Street Corning offices in the Lauvstad Center (a rehabilitated building) at 710 Davis Avenue. You can still get a Green River phosphate at either of the two old-fashioned soda fountains in Corning. Other attractions are the Icarian School House, a structure left from the utopian days, and NASCAR races every Saturday night, information on which is available at the Lauvstad Center and at area businesses.

GETTING THERE: Corning is in southwestern Iowa, south and east of Interstates 80 and 35. It's located on US Highway 34, accessible off exit 33 of I-35 or exit 70 of I-80, taking State Highway 148 south.

FOR MORE INFORMATION: Main Street Corning, 710 Davis Avenue, Corning, IA 50841, 515/322-5229

FORT DODGE, IOWA

Fall Fest

Fall Fest is a time for folks in Fort Dodge to kick back and have some fun after a hard working summer in this farming community. The day-long festival of events includes an arts festival showcasing local artists, a car show, kids' games, live performances, good food, a dog show, and gypsum rock races (you'll have to ask a local).

ADMISSION: *None*
DATE: *Third Saturday in September*

About Fort Dodge

FORT DODGE BEGAN as an Indian fort and evolved into a retail and trading center. Industry and wholesaling created growth, fueled by the construction of four railroads intersecting Fort Dodge. The Main Street program has helped revitalize downtown Fort Dodge. Its stately historic buildings, many of which have undergone rehabilitation, are home to a mix of retailers, professionals, and service providers. Brickwork designs on streets and sidewalks, ornamental lampposts, wood benches, and landscaping were all facilitated by the Main Street program, which strives to improve the visual and economic health of the downtown.

WHAT TO EXPLORE WHILE IN TOWN: The Fort Dodge Historical Museum offers a background in the history of conflict and the presence of the military here, and visitors may also want to visit the Blanden Memorial Art Museum, listed on the National Register of Historic Places, located on Third Avenue South. Information on Fort Dodge can be obtained at the Mainstreet Fort Dodge office, 819 First Avenue South.

GETTING THERE: Located in central Iowa, Fort Dodge is accessible via Interstate 35 by taking exit 142, heading west on US Highway 20 for 30 miles, then north on US Highway 169 for 3 miles.

FOR MORE INFORMATION: Mainstreet Fort Dodge, 819 First Avenue South, Fort Dodge, IA 50501, 515/573-5097

IOWA FALLS, IOWA

Riverbend Rally

This event, held on the Fourth of July, has become so popular that people now plan class and family reunions around it. It's a general celebration featuring contests, food, races, and fun, all held on the banks of the Iowa River. Events include the Miss Iowa Falls Pageant, a water skiing show, a kids' fishing contest, art in the park, live entertainment, dragon boat races, food, and, of course, fireworks over the river on Independence Day evening.

ADMISSION: *None—but a bucket may be passed for donations*
DATE: *July 3-5*

About Iowa Falls

IOWA FALLS HAS A WONDERFUL ASSET: the Iowa River winds its way between sheer limestone bluffs through the heart of the "Scenic City." Established in 1856, it has become a bustling little town of 5,500. Downtown Iowa Falls had 13 empty buildings in 1990, but today it is a thriving business district with the help of the Iowa Falls Main Street program. With 11 structures on the National Register of Historic Places, it has also maintained its historic character with preservation loans, grants, and other assistance from the program.

WHAT TO EXPLORE WHILE IN TOWN: Iowa Falls has some remarkable structures, and walking tour brochures can be picked up at the Chamber/Main Street office. The Princess Cafe and Sweet Shoppe, built in 1929, has a fabulous 25-foot Carrara marble soda fountain counter, mahogany booths, and original fixtures. The historic Metropolitan Playhouse, built in 1899 and converted to a two-screen movie theater in 1993, is a magnificent building. The rehabilitation of these two structures created a snowball effect for the improvement of additional buildings downtown. Other structures of note are the Ellsworth and Jones Building at 511 Washington, which contains an enormous three-story vault, and the Oak Street Bridge, at one time the longest single-arch structure in Iowa. The Iowa Falls Historical Museum at 320 Stevens exhibits memorabilia from local history.

GETTING THERE: Iowa Falls, located in central Iowa, is accessible via Interstate 35, taking exit 142 and heading east on US Highway 20, which turns north and runs through Iowa Falls.

FOR MORE INFORMATION: Iowa Falls Chamber/Main Street, 412½ Washington Avenue, Iowa Falls, IA 50126, 515/648-5549

OGDEN, IOWA

Ogden Fun Days

The first Fun Days celebration, held in 1931, was designed to help people in the vicinity of Ogden forget their Depression troubles by "entering into entertainment for a day," which included greased pig catching contests and three-legged races. That tradition continues with an agenda of fun: an antique tractor pull, barber shop quartets, homemade ice cream, a dart contest, and a parade grand-marshalled by two centenarian citizens.

Participants at Fun Day.

ADMISSION: *None*
DATE: *First Monday through Wednesday of July*

About Ogden

OGDEN'S BIRTH IN 1866 was not without controversy: two corporations claimed the land, and after a four-year legal battle it was named in honor of a railroad official and capitalist. Odgen experienced its share of boom and bust during the last part of the nineteenth and early twentieth centuries. In the 1920s the nation's first transcontinental highway, the Lincoln Highway, was succesfully lobbied to be routed through Ogden. The original pavement still exists on Main Street, and the community has taken steps to preserve it for future generations. Ogden Rural Main Street has been instrumental in facilitating improvements to its historic building facades, installation of new signs, and further improvements on most of Main Street's commercial buildings.

WHAT TO EXPLORE WHILE IN TOWN: Information can be obtained at the Ogden Rural Main Street program office at 218 West Walnut. Take a stroll around this town to encounter its unique architecture and friendly store owners. One can see the footprints made by a boy in 1929, when he walked through the wet pavement of the Lincoln Highway to get to a store across the street. Four blocks south of Main is a 1896 Sears Catalogue house that was moved into Ogden in 1991. Outside town, the Kate Shelley High Bridge was the longest and highest double-track rail bridge in the world when it was built in 1901. The Scenic Valley tourist railroad is a steam train that follows a historic railroad route.

GETTING THERE: Ogden is located in central Iowa, just off of US Highway 30. It is accessible by Interstates 35 and 80: on I-35 take exit 111 and head west on US-30; on I-80 take exit 110 heading north on US Highway 169.

FOR MORE INFORMATION: Ogden Rural Main Street, Box 3, Ogden, IA 50212, 515/275-2902

Michigan

HOLLAND, MICHIGAN

Tulip Time Festival

Holland celebrates its Dutch heritage amid the thousands of tulips that bloom throughout the city during the traditional Tulip Time Festival. Holland residents can be found wearing authentic Dutch costumes and wooden shoes while participating in Klompen dancing or riding on one of the many floats in three parades: the Volksparade is held after the streets have been dutifully scrubbed by thousands of Dutch-costumed particpants; the Children's Parade features 5,000 children in Dutch costumes carrying their art and displays of customs and traditions of the Netherlands; and the Parade of Bands includes more than 50 high school and civic bands.

    ADMISSION: *Parades are free; other events have fees*
    DATE: *Second through third weekend in May*

Celebration: Bridging Cultures Through the Arts

This festival serves as a way to celebrate Holland's growth and community diversity through the arts. Located in downtown's Centennial Park, the Celebration is held each year in recognition of the area's artistic and cultural diversity, drawing musicians, sculptors, illustrators, and puppeteers. Children can participate in a variety of creative activities, which in past years have included bubbology (the art of making bubbles), paper flower making, marble painting, and fish printing. In addition, numerous food booths offer cuisines from around the world. The Doo-Dah Parade takes "not taking things seriously," seriously by celebrating individualism and humor.

    ADMISSION: *None*
    DATE: *Third weekend in June*

About Holland

HOLLAND WAS FOUNDED IN 1847 by Dutch settlers. In 1871 a fire destroyed nearly 80 percent of the city, including many downtown buildings. As a result, many of the buildings are Victorian in style, reflecting the rebuilding era. The city's location on the shores of Lake Macatawa and Lake Michigan has made it a popular tourist attraction since the turn of the century. Holland's Main Street program has had great success in encouraging reinvestment downtown, with many building rehabilitations and upper stories being developed for residential and office uses.

WHAT TO EXPLORE WHILE IN TOWN: A downtown shopping guide and a guide to the historic buildings of downtown are available from the Holland Area Chamber of Commerce and the Main Street office at 194 1/2 South River Avenue. Local attractions include the Holland Museum, Cappon House Museum, Window on the Waterfront Park, and various downtown sculptures.

GETTING THERE: Located in southwestern Michigan near the shore of Lake Michigan, Holland is situated at the junction of US-31, Interstate 196, and Michigan Route 40.

FOR MORE INFORMATION: Main Street/Downtown Develoment Association, 194 1/2 South River Avenue, Holland, MI 49423, 616/355-1050

Dutch costumed participants in the Volksparade in downtown Holland.

Missouri

BRANSON, MISSOURI

Plumb Nellie Days and Craft Festival

Plumb Nellie Days is a celebration of "plumb nellie" ("nellie" is a colloquialism for "nearly") anything that you would expect to find at an old-fashioned country fair. Games, music, dancing, and demonstrations of traditional arts take place throughout the historic downtown district during the two-day event. Kids may bring their fastest turtle or bravest jumping frog to participate in contests on Main Street. Gentlemen may participate in a Best Beard Contest, and ladies may enter their bonnets in the Outrageous Hat Contest. An outhouse race challenges the town's most creative engineers to produce a winning design for this intense competition. Juried artists and crafters participate in the Heritage Craft Show featuring traditional arts and crafts, with no commercially manufactured items allowed.

One of the Outrageous
Hat Contest participants.

ADMISSION: *None*
DATE: *Third weekend in May*

About Branson

RAPIDLY BECOMING KNOWN as the "Performance Music Capital of the World," Branson is a town of 5,000 that also has historic charm and friendly people. Many buildings in Branson's historic district have been recently rehabilitated, and new buildings have been designed to blend in with the old. The local Main Street organization, the Downtown Branson Betterment Association, works to improve the historic downtown as well as to guide and mitigate the detrimental effects of thousands of visitors each year resulting from the burgeoning entertainment trade. Working with the city, it has developed comprehensive plans to improve traffic flow at major intersections, provide more parking for visitors and buses, and install new sidewalks and signs to guide visitors to downtown businesses. It has also developed a sign grant package to guide business owners in the removal of nontraditional signs and the refurbishment of existing traditional signs.

WHAT TO EXPLORE WHILE IN TOWN: The Branson Scenic Railway, leaving from the historic downtown depot, offers two-hour sightseeing excursions through the Ozark Hills on luxurious, 1950s-era passenger cars. For nostalgic atmosphere, there are three restaurants to visit: The Branson Cafe, The Farmhouse, and The Shack, all located near West Main and South Commercial Streets. Each serves hefty portions of traditional Ozark food with a side dish of local gossip. Visitors can experience the beauty of Lake Taneycomo, only two blocks from the center of the historic district. A walking tour map of the historic downtown is available at the Downtown Branson Betterment Association office at 108 1/2 South Commercial.

GETTING THERE: Branson is located in southern Missouri, near the Arkansas border in the Ozarks. Situated on US-160, it is near US-65. From Interstate 44 at Springfield, head south on US-65 for 45 miles, or just follow the tour buses, turning east onto US-160.

FOR MORE INFORMATION: Downtown Branson Betterment Association, P.O. Box 1261, Branson, MO 65615, 417/334-1548

CLARKSVILLE, MISSOURI

Eagle Days

Clarksville is renowned for some of the best bald eagle watching in the lower 48 states, and although eagle watching season runs from December through the end of February, Eagle Days offers a close-up look at these amazing birds of prey as well as spectacular viewing along the river. There are daily educational sessions, featuring a captive American bald eagle, with a handler who provides interpretation of its natural habitat, power, and hunting prowess. At the Mississippi River, just steps from downtown, scopes are set up with Missouri Department of Conservation personnel to view these majestic birds soaring over the river and sitting in the trees. A variety of hot food is offered by restaurants, a tea house, churches, and civic organizations for this eagle watching weekend.

ADMISSION: *None*
DATE: *Last weekend in January*

Big River Days

This event gives visitors an opportunity to discover the important role of rivers in the history of Clarksville, and in the history of the United States as well. Traditional foods, Native American encampments, historic reenactors, storytellers, riverboat music, and river crafters making nets, hooks, buttons, and other items of bygone days make up the historical portion of the event. Children's activities, such as mussel hunts, and an aquarium displaying local fish help to educate visitors about life in the Mississippi River. It's all topped off with a one-hour riverboat excursion, enabling visitors to get a real feel for the river.

ADMISSION: *None*
DATE: *Third weekend in September*

About Clarksville

CLARKSVILLE IS THE ONLY REMAINING Missouri town whose downtown business district faces the Mississippi River. Founded in 1817, it is listed on the National Register of Historic Places. Once a busy riverport, it still has a small town feel. Its historic downtown commercial buildings contain antique and specialty shops and studios for working artisans who practice traditional craftsmanship. The city and its environs are known as an outstanding locale for nature tourism in Missouri. Central to this recognition are the spring and fall migrations of waterfowl and, in the winter, some of the best bald eagle viewing in the lower 48 states.

WHAT TO EXPLORE WHILE IN TOWN: No matter when you're in Clarksville, you should try your hand at viewing the wildlife along the river. The Visitors Center at Lock & Dam No. 24 provides binoculars and telescopes, as well as daily counts of bald eagles and other wildlife, and has staff to answer questions. Visitors can watch river traffic passing through Lock & Dam No. 24 as well as enjoy picnicking at the riverside park.

GETTING THERE: Clarksville, in eastern Missouri, is 70 miles northeast of St. Louis. Situated on Illinois Route 79, it is 45 miles north of Interstate 70.

FOR MORE INFORMATION: Clarksville Information Center, 204 North Highway 79, Clarksville, MO 63336, 573/242-3132

HANNIBAL, MISSOURI

River Arts Festival

The Great Mississippi River Arts Festival is staged on North Main Street in the heart of Hannibal's downtown Historic District. Featuring the works of more than 50 midwestern artists, who display and sell their original

Local musicians at the Great Mississippi River Arts Festival.

works, visitors are sure to find something to their liking. Loads of food booths, a variety of entertainment groups, and children's activities round out this fun-filled holiday weekend.

ADMISSION: *None*
DATE: *The Saturday and Sunday of Memorial Day weekend*

National Tom Sawyer Days

Grab your straw hat and fishing pole for National Tom Sawyer Days, held over the Fourth of July weekend. The Hannibal riverfront and historic downtown provide the setting for fence painting and frog jumping contests, the Tomboy Sawyer Competition, Mississippi Mud Volleyball, bingo, live entertainment, and the Hannibal Cannibal 10k run. Visitors can adopt a fake frog, complete with adoption certificate, at the Hannibal Main Street Program's Frog Toss. A hometown Fourth of July parade and fantastic fireworks on the banks of the mighty Mississippi provide a perfect conclusion.

Historic Hannibal with the riverboat
American Queen **in port.**

ADMISSION: *None*
DATE: *Fourth of July weekend*

Autumn Historic Folklife Festival

This festival celebrates local cultural heritage by showcasing historic crafts, food, music, performing arts, and culture of the mid-nineteenth century. Visitors can stroll along the historic downtown's streets amid artisans demonstrating life-styles and folk art. Performers play traditional tunes, kick up their heels, and tell tales of a simpler time. Bring your appetite, the smell of the homemade food at this event is irresistible.

ADMISSION: *None*
DATE: *Third weekend in October*

About Hannibal

FAMOUS AS THE HOMETOWN of Samuel Clemens (better known by his pen name, Mark Twain), Hannibal also has a strong community history rooted in the Mississippi River and the railroad industry. At the turn of the century, lumber barons left their mark with majestic public buildings, impressive commercial storefronts, and elaborate homes. Local property owners have used incentives provided by the Hannibal Main Street program to rehabilitate their historic structures and create a viable business district.

WHAT TO EXPLORE WHILE IN TOWN: A local landmark is the recently refurbished Mark Twain Memorial Lighthouse, located at the top of Cardiff Hill. With a grant from the state and matching donations from the community, the Hannibal Main Street program restored the structure in 1994, which was rededicated via telephone by President Clinton. The Mark Twain Boyhood Home and Museum at 208 Hill Street is a must for any visitor. Take a stroll along the historic riverfront, complete with Mississippi riverboat. A visitor's guide and residential walking tour map are available at the Hannibal Convention and Visitor's Bureau, 505 North Third (Highway 79), for touring Hannibal's residential area, just west of downtown, which is on the National Register.

GETTING THERE: Hannibal is located in northeastern Missouri, on the Mississippi River. It is accessible by US Routes 36 and 61. The nearest interstate is 70, about 75 miles south on US-61.

FOR MORE INFORMATION: Hannibal Main Street Program, 623 Broadway, Hannibal, MO 63401, 573/221-2677

PARKVILLE, MISSOURI

Parkville Jazz and Fine Arts River Jam

This popular two-day event is held on the riverfront park, combing Parkville's unique waterway location with its musical heritage and art. A fine-arts exhibition showcases local talent in a juried competition, and jazz, jazz, jazz from area musicians is performed both days. Music, art, the river, and the historic integrity of the downtown and its unique shops along Main Street combine to create a special atmosphere.

ADMISSION: *None*
DATE: *Third Saturday and Sunday in June*

Christmas on the River

Christmas on the River is a family-oriented event, a wonderful start to the holiday season. It includes a performance by a 1,000-voice children's choir, a hot air balloon lift-off, a spectacular fireworks display over the Missouri River, sleigh rides, and a special arrival by Santa Claus. The merchants of Main Street have late evening open houses for browsing and beginning your shopping season. This event is very popular in the region and has become a local holiday tradition.

ADMISSION: *None*
DATE: *First Friday in December*

About Parkville

ORIGINALLY SETTLED IN 1839, the land for the town of Parkville was purchased in 1840 by Colonel George S. Park, a veteran of Sam Houston's cavalry who recognized the value of riverfront land for steamboat trade. As trade and commerce grew along the river, so did Parkville. Following the Midwest's devastating floods in 1993, the city is beginning to enjoy renewed vitality with the assistance of the Main Street Parkville Association. Its present-day success and steadfast determination to revive itself in the face of that huge natural disaster are continued testimony to the tenacity of its residents. Main Street Parkville has organized zero-interest loans for facade improvement, to restore or repair many buildings downtown, and has recruited nine new businesses. It has also purchased and coordinated the banners and planters downtown.

WHAT TO EXPLORE WHILE IN TOWN: A walking tour brochure can be obtained at the Main Street Parkville Association office at 207 Main Street, and tours can be scheduled by calling ahead. At the Park College campus, history and architecture buffs may want to investigate Mackay Hall and the Scott Memorial Observatory, both constructed by students in the 1890s and on the National Register of Historic Places.

GETTING THERE: Located just north of Kansas City in western Missouri, Parkville sits on the Misssouri River. It is located on Missouri Route 45, and is also accessible by Interstates 435, 70, and 35, which cross through Kansas City.

FOR MORE INFORMATION: Main Street Parkville Association, 207 Main Street, Suite B, Parkville, MO 64152, 816/505-2227

WASHINGTON, MISSOURI

Art Fair and Winefest

This celebration is the largest all-Missouri wine tasting event in the state. Here you'll get a chance to view the juried work of 65 midwestern artists and sample as many as 50 different Missouri-grown wines. The event includes a mix of music and entertainment, plus a large variety of specialty foods and beverages. Admission fee to the Winefest includes a special commemorative glass.

> ADMISSION: *Art Fair is free; Winefest is $15*
> DATE: *Friday through Sunday on the third weekend in May*

Fall Festival of the Arts

This event features two- and three-dimensional creations of artists from all over the United States. These artists give demonstrations of their work, and visitors have an opportunity to browse among their offerings. Specialty foods, live music, and entertainment round out the experience. For kids, there's a hands-on art activity area. The setting is beside the river at beautiful Rennick Riverfront Park.

ADMISSION: *None*
DATE: *Last weekend in September*

About Washington

FOUNDED IN 1839 by Lucinda Owens, Washington is located on the banks of the Missouri River. A strong German heritage is evident in Washington, which has become famous for its nineteenth-century brick architecture, with two separate historic districts on the National Register of Historic Places. Since the inception of the Main Street program, called Downtown Washington Inc., the downtown has witnessed more than $3 million in public and private reinvestment. Rehabilitation of many of Washington's historic buildings was made possible through Downtown Washington's building improvement loan program. Downtown Washington has also been instrumental in the renovation of the oldest buildings downtown, as well as in providing new street lights, brick crosswalks, banners, and new businesses downtown.

WHAT TO EXPLORE WHILE IN TOWN: Visitors to Washington should take a look at the Meerchaum Corn Cob Pipe Factory, the only one of its kind in the world. They may also enjoy a ride on the water-operated elevator housed in the historic Otto & Company furniture store, established more than 100 years ago. A variety of good restaurants, antique stores, B & Bs, shops, and businesses are located in downtown

Washington. A walking tour brochure can be obtained at the offices of Downtown Washington and at most downtown businesses.

GETTING THERE: Located in eastern Missouri near St. Louis, Washington is accessible by Amtrak, which makes regular stops there. It is situated at the intersection of State Roads 100 and 47. Take Interstate 44 to exit 251, then State Road 100 north for 10 miles.

FOR MORE INFORMATION: Downtown Washington, Inc., P.O. Box 144, Washington, MO 63090, 314/239-1743

A basket maker, Ramona Buss, demonstrates her craft at the Fall Festival of the Arts.

Wisconsin

CHIPPEWA FALLS, WISCONSIN

Boat, Camping, and Fishing Swap Meet

This event provides an opportunity to buy and sell new and used boats, campers, fishing equipment, and other recreational items. Winter-weary spectators can win prizes in the casting contest, Best Fish Story contest, and Guess the Gummy Worms contest. The Main Street food stand features shore lunches, cheese curds, and bratwursts. Other features include boating and fishing information from the Department of Natural Resources, antique lures, and other displays.

Fishermen haggle over lures and fish stories.

ADMISSION: *None*
DATE: *Third Sunday in April*

Pure Water Days Fun Fest

Chippewa Falls is said to be home of the purest water in the world, and the city celebrates that fact with Pure Water Days. It features Pure Fun with food, children's games, and rides. Don't miss the Pure Waddle Duck Race, the Leinenkugel Can Float, and the Golden Goose Race. A parade, a crafts sale, the Tour de Chippewa Bike Ride, and fireworks are just some of the highlights.

ADMISSION: *None*
DATE: *Third weekend in August*

Bridge to Wonderland Holiday Parade

This popular nighttime parade heralds the beginning of the Christmas season in Chippewa Falls. It features illuminated floats and marching bands, and, of course, Santa and his elves make their appearance at the end of the parade. Spectators can warm up with hot drinks and refreshments at local businesses that host open houses during the event, and kids can put in their requests to Santa at his candyland house.

ADMISSION: *None*
DATE: *First Saturday in December*

About Chippewa Falls

Early settlers arrived in Chippewa Falls in 1836, and that same year the American Fur Trade Company commissioned them to construct a sawmill. For the next 75 years lumber was the major industry in Chippewa Falls. After the lumber industry declined, the town was able to survive because of its early diversification of economy. Mason Shoe Manufacturing and the Leinenkugel Brewing Co. are two businesses that remain succesful to this day. The Main Street program began in 1989 in Chippewa Falls and has spurred major investment in downtown with building facade renovations and recruitment of new businesses. The vacant Chippewa Shoe Factory, once called an eyesore, was converted into attractive low- and moderate-income apartments, thanks to Main Street's efforts. The newly rehabilitated buildings, hanging flower baskets, and good shopping opportunities downtown are evidence of the Main Street program's effectiveness.

WHAT TO EXPLORE WHILE IN TOWN: The fifth-generation Leinenkugel family still operates Leinenkugel Brewing, which operates a gift shop and offers tours by appointment. The Cook-Rutledge Mansion, with its hand-painted ceilings and ornately carved woodwork, is open for tours in the summer. Chippewa Falls is home to the "purest water in the world," and Chippewa Springs Water and the community have preserved the original springhouse for viewing. A detailed walking tour brochure explaining local history and local landmarks is available at the Main Street office, 315 North Bridge Street, and at many businesses downtown.

GETTING THERE: Chippewa Falls is located in northwestern Wisconsin, on Wisconsin Route 29 and just off US-53. It is also approximately 10 miles north of Interstate 94.

FOR MORE INFORMATION: Main Street Chippewa Falls, 315 North Bridge Street, P.O. Box 554, Chippewa Falls, WI 54729, 715/723-6661

COLUMBUS, WISCONSIN

Redbud Festival

This annual event dates back to 1913, when the first redbuds were planted by the Women's Club to beautify Columbus. Each May, these trees bloom as the harbingers of spring and the end of the long Wisconsin winter. The festival is a celebration of spring with food, fun, and special events: the crowning of the Redbud Prince and Princess, a downtown pet parade, bake sales, and music. Food includes the traditional bratwursts, ice cream, pies, and cream puffs.

ADMISSION: *None*

DATE: *Third weekend in May*

About Columbus

NATIVE AMERICAN ARTIFACTS indicate that there were settlements in the locality of Columbus hundreds of years before its namesake arrived. A European settler, Elbert Dickason, built a home and sawmill on the Crawfish River in 1839 and is credited with "founding" Columbus. Over the next 20 years merchants, money lenders, tradesmen, and developers built homes that today stand as testament to their prosperity. In the late 1800s, two major roads and a railway served Columbus. As the twentieth century progressed, economic and social changes shifted the prosperity of the downtown. In 1992, Columbus became a Main Street community, with a committed group of volunteers working to save the historic Whitney Hotel located at the town's main intersection. The Whitney now houses eight charming apartments and two commercial spaces. Columbus's downtown, now a National Register Historic District, proudly boasts rehabilitated buildings and new streetlights.

WHAT TO EXPLORE WHILE IN TOWN: One building you don't want to miss is the Farmer's and Merchants Union Bank, one of the last eight banks designed by Louis Sullivan. It maintains a small museum related to Sullivan and to the bank's history. Those who enjoy Prairie architecture should visit the 1912 Carnegie library. A walking tour guide is available at the Main Street office, 105 North Dickason Boulevard, and at city hall, the chamber of commerce, and several businesses.

GETTING THERE: Columbus is located in southern Wisconsin, northeast of Madison, on US-151.

FOR MORE INFORMATION: Columbus Main Street, 105 North Dickason Boulevard, P.O. Box 23, Columbus, WI 53925, 414/623-5325

DE PERE, WISCONSIN

Celebration 108

Celebration 108 remembers the union of east and west De Pere as it honors America's veterans. This is a community event on Memorial Day weekend that provides fun, food, entertainment, organized by more than 2,000 volunteers. Events include national and regional entertainment on three stages, a three-on-three basketball tournament, a four-mile run, duck races, and homemade boat races. For kids, there's a large children's area with camel, elephant, and llama rides, games, and performers. Civic groups sell food, and the highlight of the day is a parade with more than 100 units, the largest Memorial Day parade in Wisconsin.

ADMISSION: *Weekend pass $12, each day $6*
DATE: *Memorial Day weekend*

About De Pere

IN 1634, A MERE 14 YEARS after the Pilgrim landing at Plymouth Rock, Jean Nicolet ended a 1,000-mile voyage from Montreal to Red Banks and became the first European to reach the De Pere area. After being welcomed by a tribe of Winnebago Indians, he proceeded up the Fox River to what is now the town of De Pere. A mission was later founded at the foot of the rapids; this site became a religious outpost and fur trading way station. In 1673 the explorers Marquette and Joliet stopped at the mission for three days on their historic journey to find the Mississippi River. The development of De Pere has hinged on its proximity to the river, with industries finding its rapids an ideal source of power. Flour mills, sawmills, and knitting mills, were located here and helped expand the economy. These structures, along with dams, locks, bridge tenders' houses, and other relics of the river economy still exist today and are now showcased as part of De Pere's heritage. Main Street De Pere has played a huge role in recognizing the value in the old structures of De Pere and in lobbying support to reuse, rather than destroy them. The Lawton Foundry Apartments building was weeks away from the wrecking ball but now stands, offering unique apartments. A former flour mill is now a luxurious inn.

WHAT TO EXPLORE WHILE IN TOWN: The Lee Building, at 124 North Broadway, was first a hotel, then a department store. It has been completely renovated and now houses retail businesses and offices. Egan Brewing Company, at 330 Reid Street, is De Pere's first microbrewery. The James Street Inn, at 201 James Street, is a former flour mill turned into a luxurious inn. A wonderful walking tour brochure and business directory can be obtained at the Main Street office located in the Associated Bank, 206 North Wisconsin Street.

GETTING THERE: De Pere is located in northeast Wisconsin, inland from Green Bay on the Fox River. It is situated near Interstate 43 and US-41.

FOR MORE INFORMATION: Main Street De Pere, 206 North Wisconsin, P.O. Box 311, De Pere, WI 54115, 414/433-7767

DODGEVILLE, WISCONSIN

Farmers Appreciation Day

Farmers Appreciation Day celebrates the important role farming plays in the community. The day starts off with a parade and includes a draft horse show, hayrides, an antique farm equipment exhibition, and a tractor pull. The day's highlight is the International Hog and Cow Calling Contest, in which kids and adults both compete for the best "Sooo-wee" and "Here, Bessie."

ADMISSION: *None*

DATE: *July 2*

Judges rate the entrant's ability, while spectators listen and learn to call a cow or hog at Farmers Appreciation Day.

About Dodgeville

A TRUE ADVENTURER AND EXPLORER, Henry Dodge, founded Dodgeville in 1827 as a mining town when he discovered the area to be unusually rich in lead ore.

The community prospered as a business and retail center for the area. By the 1980s, Dodgeville had lost much of its business to nearby Madison's regional shopping malls. In 1991, a Main Street program was begun to head off the downtown's deterioration; it has won that battle, bringing the vacancy rate down to 3 percent. Dodgeville Revitalization, as the program is called, offers comprehensive design assistance for building owners, leading to 90 percent of the buildings downtown being improved in some way. It has worked with area businesses to enhance the availability of goods and services downtown, thus creating a healthy retail mix.

WHAT TO EXPLORE WHILE IN TOWN: A visit to Dodgeville wouldn't be complete without a visit to the Corner Drug Store for cherry phosphates, lemon cokes, and square ice cream. Dodgeville also has the oldest working courthouse in the state; the impressive Greek Revival structure has been a landmark in the community since its construction in 1859. The historic slag furnace recalls Dodgeville's origins as a mining town. A lavish walking tour brochure is available at the Visitor Information Center on Highway 23 north and at local bookstores.

GETTING THERE: Dodgeville is located in southern Wisconsin, southwest of Madison, on US-151.

FOR MORE INFORMATION: Dodgeville Revitalization, 178 1/2 North Iowa, Dodgeville, WI 53533, 608/935-9200

MARSHFIELD, WISCONSIN

Dairyfest

Dairyfest is Marshfield's salute to the local dairy industry. Held the weekend after Memorial Day, this festival is in its 17th year. It features all sorts of events, including a gigantic parade, an old-fashioned ice cream social at a historic mansion, and the Dairyfest Cheese Chase. There will also be a pig roast, a car show, arts and crafts, and children's games. Music and food round out this jam-packed day of fun in Cheese Country, USA.

ADMISSION: *None*

DATE: *The weekend after Memorial Day*

About Marshfield

IN 1872, THE WISCONSIN CENTRAL RAILROAD came through Marshfield, and by 1883 the city was incorporated. In 1897 the city was nearly destroyed by a fire that swept through town, but businesses pulled together and rebuilt. Today, Marshfield is a

community of 20,000 and its revitalization program, Main Street Marshfield, has mobilized business, retailers, government, property owners, and civic groups to work together to improve the downtown and make it a friendly place to shop, highlighting its special market niche: bridal needs. Enhancements to buildings, signs, window displays, landscaping, and pedestrian amenities have all been due to Main Street Marshfield.

WHAT TO EXPLORE WHILE IN TOWN: Visitors can enjoy the Daily Grind, a local institution sporting old furnishings and photos of the restaurant's early years. There are many buildings in downtown Marshfield that have been rehabilitated to residential use: the Charles Apartments, once a grand hotel; the old high school that is now senior residential housing; and Tower Hall, a former old city hall building that has been converted to residences. Rogers Cinema, which has been downtown for 25 years, offers movies daily.

GETTING THERE: Located in north central Wisconsin, Marshfield is situated on Wisconsin State Highway 13. It is accessible by two major highways: Interstate 94, which is approximately 60 miles to the west, and US-51, which is 33 miles to the east.

FOR MORE INFORMATION: Main Street Marshfield, 222 South Central, #404, Marshfield, WI 54449, 715/387-3299

Midwest Cornish Festival

Mote than 160 years ago immigrants from Corn-
wall, England, flocked to Mineral Point to mine
the rich veins of lead ore found in the area. They
used locally quarried limestone to construct stone
cottages, much like those they left behind in Corn-
wall. The annual Midwest Cornish Festival celebrates their traditions and the mark they left on
this community. Activities include bus tours of the
Historic District, Cornish and Celtic entertainment, the Taste of Mineral Point food festival, and
children's activities.

ADMISSION: *None*
DATE: *Last weekend in September*

**The Zor Shrine pipes and
drums band performs at the
Midwest Cornish Festival.**

Fall Art Tour

During the Fall Art Tour, some of Wisconsin's best-known artisans open their studios
to visitors, providing a behind-the-scenes glimpse of how their work is created. The
region around the communities of Mineral Point, Spring Green, and Baraboo are
known for the many artisan studios tucked away in its scenic hills. This is an area of
rolling hills and valleys, where you'll find artists working in restored breweries, schoolhouses, and stone cottages. The tour features nationally known painters, sculptors, potters, weavers, goldsmiths, and mixed media artists, who have arranged to be on-site in
their studios, demonstrating their skills. The three tour communities are filled with cafes
and bed and breakfasts, and the glorious autumn foliage of southwestern Wisconsin is
near peak during this three-day event.

ADMISSION: *None*
DATE: *Third weekend in October*

About Mineral Point

IN THE 1820s, after hearing reports of abundant lead in the area, prospective miners
with "lead fever" began pouring into southwestern Wisconsin. Finding ore just beneath
the surface, miners set up "diggings" and soon established Mineral Point. It quickly
became the regional center for land sales and government. Immigrant Cornish miners
brought advanced hard-rock and deep-mining skills and a distinctive stone-building tradition to the area. The lead industry waned in the 1860s, but zinc mining developed in
the 1880s and flourished into the twentieth century. The 1930s marked the birth of
Mineral Point's preservation movement, but it did not develop on a large scale until the
1960s, when artists, crafts people, and preservationists began to restore many of the old

mining town's limestone buildings. Mineral Point Main Street's business improvement incentive program has encouraged additional rehabilitation projects in the downtown, facilitating $2.4 million in reinvestment since the program's inception.

WHAT TO EXPLORE WHILE IN TOWN: To relive the days of Cornish immigrants, visit Pendarvis State Historic Site, where costumed guides lead you on interpretive tours of log and stone cottages built by Cornish miners in the 1840s. The Gundry House Museum is an Italianate mansion, constructed in 1867, featuring antiques and local artifacts and is open for tours. The Mineral Point Historic District contains more than 500 contributing structures, many of which have been painstakingly restored. A walking tour guide and a visitors' guide are available from the Main Street/Chamber of Commerce office at 225 High Street. Within the district, visitors will find a variety of art galleries, shops, and restaurants.

GETTING THERE: Mineral Point is in southwestern Wisconsin at the junction of Wisconsin Highways 23 and 39 and US-151. Interstate 90 is approximately 50 miles west.

FOR MORE INFORMATION: Mineral Point Main Street, 225 High Street, Box 267, Mineral Point, WI 53565, 608/987-2580 or, 888/POINT WI, e-mail: minpt@mhtc.net, http://www.mhtc.net/~minpt

RICHLAND CENTER, WISCONSIN

Frank Lloyd Wright Birthday Celebration

Richland Center honors its most famous son's birth in 1867 with this event. There are lectures and discussions with Wright historians and directors of Wright house museums. There are also architectural tours of the A.D. German Warehouse, the only Mayan style

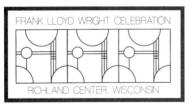

Wright structure remaining, as well as horse-drawn trolley rides through the town's historic neighborhoods. Other activities include an arts and crafts show, children's art activities, croquet, musical performances, and a birthday cake for the man of honor, who appears in the form of an unsmiling F.L.W. reenactor.

ADMISSION: *Tours, trolley rides, and birthday cake entail nominal fees*
DATE: *Weekend closest to June 8*

Centerfest

The entire community gets involved in Richland Center's fall harvest celebration, Centerfest. The two-day festival is loaded with activities, including auto and bicycle tours of the colorful hills, visits to area orchards, a quilt show, and the Cider Jig Jog (a four-mile run/walk). Don't miss the Rotary's pancake breakfast, the Girl Scouts' spaghetti supper, or the chili cook-off and tasting. Kids will love the Apple Toss and Pumpkin Bowling. There are also chorales, homecoming parades, and home tours. Be sure to bring your camera to capture the fall color of Richland County, where, locals say, "Mother Nature does some of her best work."

ADMISSION: *Some events have nominal admission fees*
DATE: *First weekend in October*

About Richland Center

CRADLED IN THE UNGLACIATED HILLS of southwest Wisconsin, Richland Center is the birthplace of world-renowned architect Frank Lloyd Wright. Located as a

travel stop between Chicago and Minneapolis, as well as Madison and LaCrosse, Richland Center has housed many entertainers and politicians who appeared at the city's Municipal Auditorium, now on the National Register of Historic Places. Both the downtown and residential architecture reflects the late 1880s and 1920s periods of growth and expansion in Richland Center. The town's Main Street program has provided assistance to merchants and building owners with low-interest loans for better designed signs and rehabiliation of their building facades. The program has also promoted preservation in the downtown area, and it organizes special events to bring people downtown and to raise awareness of its importance for the community.

WHAT TO EXPLORE WHILE IN TOWN: The only remaining example of Wright's Mayan period style is the A.D. German Warehouse, now on the National Register of Historic Places. Wright reputedly owed money to a local grocer and food merchant and agreed to design the building in lieu of payment. Unfortunately for Mr. German, the cost of the warehouse that was supposed to be about $30,000 ended up being $120,000. Other renovated buildings include the restored courthouse, built in 1889, and the Park Hotel, built in 1873, which has been rehabilitated into apartments. A walking tour brochure and other information are available at the Chamber/Main Street Information Center at 174 South Central.

GETTING THERE: Richland Center is located in southwestern Wisconsin on US-14. It is approximately 55 miles west of Madison and Interstate 90.

FOR MORE INFORMATION: Richland Main Street/Chamber, P.O. Box 25, Richland Center, WI 53581, 608/647-8418

RIVER FALLS, WISCONSIN

Art on the Kinni

Art on the Kinni (short for Kinnickinnic River) is a juried art fair held on the first Saturday in September. It seeks to highlight the talents and works of the growing number of artists who are becoming residents of rural western Wisconsin. About 50 artists exhibit, whose works must be original fine art and traditional crafts; no commercially produced work is permitted. Visitors can spend a day along the Kinni, browsing the many artists' works, enjoying the music and entertainment provided, as well as great food.

ADMISSION: *None*
DATE: *First Saturday after Labor Day*

About River Falls

RIVER FALLS IS NAMED for its falls along the Kinnickinnic River. The Kinni is a renowned trout stream originating 12 miles northeast of the city. The river narrows through the heart of River Falls and moves on to Lake George. The town is also home to the campus of the University of Wisconsin-River Falls, which is adjacent to the downtown. The River Falls Main Street program has worked to revitalize the downtown area through its many projects, including maintenance of more than 55 public gardens.

WHAT TO EXPLORE WHILE IN TOWN: River Falls is very walkable, with its many trails along the river and community gardens gracing the downtown area. A walking tour guide of the historic downtown area and other information are available at the River Falls Main Street office at 220 South Main.

GETTING THERE: River Falls is located in western Wisconsin, near the Minnesota border, approximately 30 miles from St. Paul. It is situated at the junction of Wisconsin Routes 65 and 29 and is 6 miles south of Interstate 94.

FOR MORE INFORMATION: River Falls Main Street Project, P.O. Box 144, 220 South Main Street, River Falls, WI 54022, 715/425-8901, e-mail: mainst@pressenter.com

SHEBOYGAN FALLS, WISCONSIN

Ducktona 500

The Ducktona is the most popular event in Sheboygan Falls. Here's how it works: an armada of rubber ducks, which have been sold for $3 each, is set loose on the local river. The first six ducks to float across the finish line win their owners big prizes. Other events at the Ducktona 500 include a Kiss the Pig contest, Big Wheel races for kids, and a classic car show.

ADMISSION: *None; ducks cost $3 each*
DATE: *First Sunday in July*

About Sheboygan Falls

SHEBOYGAN FALLS' EARLIEST HISTORY indicates that it was the home of several Native American tribes, as well as a post for French fur traders. Officially founded by a New Englander in 1835, Sheboygan Falls grew as a community, based on its access to the Sheboygan River and use of the falls as a source of power. Through the years, woolen mills and other industry came and left Sheboygan Falls. The Main Street program has achieved remarkable results in revitalizing the downtown, including oversight of the rehabilitation of the Brickner Woolen Mill building to apartments. It has facilitated 86 rehabilitation projects, 35 new businesses, and $7.2 million in reinvestment in the downtown. The program's successes earned it recognition with the National Trust's Great American Main Street Award.

The Ducktona 500 is a popular event in Sheboygan Falls.

WHAT TO EXPLORE WHILE IN TOWN: Sheboygan Falls is home to two historic districts, the Cole Brothers District and the Downtown District on Broadway, both of which feature many rehabilitated homes and commercial buildings. Walking tour brochures are available at the Main Street office, 641 Monroe, Suite 108.

GETTING THERE: Sheboygan Falls is located in eastern Wisconsin, near Lake Michigan. Situated near the larger community of Sheboygan, it is just off of Interstate 43.

FOR MORE INFORMATION: Sheboygan Falls Main Street, 641 Monroe Street, Suite 108, Sheboygan Falls, WI 53085-1337, 414/467-6206

VIROQUA, WISCONSIN

May Visions Arts Faire and Chalkdust Festival

This is an arts fair for both the amateur and the professional. While artisans exhibit their works for sale, adults and kids alike try their hand at drawing right on the downtown sidewalks. Quality artists participate, with works in jewelry, metalwork, photography, sculpture, pottery, wood carving, and watercolors. Many will be giving demonstrations of their work. The event also includes food, exhibitions of folk dancing, prizes, and musical entertainment.

ADMISSION: *None*
DATE: *Second Saturday in May*

About Viroqua

IN 1846, MOSES DECKER, a prospector traveling through territorial Wisconsin, happened on the area of Viroqua and became its first settler when he built a cabin. Others soon joined him, and the small community was born. This rural town has always had its economic base in agriculture. In 1989,  in response to the closing of seven stores that followed the location of a large discounter on the edge of town, Viroqua Revitalization was created. Since then, it has overseen 24 new businesses, 15 business expansions or relocations, and 104 new jobs. The Main Street program has also responded to the growth resulting from the increasing numbers of young professionals moving into the area. It has developed a comprehensive plan to limit uncontrolled sprawl on the edge of town and has created a low-interest loan pool for facade improvements and coordinated streetscape improvements downtown.

WHAT TO EXPLORE WHILE IN TOWN: Be sure to see Viroqua's new mural on Main Street, which was a community effort coordinated by the Main Street program, encompassing 2,500 volunteer hours and taking two years to complete. Viroqua has several walking tours: Main Street Meanderings, the Courthouse Trail, and the Heritage Trail. They are available at the Main Street offices at 220 South Main Street.

GETTING THERE: Viroqua is located in southwestern Wisconsin at the intersection of US Highways 14 and 61 and Wisconsin Routes 27, 82, and 56. Interstate 90 is 35 miles to the north.

FOR MORE INFORMATION: Viroqua Chamber—A Main Street City, 220 South Main Street, Viroqua, WI 54665, 608/637-2575

MOUNTAIN AND
PLAINS STATES

Kansas

Nebraska

South Dakota

Wyoming

Kansas

GREAT BEND, KANSAS

The Marigold Festival

This event is the community's celebration of fall, with activities at the local zoo, a children's carnival and circus, a festive mini-parade, demonstrations, and historical  recreations. The Great Golden Belt Chili Cook-off adds more spice to the day's events with chili-heads getting together for some friendly competition. The traditional Rainbow's End Arts and Crafts festival, showcasing community artists for more than 14 years, is also a mainstay. Quilters and quilt lovers will love the Kansas Quilt Walk and the Central Kansas Threadbenders Annual Quilt Show, held in conjunction with this event. Food, a horse-drawn trolley, entertainment, and a zoo train add up to a day of fun for everyone.

ADMISSION: *None*
DATE: *First Saturday in September*

About Great Bend

ALL THE CHARACTERS of the Wild West—Plains Indians, fur traders, bull whackers, and cowboys—were part of the foundation of Great Bend. At the confluence of the Arkansas River and Walnut Creek, the area was well watered, attracting huge herds of buffalo, which in turn attracted Native Americans from across the Great Plains. They were joined later by fur traders, including Kit Carson, Jedediah Smith, and the Bent brothers. When the buffalo were decimated and replaced with longhorn cattle on the plains, Great Bend served as a railhead for shipment of the cattle back east. The rip-roaring cow town days were soon replaced by a steady economy produced by farmers and merchants, and Great Bend became the regional trade center it is today.

WHAT TO EXPLORE WHILE IN TOWN: The Kansas Quilt Walk, a collection of quilting designs set into the sidewalk around the square, was coordinated by the local Main Street program, Downtown Development, Inc. Great Bend boasts a local zoo, the Barton County Historical Village, the Kansas Oil and Gas Museum, and the renovated Crest Theater, offering live performances. A walking tour guide as well as a "Tours on a Tankful" driving guide of the area are available from the Chamber of Commerce at 1307 Williams.

GETTING THERE: Great Bend is located in central Kansas at the juncture of US-281, US-

56 and Kansas Highways 96 and 156. It is south of Interstate 70, 39 miles on US-281.

FOR MORE INFORMATION: Downtown Development, Inc., 1920 16th Street, Suite 105, Great Bend, KS 67530, 316/793-7700

FORT SCOTT, KANSAS

Good Ol' Days

Step back a century with the Fort Scott folks for an 1890s street fair. Enjoy five stages of live entertainment, more than 200 craft booths, and an evening street dance. There are also melodramas, horseshoe pitching, a gun show, and a railroad exhibit. Visit the Red Garter Saloon show, complete with singing bartenders and high-kicking dancers. For kids, there's the huge Children's Fair for hours of old-fashioned fun.

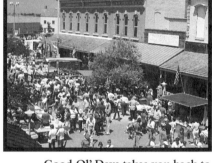

Good Ol' Days takes you back to the Fort Scott of the 1890s.

ADMISSION: *$1*
DATE: *First full weekend in June*

About Fort Scott

FORT SCOTT WAS ESTABLISHED as a U.S. army fortification in Indian territory in 1842, but was abandoned in 1853. The buildings were sold to a settler, and the former post became the center of one of the largest towns in the Kansas Territory. Between 1855 and 1861 the citizens of Fort Scott experienced the violent unrest occurring on the Kansas-Missouri border that preceded the Civil War. Described as "Bleeding Kansas," this period of conflict resulted from the controversy over extending slavery into new territories. Murder, mayhem, and robbery were committed by both free-state and pro-slavery advocates. In 1861, Kansas entered the Union as a free state, but the turmoil continued through the Civil War. After the Civil War, Fort Scott competed with Kansas City to become the largest railroad capital west of the Mississippi. After the turn of the century, it became the agricultural and industrial center it is today. The community's pride in its past is reflected in its Main Street program and preservation efforts.

WHAT TO EXPLORE WHILE IN TOWN: Fort Scott has much that recalls its past. The Fort Scott National Historic Site is a restored fort that's open for self-guided tours. Fort Scott also has a trolley that can convey you past Victorian mansions and the city's parks. Its National Cemetery was one of 12 cemeteries designated by President Lincoln, and other sites of interest include the Ralph Richards Museum, Fort Lincoln School, and the Old Congregational Church. A Visitors Center in the Chamber of Commerce is open seven days a week, offering information on the town and the entire area.

GETTING THERE: Located near the Missouri border in southeastern Kansas, Fort Scott is at the junction of US Routes 69 and 54.

FOR MORE INFORMATION: Fort Scott Downtown Program, P.O. Box 226, Fort Scott, KS 66701, 316/223-6088

WAMEGO, KANSAS

Tulip Festival

Wamego celebrates spring with its annual Tulip Festival. Thousands of Holland tulips are in colorful bloom as friends, families, and visitors gather in Wamego City Park for crafts, foods, and entertainment. Other highlights of the two-day festival include an antique auto tour of the community, a 4-H petting zoo, a fishing derby, the Dutch Mill Bike Ride, and rides through the park on Wamego's miniature train, the "Tulip Blossom Special."

ADMISSION: *None*
DATE: *Third weekend in April*

July Fourth Celebration

For more than 100 years, Wamego has observed Independence Day in a bang-up fashion, but with a traditional, old-fashioned spirit. Its Fourth of July parade is recognized as one of the largest in Kansas, annually attracting more than 10,000. It traditionally includes Shrine units, antique cars, local dignitaries, and hometown folks putting their patriotism on display. The celebration also features a four-day carnival (July 1-4), a community picnic, an antique and classic car show, an antique tractor and steam engine show, and a giant fireworks display.

ADMISSION: *None*
DATE: *July 1-4*

Fall Festival

One of the most popular fall events in Kansas is Wamego's Fall Festival. It features a large craft show with a variety of ethnic foods along Wamego's Lincoln Avenue downtown. In the afternoon, a cabaret and beer garden treat visitors to refreshments and local entertainment. There are also bingo, a quilt show, a biathalon, and games for kids. The music continues into the night, with dancing to live bands for adults and a separate dance for the teens.

ADMISSION: *None*
DATE: *First Saturday in September*

About Wamego

WAMEGO, A SMALL RURAL TOWN on the banks of the Kansas River, was founded by seven men with a purpose to develop a new settlement. The town observed many Oregon Trail travelers, who had to cross the Kansas River near Wamego. During the Civil War and the "Bleeding Kansas" years, Wamego saw conflict arising from the dispute over making Kansas a slave state. Antislavery activists came from Connecticut to keep it a "free" state, bringing rifles and Bibles and creating outposts such as the Beecher Bible and Rifle Church, built in 1862 outside Wamego. The town prospered after the war and into the twentieth century, as theaters, banks, churches and other institutions were constructed. With the initiation of the Main Street program in 1988, Wamego has turned back to its history as a foundation for the downtown's revitalization. It has initiated an investment of more than $2.5 million for rehabilitation projects and created 75 jobs for downtown Wamego.

WHAT TO EXPLORE WHILE IN TOWN: Because of its location on the Oregon Trail, Wamego has some interesting local sites. The Louis Vieux Elm, just outside town, is the largest American elm in the United States. It stands where Louis Vieux, a Pottawatomie Indian, once operated the first ferry along the Oregon Trail. Nearby is a cemetery where many Oregon Trail travelers are buried. The Columbian Theatre holds six large oil paintings purchased by its owner at the Columbian Exposition of 1893, which are the only known survivors of decorative art from the Exposition. The theater is now restored to a live performance venue, thanks to initial coordination by the Main Street program. The Beecher Rifle and Bible Church outside town is a reminder of Kansas's antislavery conflict. A walking and driving tour of sites of interest is available at the Chamber/Main Street office.

GETTING THERE: Wamego is located in eastern central Kansas, northwest of Topeka at the junction of Kansas Route 99 and US-24. It is accessible from Interstate 70 by taking exit 328, heading north on Kansas Route 99 for 10 miles.

FOR MORE INFORMATION: Wamego Main Street Program, P.O. Box 34, Wamego, KS 66547, 913/456-7849

Nebraska

ALLIANCE, NEBRASKA

Sandhills Celebration

This is a community event that allows people to get together during the busy summer in Alliance. It features square dancing, a junior rodeo, a village set up by the local Mato Jamni Indian Tribe, and other events that reflect the heritage of the Nebraska Sandhills. Kids enjoy Art in the Park, where hands-on activities are planned just for them. An international food festival, a dinner theater, local entertainment in the park, and free watermelon are all in store. The highlight of the event is a country-western music concert with a nationally known performer. There is a farmers market, and guided heritage walking tours are also available during the event.

ADMISSION: *None*
DATE: *Second week of July*

About Alliance

ALLIANCE ONCE SERVED as a land office for homesteaders, attracting agriculture and livestock producers to the area. Later, it became a major stop on the railroad. Trains unloaded their passengers and freight, generating development to the east and west of the depot. After three fires during 1892-93 destroyed most of the town's buildings, new development began, establishing Box Butte Avenue. Box Butte Avenue is a brick-paved street with many historic buildings dating from the growth period of 1883-1930. These buildings are included in a walking tour. Alliance was selected as a pilot community for the Nebraska-Lied Main Street program in 1994. As a result, merchants are beginning to restore and rehabilitate their buildings, and Alliance Main Street looks forward to guiding the revitalization of the downtown as its efforts progress and take hold.

WHAT TO EXPLORE WHILE IN TOWN: For a brochure on a walking tour of the historic buildings of Box Butte Avenue and the history of the town, stop by the Main Street office at 204 East Third Street. Don't miss the Box Butte County Courthouse, listed in the National Register of Historic Places, and the Art Deco Alliance Theater.

GETTING THERE: Located in western Nebraska, Alliance is at the junction of US-385 and NE-2. The nearest interstate is 80, about 80 miles south on US-385.

FOR MORE INFORMATION: Alliance Main Street, P.O. Box 802, Alliance, NE 69301, 308/762-1800

Red Cloud Streetcar Days

This event celebrates the horse-drawn streetcar era in Red Cloud. Red Cloud began operating a "horse street railway" in 1888, which ran from the Burlington and Missouri Railroad depot to the downtown hotels. The line was in operation until 1917 and was the last horse-drawn streetcar in the United States. Activities at this event includes farmers' olympics, horseshoe pitching, a toad and frog jumping contest, sack races, a parade down Main Street, a country-western dance, a firemen's barbecue, and more.

ADMISSION: *Fee for admission to some events*
DATE: *Second weekend in August*

About Red Cloud

RED CLOUD, NAMED FOR the famed chief of the Oglala Sioux, is probably best known as the home of author Willa Cather, who wrote about life on the Nebraska prairie in the late 1800s. The town has a Willa Cather Historic District, which includes buildings important to the author. Historic preservation has been active in Red Cloud, saving Willa Cather structures as well as others. It recently organized a downtown revitalization program and became part of the Nebraska Main Street program, which has begun building on its preservation efforts with revitalization strategies.

WHAT TO EXPLORE WHILE IN TOWN: Your first stop should be the Willa Cather Pioneer Memorial at 326 North Webster Street, which can provide walking tour brochures of the area, highlighting the Willa Cather buildings, and other tourist information. Related sites are the Willa Cather Home and the 1885 Opera House, which Cather mentioned in her books and which served as the site of her high school graduation ceremony in 1890. The restored 1897 Burlington and Missouri Depot was impor-

Willa Cather Pioneer Memorial

tant in Red Cloud's history, and now features an exhibit on the area's colonization and development. The Starke Round Barn, built in 1902, measuring 130 feet in diameter and three stories high—making it one of the largest of its kind in the nation—is also on the National Register. The Nature Conservancy owns the Willa Cather Memorial Prairie, a 610-acre tract of unbroken prairie, combining charactertistics of both the tallgrass prairie of the east and shortgrass prairie of the west.

GETTING THERE: Red Cloud is located in southern Nebraska in the Republican River valley. It is situated at the junction of US-281 and US-136. The nearest interstate is I-80, about 58 miles to the north.

FOR MORE INFORMATION: Historic Red Cloud Main Street, 540 North Webster, Red Cloud, NE 68970, 402/746-2303

South Dakota

BELLE FOURCHE, SOUTH DAKOTA

Annual Black Hills Roundup

This event, celebrating its 79th birthday in 1998, is an American original. The original roundup was organized to give area residents a chance to get together to celebrate the nation's birthday and demonstrate their ranching skills in a competitive arena. The Roundup is comprised of an array of events for the whole family to enjoy and partici- pate in, including three days of professional rodeo action, a Fourth of July parade, the Miss South Dakota Rodeo Pageant, a carnival, and fireworks.

The Annual Black Hills Roundup has been a Belle Fourche tradition for almost 80 years.

ADMISSION: *Fees for rodeo admission and carnival rides*
DATE: *July 2-4*

About Belle Fourche

BELLE FOURCHE (French for "beautiful fork") was named by French explorers in the mid-1800s. With the arrival of the railroad in 1895, Belle Fourche became the world's largest livestock shipping point. Despite a fire that destroyed much of the downtown business district in 1895, as well as the ups, downs, and changes in the agri- cultural industry over the past 100 years, Belle Fourche has grown and survived as a major agricultural hub. It also acts as the gateway to the beautiful Black Hills. With the addition of Alaska and Hawaii as states, Belle Fourche became the geographic center of the United States.

WHAT TO EXPLORE WHILE IN TOWN: A large portion of the downtown business dis- trict has been included in the National Register of Historic Places. A walking tour and information are available at the Center of the Nation Building. Bob's Cafe and Prime Time, a notable local eatery, has received praises from as far away as Chicago.

GETTING THERE: Belle Fourche is in western South Dakota, situated on US-85, a scenic highway. It is accessible by Interstate 90, which is about 10 miles to the south at exit 10.

FOR MORE INFORMATION: Belle Fourche Chamber of Commerce, 415 Fifth Avenue, Belle Fourche, SD 57717, 605/892-2676

Wyoming

LARAMIE, WYOMING

Jubilee Days

See the Old West come alive during Laramie's Jubilee Days, the annual celebration of Wyoming's entry into statehood. This is a celebration of world-class professional rodeos, cattle drives, parades, and fun. Bring your appetite for barbecue and the free pancake breakfast, with volunteers serving more than 2,300 people in a little over two hours' time. The four days of fun provide entertainment such as cowboy poetry, western music karaoke, the Great Prison Break 5k run, and Fourth of July fireworks. Try the two-step or the Cotton-Eyed Joe at the country-western dance under the stars. And don't miss the cattle drive, which "gets those little doggies along" down Main Street. Jubilee Days is your chance to see the West the way it used to be—and still is—in Laramie.

ADMISSION: *None for general events; rodeo is $8*
DATE: *Third weekend in July*

Volunteers flipping hotcakes for the free pancake breakfast at Jubilee Days.

About Laramie

IN THE SPRING OF 1868, the Union Pacific Railroad's chief surveyor chose Laramie's townsite for its water supply, as well as other resources that would benefit the Union Pacific, naming it for French trapper Jacque LaRamie. Laramie was created

amid the great push toward settlement of the American West. The Downtown Development Authority (DDA) of Laramie has been in place since 1989, improving the downtown, working with building owners to maintain the historic character of their buildings and the community as a whole. The DDA has been involved with over

Jubilee Days parade is one of the many events held in historic, revitalized, downtown Laramie.

$3.5 million worth of reinvestment in the downtown, and has issued more than $1 million in low-interest loans and grants for rehabilitation projects.

WHAT TO EXPLORE WHILE IN TOWN: Much of the downtown area is a National Register Historic District, and a walking tour brochure is available at the DDA office at 316 South Third Street and at the chamber of commerce at 800 South Third Street. Make sure to see the site of Laramie's first jail where, among others of its notorious prisoners, Jack McCall, Wild Bill Hickok's murderer, was held. The great Victorian depot in town is still used by Amtrak. The Wyoming Territorial Park is a living history museum of the Wyoming Territorial Prison, which once housed Butch Cassidy and is one of the few surviving territorial prisons that were built in the country's early days. The American Heritage Center at the University of Wyoming draws scholars from around the world to its collection on western history. Within an hour's drive of Laramie are more than 800,000 acres of National Forest lands, teeming with wildlife and offering prairie vistas.

GETTING THERE: Laramie is located in southeastern Wyoming on US-287, just off Interstate 80. It is also 47 miles from Interstate 25.

FOR MORE INFORMATION: Downtown Development Authority, 316 South Third Street, Laramie, WY 82070, 307/721-8881, e-mail: dda@lariat.org

Chili Round Up

The Chili Round Up is the state chili championship competition, sanctioned by the International Chili Society. The event takes place on Grinnell Street right in the heart of historic downtown Sheridan. Music, arts and crafts, and games for kids await visitors. Talk to the maestros of chili concoction as they hone their culinary craft in preparing for the competition. Afterward, brave visitors will be able to purchase samples of the fiery dishes.

Competitors at the Chili Round Up prepare their brew.

ADMISSION: *None*
DATE: *Second Saturday in July*

Christmas Stroll

Celebrate the beginning of the Christmas season in downtown Sheridan with a stroll down Main Street. Carolers set the mood, and horse-drawn wagons offer tours of the historic downtown area. There is also a petting zoo for kids. Downtown merchants hold open houses, displaying their Christmas merchandise, and Santa is scheduled to make an appearance.

ADMISSION: *None*
DATE: *Friday after Thanksgiving*

About Sheridan

SHERIDAN WAS PLANNED by John D. Loucks in 1882 on the back of a sheet of wrapping paper, which was all he had to write on at the time. Named after Loucks's Civil War commander, General Philip Sheridan, it was incorporated in 1884. The town grew with the coming of the railroad, the opening of many coal mines, and the development of area ranchlands. By 1900 the population reached 1559, and many of the false front, wood frame buildings constructed in the settlement years were replaced between 1910 and 1920 with sturdier structures of brick and stone. The Bozeman Trail, created as a result of the gold rush in Bozeman, Montana, passed through what is now Main Street in downtown Sheridan. Many colorful characters, including Buffalo Bill, have frequented this western town during its history.

WHAT TO EXPLORE WHILE IN TOWN: Visit the historic Sheridan Inn at 865 Broadway, home of Buffalo Bill. The Trail End Historic Center, at 400 Clarendon Street, is a house museum dating from the cattle baron days. Tour the Quarter Circle Ranch located in Big Horn, 12 miles south of Sheridan. A walking tour brochure is available from merchants in the downtown area.

Take a western hayride at Sheridan's Christmas Stroll.

GETTING THERE: Sheridan is located in north central Wyoming, just off Interstate 90.

FOR MORE INFORMATION: Uptown Sheridan Association, P.O. Box 13, Sheridan, WY 82801, 307/672-8881, e-mail: uptown@wave.sheridan.wy.us, http://wave.sheridan.us.wy/~uptown

SOUTHWESTERN
STATES

Arizona

New Mexico

Oklahoma

Texas

Arizona

COTTONWOOD, ARIZONA

Sizzling Salsa Saturday

This Cinco de Mayo celebration honors the area's Mexican heritage. The main event is a salsa tasting competition among Verde Valley restaurants, with entries in the medium, hot, and most unusual categories. Festivities are held on two blocks of Old Town Cottonwood's Main Street and include mariachis, Ballet Folklorico, charros (Mexican cowboys), and lots of food. The day culminates in a live Latin music street dance.

ADMISSION: *None*
DATE: *First Sunday in May*

The Chocolate Lovers Dessert Walk

This event is a chocoholic's dream come true, allowing you to sample chocolates from the best bakeries, restaurants, and home kitchens in the Verde Valley. The festivities are held in Cottonwood's Old Town, and visitors stroll along four blocks of Main Street, sampling chocolate goodies at participating shops. Enjoy holiday lights and decorations, carolers, and seasonal music, and relax with hot cocoa or cider. Call ahead for ticket availability—this is a popular event.

ADMISSION: *$10*
DATE: *First Friday in December*

About Cottonwood

AN OASIS IN THE DESERT by the lush Verde River, amid the shady trees that are its namesake, Cottonwood began as a farming settlement in the 1870s. With the advent of copper mining in the surrounding area, it soon became the commercial hub of the Verde Valley. When a bypass was built in the 1970s, traffic was diverted from Cottonwood's historic business district, which led to the development of several shopping malls on its outskirts. Subsequently, the Old Town area fell on hard times. Through the efforts of the Old Town Association and the Arizona Main Street program, Old Town is being revitalized and is on its way to becoming a tourist attraction as an authentic western town. Old Town now hosts a wide variety of art, antiques, services, and unique shops, and renovated historic buildings.

WHAT TO EXPLORE WHILE IN TOWN: Tourist information is available at the Old Jail, which houses the Old Town Association. The Clemenceau Museum chronicles the area's early history, its mining and farming days, and the railroads that served the area.

Dead Horse State Park, which offers camping and fishing, is a stone's throw from Old Town, or dig in to a chuckwagon supper or western stage show at the adjacent Blazin' M Ranch. With the Tuzigoot National Monument and its Sinagua Indian ruins, as well as the Verde Canyon train ride as other options, you'll have no problem getting a taste of the Old West.

GETTING THERE: Cottonwood is located in central Arizona in the Prescott National Forest, accessible by State Highway Alternative 89, off Interstate 17.

FOR MORE INFORMATION: The Old Town Association/Main Street Program, 1101 North Main Street, Cottonwood, AZ 86326, (520) 634-9468

New Mexico

CARLSBAD, NEW MEXICO

Western Week Celebration

Join the stampede to Carlsbad MainStreet and soak up some western culture during fun-filled Western Week. The event begins with a parade, then proceeds to the court-house area, where you'll find cowboy poets and singers, a home-style barbe-cue, a petting zoo, stick horse races for the little ones, and a dunking booth fea-turing local notables. Other activities include an American Junior Rodeo Association rodeo competition, a street dance, and a pancake breakfast.

ADMISSION: *None*
DATE: *Wednesday through Saturday of the first weekend in July*

Hometown Christmas

At Christmastime downtown Carlsbad is filled with white-faced high school mimes seeking an audience for balloon giveaways and silent performances. Hometown Christ-mas activities at the courthouse area culminate with the annual lighting of the city's giant Christmas tree, followed by the annual light parade with more than 25 floats.

ADMISSION: *None*
DATE: *The day after Thanksgiving*

About Carlsbad

IN A TRULY AMERICAN FASHION, Carlsbad was born in 1888 when a daughter of one of the area's developers bashed a bottle of champagne on the banks of the Pecos River to christen the proposed new city. By naming the town Carlsbad, after the famous European health resort, Karlsbad, Bohemia (now Czechoslovakia), its developers were hoping to attract residents and visitors because of the mineral content and related healing properties of its water. In 1922 an organized expedition explored the large caverns southwest of town, which were so impressive that President Coolidge proclaimed the site Carlsbad Caverns National Monument the following year. By 1930 it was named a National Park, which has continued to fuel tourism. Lately, the Main Street program has been successful in improving the image of downtown by coordinating banners and working with businesses to improve their building facades.

WHAT TO EXPLORE WHILE IN TOWN: Take a scenic drive through town and its surroundings with the Explore Carlsbad visitors guide available at the Chamber of Commerce at Canal and Greene Streets. Also available is information on not-to-be-missed sites such as Carlsbad Caverns National Park, Living Desert State Park, the Carlsbad Museum and Art Center, and recreational activities on the Pecos River.

GETTING THERE: Carlsbad is located in southeastern New Mexico at the junction of US-285 and US-62/180. It is approximately 160 miles northeast of El Paso and 275 miles south of Albuquerque.

FOR MORE INFORMATION: Carlsbad MainStreet, P.O. Box 910, Carlsbad, NM 88220, 505/887-6516

LOS ALAMOS, NEW MEXICO

MainStreet Earth Day Celebration

Earth Day in Los Alamos, of all places, truly brings the community together. It's a day of events for young and old, taking place throughout the downtown. It demonstrates what various community groups can do to show the impact they have on the care of the earth and the life it sustains. Exhibitions and demonstrations are held by groups as disparate as the county landfill recycling experts, search and rescue teams and their

An exhibitor at Los Alamos' MainStreet Earth Day Celebration.

canines, a young girl and her snake collection, the local weaving guild, Hazmat equipment operators, astronomers, forest fire fighters, fly-fishers, and scientists. There are hands-on learning activities, food, and music as well.

ADMISSION: *None*
DATE: *Saturday after the observed Earth Day*

About Los Alamos

FOR RESIDENTS AND VISITORS ALIKE, Los Alamos is known as Atomic City, because of its connection to Los Alamos National Laboratory—home of the atomic bomb. But Los Alamos is much more, and the Laboratory and the county government have joined to diversify the economic base by capitalizing on outstanding educational facilities and research opportunities. Los Alamos is also a Main Street community, working with the New Mexico Main Street Program. Los Alamos MainStreet has been active in recruiting businesses for downtown, helped to relocate the National Laboratory's museum to downtown Los Alamos, and pro-

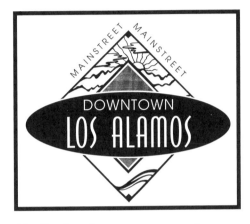

vided leadership, direction, and organized funding for a downtown streetscape improvements project on Central Avenue.

WHAT TO EXPLORE WHILE IN TOWN: There are plenty of attractions for visitors, chronicling Los Alamos from ancient times to the Manhattan Project. The Los Alamos Historical Museum offers a history of Los Alamos, from its early habitation to the Atomic Age. The Los Alamos National Laboratory's Bradbury Science Museum provides insight on the history of the Laboratory's past projects and information on its current ones. Visitors can also explore Fuller Lodge and the surrounding ranch schoolhouses. Outside Los Alamos, there are Bandalier National Monument (a must-see), the Tewa Indian ruins, and the Santa Fe National Forest. Walking tour brochures and other tourist information can be obtained at the Tourist Information Center at 800 Trinity Drive, Suite C, and at the Historical Museum at 1921 Juniper Street.

GETTING THERE: Los Alamos is located in north central New Mexico, north and west of Santa Fe. It is situated on NM Route 4 near the major NM Route 68. It is also close to Interstate 25, which is about 25 miles to the south.

FOR MORE INFORMATION: Los Alamos MainStreet, 800 Trinity Drive, Suite C, P.O. Box 460, Los Alamos, NM 87544, 505/662-9204

ROSWELL, NEW MEXICO

Roswell UFO Encounter

This annual get-together of believers takes the incident at Roswell very seriously, with a week-long event featuring speakers and theorists providing lectures on their theories and findings in encounters with those Not of This Earth. But it also offers a lot of fun, pushing some ideas a bit beyond believability. Along with crash site tours, there are the Flying Saucer Pancake Eating Contest and the Alien Chase 5k/10k walk-run. If your unidentified flying object has two wheels and is human-powered, you can enter the UFO Cycling Classic to benefit Habitat for Humanity. And not to be missed is the Crash and Burn Extravaganza, challenging participants to create a human-powered space craft that relies on wheels and a really big hill to get its energy.

ADMISSION: *Some activities have fees; most are free*
DATE: *First week in July*

The Pecos Valley Chile and Cheese Festival

This hot, hot, hot event is held as a big "thank you" to the farmers and ranchers of the Pecos Valley for their tremendous contribution to the region's economy. The best wool

and alfalfa in the world are said to be grown here, the high-quality alfalfa allowing dairy farmers to get more milk from their cows. The area is also fast becoming world famous for its chile products, some of which are being used in new and unusual applications: as additives in paint to keep livestock from chewing fences, and on boat hulls to keep barnacles off. This event features lots of fun and food; there are arts and crafts, a fiddler's competition, an outdoor dairy classroom, world champion yodeling, a chile ristra workshop to make the chile pepper strings so notable in the Southwest, a growers market, and horse-drawn depot wagon rides. Don't miss the bus tours to the local chile fields and world's largest mozzarella plant. And don't forget to buy your chiles—more than 10 tons of chile has been sold at past events.

ADMISSION: *None*
DATE: *Last weekend in September*

About Roswell

THE MAIN STREET APPROACH to downtown revitalization is nothing if not resourceful. Never one to pass up a good economic development opportunity, Main-Street Roswell has unabashedly used the UFO incident of 1947 as a tourism generator. The UFO Museum downtown attracts thousands of visitors, and Roswell is all hospitality. "We love aliens, as you might imagine," quips Dusty Huckabee, director of

Main Street Roswell. But Roswell has another history, before 1947, dating back to its origins as a campsite on the Goodnight-Loving Trail, which in 1868 brought Anglo ranchers to the area, thus initiating the ranching industry. In 1890 artesian water was discovered, and with this groundwater source, the economy turned to agriculture. The railroad brought settlers, who introduced all sorts of architectural styles. The resulting Roswell Historic District is an eclectic mix of styles, melding Hispanic and Anglo cultures. MainStreet Roswell, after years of a declining downtown, has facilitated new business as well as $13 million in new streets, lighting, and landscaping. It has also coordinated 31 building rehabilitations through its low-interest loan program and partnerships with local businesses and banks.

WHAT TO EXPLORE WHILE IN TOWN: Roswell's tourism brochure claims, "Some of our most famous visitors . . . came from out of state"—alluding to the famous "visit" of 1947. You can certainly soak up the UFO kitsch here with visits to the International UFO Museum and Research Center, at 400 North Main Street, and the UFO Enigma Museum, 6108 South Main Street. The Robert H. Goddard Planetarium gives shows and star talks. But in case you have had enough encounters for the day, there are other places where you can ground yourself: The Roswell Museum and Art Center houses New Mexico Modernist, Native American, and Hispanic art and artifacts; the Historical Center for Southeast New Mexico presents life in the Pecos Valley at the turn of the century; and the Roswell Community Little Theater gives theatrical performances throughout the year. Visit the Visitor and Tourism Bureau at 912 North Main for more information on what to see and do while in Roswell.

GETTING THERE: Roswell is located in southeastern New Mexico, at the junction of US-70/380 and US-285. The nearest interstate is 150 miles away.

FOR MORE INFORMATION: MainStreet Roswell, P.O. Box 1328, Roswell, NM 88201, 505/622-6706

Oklahoma

ARDMORE, OKLAHOMA

Ardmoredillo Chili Cookoff Festival

If you want the real Oklahoma, this is it: the Ardmoredillo Chili Cookoff, held downtown in conjuction with a local rodeo. This competition tests the locals' talent in concocting the best chili, salsa, and red beans, and with the purchase of a taster's cup, you can enjoy the fruits of their labor. Not to be missed is the special "showmanship" category of cooking, in which local businesses vie for style, such as one local church group's theme of the "ten cayennements." Events are planned for the entire family,

including cowboy poetry reading, country and western dancing, pony rides, and petting zoos. A children's rodeo clown costume contest, judged by professional rodeo clowns, is always a crowd pleaser. Enter the Ugly Cowboy Boot contest, the Ugly Pickup Truck contest, or, if you dare, the jalapeño eating contest.

Participants in the rodeo clown contest.

ADMISSION: *None*
DATE: *First weekend in April*

Taste of Ardmore and Art in the Park

This food and art event is an opportunity for both local restaurants and local artists to show their talents. Area restaurants provide samples of their best cuisine, available for a small charge. Art in the Park is a juried show held in the heart of the historic district. There are craft activities for kids, as well as puppet making. Young artists get to showcase their talents in the sidewalk chalk contest, as sidewalks become the canvas for their creative interpretation of "Downtown as Funtown." Live entertainment and fun for the entire family is featured, including a kids' area with pony rides, petting zoos, and carnival rides.

ADMISSION: *None, small fee for food samples*
DATE: *Last Thursday through Sunday in September*

About Ardmore

ARDMORE WAS FOUNDED IN 1887, as a refueling rest stop for the Santa Fe Railroad, on a site that was part of the Chickasaw Indian Nation. It is named for Ardmore, Pennsylvania, which was in turn named for Ardmore-by-the-Sea, Ireland. During the mid-1980s, the oil bust brought economic hardship, the community was losing population, and the downtown had a 40 percent vacancy rate. A strong city government supported the organization of a Main Street program, which, since its inception in 1989, has generated $10 million in reinvestment for the downtown, lowered the vacancy rate to 3 percent, brought in 77 new businesses, and increased retail sales by 46 percent. Most important, it has brought together partners for downtown's future, and downtown has returned as the heart of the community.

WHAT TO EXPLORE WHILE IN TOWN: The Southwest Historical Museum can provide local history. Several of Ardmore's oil baron mansions are open for tours. Ardmore is the home of the Noble Foundation, a medical research organization, which conducts tours through its facility. A walking and driving tour brochure is available at the Main Street office at 9 A Street and at downtown businesses.

GETTING THERE: Located in southern Oklahoma halfway between Oklahoma City and Dallas, Ardmore is situated just off Interstate 35 on US-70 and State Road 199.

FOR MORE INFORMATION: Ardmore Main Street Authority, 9 A Street, S.W., Ardmore, OK 73401, 405/226-6246

CHECOTAH, OKLAHOMA

Okrafest

To celebrate that much maligned, itchy vegetable, okra, Checotah Main Street blocks off the streets in downtown and holds a giant one-day food festival. The cook-off competition attracts more than 30 cooks, who prepare okra in unusual ways—okra grits, okra quesadillas, okra sausage, and okra pecan pie—as well as the traditional gumbos and fried okra. All entries are available for public tasting. Excitement builds for

participants and spectators alike in the Okra Eating Contest, the Okra Slime Balloon Toss, and the Okra Olympics. Live music emanates from two Okrayland stages, where "Karaokra" is a major crowd pleaser.

ADMISSION: *None*
DATE: *Second Saturday in September*

About Checotah

THE AREA AROUND CHECOTAH became home to the Creek Indians when they were relocated from the east in the 1830s. It was in 1872, when the M-K-T Railroad built a line south through Indian territory, that the railroad honored a Creek chief by naming its railhead "Checote Switch." Later, a mapmaker's error renamed the town Checotah. After a fire in 1992 that destroyed one-fourth of the downtown's National Register Historic District, the Main Street program served as catalyst in rebuilding the burned-out block, assisted other building owners in the rehabilitation of their buildings, and has promoted the downtown to achieve its fullest economic potential and vitality.

WHAT TO EXPLORE WHILE IN TOWN: The first stop in Checotah should be at the Katy depot. Built in 1890 and listed on the National Register, it was restored in 1988 and now serves as a museum and tourist information center. A Civil War battle was fought here in 1863, known as the Battle of Honey Springs, which was a decisive Union victory. It was historically significant because of its diverse participants: Native Americans, Hispanics, blacks, and whites. Its Visitors Center and memorial can provide background information on the participants and the battle.

GETTING THERE: Checotah is located in eastern Oklahoma on US Highway 69, just north of Interstate 40.

FOR MORE INFORMATION: Checotah Main Street, P.O. Box 96, Checotah, OK 74426, 918/473-4178

EL RENO, OKLAHOMA

Onion Fried Burger Day Festival

Served up by El Reno Main Street, this festival celebrates El Reno's world renowned "onion fried hamburger." The focal point of the celebration is the Big Burger, more than 8 1/2 feet in diameter, weighing more than 650 pounds, and cooked over an open pit fire. If you are there early enough, you can get a free bite of the big one. Downtown El Reno bustles with family fun: live entertainment, an arts festival, a classic car show, and lots of kids' activities. Early in the morning, you can compete in the "Bun Run," a 5k and 10k walk/run.

ADMISSION: *None*
DATE: *First Saturday in May*

About El Reno

LOCATED AT THE INTERSECTION of two historic highways, Route 66 and the old Chisholm Trail (which is Highway 81), El Reno reflects Oklahoma's history. Founded on the date of a land rush, April 22, 1889, the city later played host to thousands of land seekers in two later land runs. The construction of the Rock Island Rail-

road through El Reno caused residents to abandon nearby Reno City, moving their posessions, even their houses, south to El Reno. A three-story hotel building was moved, then stranded on a riverbed, but operated continuously. Later it was moved to more stable ground. In recent years El Reno experienced economic decline, but since 1988 the El Reno Main Street program has diligently worked to restore downtown as the heart of the community, with more than 50 buildings undergoing rehabilitation and new businesses being recruited to the downtown annually.

WHAT TO EXPLORE WHILE IN TOWN: The Canadian County Historical Museum is housed in a restored Rock Island passenger terminal. On the grounds, you'll also find a number of buildings pertinent to local history—General Sheridan's cabin dating from the Indian wars, the original El Reno Hotel, and the first Red Cross Hut—all of which are on the National Register. Information can be obtained at the chamber of commerce, located at 206 North Bickford in downtown El Reno.

GETTING THERE: El Reno is located in central Oklahoma, just off Interstate 40. It is situated west of Oklahoma City at the junction of US Highways 40 and 81.

FOR MORE INFORMATION: El Reno Main Street, P.O. Box 606, 117 North Choctaw, El Reno, OK 73036, 405/262-8888

STOCKYARDS CITY, OKLAHOMA CITY, OKLAHOMA

Stockyards Stampede Festival

This award-winning festival is held to celebrate Oklahoma's rich western heritage. It features gunfighter reenactments, a bull riding competition (with real bulls), storytellers and liars competitions, horseshoe pitching, and activities for kids. For food, there are barbecue and chili cook-offs. This event is held in historic Stockyards City, a district that preserves a vital part of the state's western heritage.

ADMISSION: *None*
DATE: *First weekend in June*

About Stockyards City, Oklahoma City

STOCKYARDS CITY, LOCATED IN Oklahoma City, was founded in 1910 and built to service the nation as a primary source for meat processing and packing. By 1915, Stockyards City was home to three established packing facilities to slaughter and process cattle, hogs, and sheep, which were transported to the area first by cattle drive, then later by rail and truck. When the meat-packing plants moved from Stockyards City, the area began a downward trend. Through the efforts of the Main Street program, many business and property owners were encouraged

Western activites abound at the Stockyards Stampede Festival.

to invest their money in rehabilitating their buildings. Once these renovations started, a domino effect occurred. The area now has a low vacancy rate and boasts more than 130 new jobs.

WHAT TO EXPLORE WHILE IN TOWN: Stockyards City has built its revival on its western heritage. Here you can find hand-crafted saddles, boots, and hats, and in some cases you can actually watch the artisans at work. It's also home to the Oklahoma National Stockyards, the largest stocker and feeder cattle market in the world. Cattle auctions are held each Monday and Tuesday, where you can get a glimpse of the operation and some of the more than 105 million head of cattle that have passed through its historic iron gates.

GETTING THERE: Stockyards City, in Oklahoma City, is in the dead center of the state. It is accessible by many major roads, including Interstates 35 and 40, and US-44.

FOR MORE INFORMATION: Stockyards City Main Street, 2501 Exchange Avenue, Room 118, Oklahoma City, OK 73108, 405/235-7267

PERRY, OKLAHOMA

Cherokee Strip Celebration

The Cherokee Strip Celebration remembers the "hopes and dreams" of the 100,000 participants in the largest land run in history, held on September 16, 1893. The day is planned to be full of events such as the Ugliest Truck contest, a rodeo, a carnival, and many other community activities. During the Li'l Settlers Land Run, children aged two to four, dressed in period costume, race to stake their claims. The morning continues with a parade of more than 100 entries, stagecoach rides, horseshoe pitching, staged gunfights, and day-long musical entertainment. The day concludes with a street dance.

Parade entries in the Cherokee Strip Celebration.

ADMISSION: *None*
DATE: *Second Saturday in September*

About Perry

PERRY, OKLAHOMA, SPRANG UP following the gunshot that started the Cherokee Strip Land Run of September 16, 1893. Since its early days as "Queen of the Cherokee Strip," Perry has settled into a calmer, largely agricultural existence as the center of Noble County government and headquarters of a large machine works. The attractive and historic downtown square remains the hub of social, business, and retail activities for the more than 5,000 residents. Over the past two years, Perry Main Street has worked to recharge the economy of the town. These efforts are reflected in the facade renovations on the square, which were initiated with Main Street design assistance.

WHAT TO EXPLORE WHILE IN TOWN: Stop in at the Kumback Lunch, the oldest cafe in continuous existence at one location in Oklahoma. Foster's Corner Drug still serves at an authentic soda fountain complete with 1950s neon lighting. The Cherokee Strip Historical Museum, on West Fir Avenue, houses an extensive photo collection and other exhibits. Information and a walking tour brochure are available at the Perry Main Street offices, at the southeast corner of the square in the J.P. Foucart Building.

GETTING THERE: Perry is located in northern Oklahoma, situated on US-64. It is directly off Interstate 35 at exit 186 and is accessible by US-412 (the Cimarron Turnpike) and US-44 (the Turner Turnpike) as well.

FOR MORE INFORMATION: Perry Main Street, P.O. Box 128, Perry, OK 73077, 405/336-1212

Texas

BRYAN, TEXAS

Mardi Gras Brazos Style

Bryan celebrates Mardi Gras in its own Texas style, as downtown comes alive with the special sights and sounds of this festival. Local bands play at the Palace Theater, and foods, crafts, and games abound in the downtown streets. A barbecue competition heats up with awards in the beans, chicken, ribs, and brisket categories. There's the traditional Mardi Gras beads giveaway, and children stay busy in the kids' area with games, clowns, and train rides.

ADMISSION: *None*
DATE: *Second Saturday in February*

Diez y Seis

This is a celebration of the local Hispanic culture of the Bryan area. Diez y Seis features music and dancing, and food and craft vendors offer a variety of Hispanic and Tex-Mex favorites. Apearances by Tejano bands, Ballet Folklorico dancers, and mariachis set the festive mood for about 5,000 attendees in downtown Bryan.

ADMISSION: *None*
DATE: *Saturday closest to September 16; call ahead for exact date*

Hometowne Christmas Celebration

The aim of this Christmastime event is to bring families and neighbors together to share an evening in the holiday spirit. It's a time when merchants stay open late at night, horse-drawn carriages ply the streets, carolers sing from street corners, and Santa visits to take requests. The key to this event's success is full community involvement, from Girl Scouts and schoolchildren serving as carolers, to the local T.V. station doing weather broadcasts on location at the event.

ADMISSION: *None*
DATE: *First Friday in December*

About Bryan

THE CITY OF BRYAN was incorporated in 1871, and in the following years the once small-town stop along the railway flourished into a thriving community. Agricultural and mercantile businesses in Bryan were linked by rail to major markets across the country, and downtown Bryan grew to become the business center for the surrounding area. In the 1950s shopping centers were built in the area, which eventually drew many businesses from the downtown, leaving it virtually empty for years. In 1992, Bryan became a Texas Main Street city, and through public and private partnerships, buildings have been rehabilitated, businesses recruited, and improvements made to public facilities such as benches and trash receptacles.

WHAT TO EXPLORE WHILE IN TOWN: A walking tour brochure is available from downtown merchants and the Main Street office at 405 West 28th Street, along with other tourist information. Downtown Bryan is home to the oldest Carnegie Library in Texas, soon to become a museum of history. There are two community theaters, offering performances on a regular basis in downtown Bryan, as well as two live music venues doing the same.

GETTING THERE: Bryan is located in east Texas, northeast of Austin on Texas Highways 6 and 21/190. The nearest Interstate is I-45, about 40 miles to the east.

FOR MORE INFORMATION: Bryan Main Street Project, P.O. Box 1000, 405 West 28th Street, Bryan, TX 77805, 409/821-3409

ELGIN, TEXAS

Hogeye Festival

Elgin celebrates its title as the sausage capital of Texas with its one-of-a-kind Hogeye Festival, whose motto is "A time for warm hearts and hot guts." Elgin lives high on the hog as it pays tribute to its industry and its historic downtown. Thousands come to enjoy

Elgin hot sausage, unique arts and crafts, and live music on two stages. There's a hog calling contest and prodigious amounts of pithy porcine puns. The grand finale is Cow Patty Bingo, billed as "a departure from your average church bingo." Some lucky "hog" wins a jackpot depending on where Bessie does her business on a grid-lined street.

ADMISSION: *None*
DATE: *Fourth Saturday in October*

About Elgin

THE CITY OF ELGIN was created by the Houston and Texas Central Railroad on August 18, 1872, and was named for Robert Morris Elgin, the railroad's land commisioner. Early industries included cotton ginning and brick making. Now known as the Sausage Capital of Texas, the town ships its famous Elgin Hot Sausage nationwide. The historic downtown area continues to benefit from the Elgin Main Street program, whose motto is "Old town, new spirit." More than 40 buildings have been restored and are excellent examples of regional turn-of-the-century brick architecture.

WHAT TO EXPLORE WHILE IN TOWN: Walking tour brochures and other tourist information are available at the chamber of commerce, at 15 North Main, and at the city offices at 310 North Main. The City Cafe at 19 North Main opened in 1910, and its new owner has just completed a major renovation of the building. Simon's Department Store is the oldest retail establishment in Elgin, dating from 1912. Outside downtown, one can tour a brick factory, sausage companies, and breeding services. World-famous barbecue is available at Biggers BBQ and Southside BBQ, both on Highway 290, and Crosstown BBQ on Central Avenue.

GETTING THERE: Elgin is located just northeast of Austin, at the junction of US-290 and Texas Highway 95. It is about 20 miles east of Interstate 35.

FOR MORE INFORMATION: Elgin Main Street, P.O. Box 591, Elgin, TX 78621, 512/285-5721

Spring Ho

The name of this festival is derived from the expression of wagon train scouts upon finding water, and due to the rich mineral spring water supply in Lampasas. This event features all sorts of craziness: cow chip throwing contests, washer pitching contests, a diaper derby, and a greased pig contest. It also includes a parade, a barbecue cook-off, a talent show, a children's fishing contest, street dances, gospel singing, and much more. This event is so popular that most high school and family reunions are held during the week of the festival, which is expected to attract more than 40,000.

Participants in the Diaper Derby.

ADMISSION: *Some events require purchase of a badge for admission; others are free*
DATE: *First full week in July*

Lampasas Quilt Extravaganza

After discovering that so many local ladies were skilled in the art of quilting, locals decided to honor their work with an annual quilt show. That was 20 years ago, and this event is now better than ever. Visitors will see a combination of beautiful antique and new quilts, each year focusing on a different theme. There is an opportunity to win one of the quilts in a raffle. Quilts are displayed in various areas of the town, including the county courthouse and several historic homes.

ADMISSION: *$3*
DATE: *Second weekend in August*

Bluebonnet Fest and Farm Heritage Day

Every year in April in central Texas, visitors and locals alike take driving tours through the Hill Country to see the bluebonnets that blanket roadsides and fields, with everyone stopping to take photos of their loved ones amid the brilliant color. Lampasas celebrates this rite of spring each year with the Bluebonnet Fest. This day-long event features an arts and crafts fair, a classic car exhibit, a petting zoo, an Easter egg hunt, and pony rides. Lampasas is situated in the heart of ranch country, and to honor this backbone of the community, Farm Heritage Day is celebrated at the same time, featuring farm exhibits of old and new equipment.

ADMISSION: *None*
DATE: *First Saturday in April*

Herb/Art Fest

This unusual art festival takes place in the downtown square. Visitors browse through an exhibit of local and regional artists including painters, photographers, sculptors, and potters. Booths feature herbs, dried flowers and grasses, herbal foods and beverages, Texas native plants, topiaries, gardening items, and more. The event also features herb experts and authors in informal herbal demonstrations. Special herbal menu items are available at downtown restaurants.

ADMISSION: *None*
DATE: *Second Saturday in October*

About Lampasas

LAMPASAS, THE COUNTY SEAT, was originally settled in 1850 by John Burleson, who received 1,280 acres in 1838 for his services in the Texas Revolution. Significant mineral springs were discovered, and by 1882 the railroad came to Lampasas and the town was filled with spas and resorts. For several years, Lampasas was a boom town where people all over the country came to bathe in the healing mineral water. When that era ended, the population dropped from 25,000 to less than 5,000. Since 1984, the Main Street program has revitalized the downtown square, working with building owners to encourage major investments in the rehabilitation of storefronts and extensive landscaping and to renew interest in shopping downtown. The program also coordinates six festivals and events to draw people back into the heart of the community.

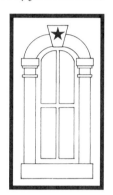

WHAT TO EXPLORE WHILE IN TOWN: Quite a few buildings remain from Lampasas' earlier days, and a walking tour brochure can be obtained at the chamber of commerce at 501 East Second Street. Notable structures include the J.N. Adkins Home, built in 1868 by Lampasas' first pioneer doctor, whose house material came from patients paying in stone rather than cash. The Keystone Hotel, built 1870, was a stagecoach stop, and the Little Hotel was built with stone left over from construction of the Keystone. You won't go hungry in Lampasas, with the Courtyard Cafe and Eve's Cafe on the square, the Third Street Coffee Shop on Third Street, a half block from the square, and Lisa's Schnitzel House, also on Third.

GETTING THERE: Lampasas is located in central Texas, northwest of Austin. It is situated at the junction of US-281 and US-183. It is also accessible via nearby Interstate 35, 55 miles to the east off US-190.

FOR MORE INFORMATION: City of Lampasas Main Street Program, 312 East Third Street, Lampasas, TX 76550, 512/556-6831

MARLIN, TEXAS

Market on Main Street

This event, which takes place twice a year in downtown Marlin, features antiques, crafts, food, and entertainment up and down the sidewalks. You can play cow patty bingo, win a raffle for a trip to Las Vegas, hear the Fort Hood First Armored Cavalry Division Band play, sing your own karaoke, take a pony ride, or build your own scarecrow in the children's area. These days of fun happen twice a year, at the changing of the seasons.

ADMISSION: *None*
DATE: *Third Saturday of March and September*

Miracle on Main Street

Miracle on Main Street is an annual Christmas celebration in Marlin featuring carriage rides through the historic downtown, a tour of homes, a breakfast with Santa, a children's workshop, a quilt show, and a lighted Christmas parade. There's even "ice skating" (if you count linoleum and a can of Pam). A Christmas food court and live music and caroling add to the ambience. The day-long event is planned to give all the Christmas spirit.

ADMISSION: *None, but nominal charges for some activities*
DATE: *First Saturday in December*

About Marlin

THE CITY OF MARLIN was established in 1866; however, it wasn't until 1893 when well drillers struck very hot mineral water that it began to bustle. By the turn of the century, Marlin was a mecca for those seeking the soothing benefits of the hot baths. Spas and clinics appeared on every street corner. With the advent of modern medicine, the popularity of the baths began to wane. The water still flows from the original Hot Water Pavilion, but the crowds are less constant. Since 1994, through the efforts of the Main Street program, Marlin has seen more than a half million dollars reinvested in the downtown, more than 45 buildings rehabilitated, and 41 new jobs. Much of this renewal has happened through its assistance to businesses to provide better lines of merchandise and incentive programs to rehabilitate their buildings. With continued emphasis on historic preservation and heritage tourism, Marlin hopes to tap into their economic benefits well into the next century.

WHAT TO EXPLORE WHILE IN TOWN: There's quite a lot of interesting local history in Marlin, and a walking tour brochure and other information are available at the chamber of commerce, housed in the Hot Water Pavilion at 245 Coleman Street. The eighth hotel in Conrad Hilton's chain was built in Marlin in 1929 during the bathhouse heyday. The Falls County Courthouse is the fourth to be built on that site, constructed in 1939 in Art Deco style. The oldest operating hardware store (since 1896) still opens its doors six days a week in downtown, under the name of RGB TrueValue Hardware, and still uses an old hand-pulled freight elevator. On Railroad Street, the Falls County Historical Museum is open Monday and Friday afternoons, adjacent to the vaudeville-era Palace Theater (1929) which stages live productions at least four times a year.

GETTING THERE: Marlin, located in east Texas, is situated at the junction of Texas Highways 6 and 7. It is between Interstates 35 and 45 and accessible by both from Highway 7.

FOR MORE INFORMATION: Marlin Main Street Project, 245 Coleman Street, P.O. Box 980, Marlin, TX 76661, 817/883-9203

MINEOLA, TEXAS

Iron Horse Heritage Days

This festival honors the railroad heritage of Mineola, and the importance of the railroad in the town's development and economy, with activities such as a trackside "Hobo Stew" supper, railroad memorabilia displays, and Railroad Museum tours. It lives up to its billing as "a family affair with something for everyone," with events planned for grown-ups (broadcasts of football games at the local furniture store, a classic car show, and horseshoe tournaments; an arts and crafts show, a chili cook-off, and a pie baking contest) and for kids (a petting zoo, pony rides, model train displays, and a mini art camp). Volunteers working with Main Street, from kids to senior citizens, have fun making this event happen.

ADMISSION: *None*
DATE: *Second weekend of October*

About Mineola

THE RAILROAD HAS ALWAYS PLAYED a vital role in Mineola's development and livelihood. The town was settled in the 1840s, but its boom came when the Northern and Texas Pacific railroads arrived in 1873, providing a vital link in the area's commerce. Along with many retirees, there are a large number of presently employed Union Pacific workers residing here. As a result of the oil bust in the region, Mineola suffered greatly; its downtown was a sad sight, with at least 60 percent of the buildings vacant. The Main Street program was established in 1989, giving Mineola the courage to move forward, offering tax abatements and incentives for businesses to renovate and relocate here. It achieved a 2 percent vacancy rate, which remains today. Downtown and Main Street are now the "heartbeat of Mineola."

WHAT TO EXPLORE WHILE IN TOWN: Mineola's buildings reflect a craftsmanship and artistry not found in today's construction, with decorative cast iron columns from the turn of the century standing with Carrara glass facades of the 1930s. Hotels built in the heyday of the railroads, as well as several historic homes, have been rehabilitated and serve as B & Bs as well as unique retail locations. The 70-year-old Select Theater, the only remaining movie house in the county, still offers first-run films on weekends. A walking tour guide brochure, along with a city map and other information, is available at area businesses and at the Chamber of Commerce.

GETTING THERE: Mineola is located in east Texas, east of Dallas at the junction of US-80 and US-69. It is about 20 miles north of Interstate 20 on US-69.

FOR MORE INFORMATION: Mineola Main Street/Tourism Project, 300 Greenville Highway, Mineola, TX 75773, 903/569-6944

MOUNT PLEASANT, TEXAS

Children's Patriotic Festivities

Bring your little ones to Mount Pleasant for a morning of fun on Independence Day. In the cool shade beneath the trees of Caldwell Park, this event just for kids features the hilarious 20-year-old Mount Pleasant Daily Tribune Turtle Race. Kids from all over race their favorite turtles in hope of winning first prize. Afterward they can enter a number of other events, including the cardboard boxcar races, a hula hoop-off, a watermelon seed spitting contest, and an apple pie bake-off. A number of other games keep kids entertained throughout the entire morning.

Cardboard boxcar racers warm up.

ADMISSION: *None*
DATE: *July 4*

About Mount Pleasant

ORIGINALLY CALLED PLEASANT MOUNT by the indigenous Caddo Indians, Mount Pleasant was founded on May 11, 1848, and serves as the seat for Titus County. Standing at the center of the downtown business district, the Titus County Courthouse was restored to its original 1940s appearance in 1991, sparking interest and pride in the appearance and vitality of the downtown area. This movement, along with the efforts of the Main Street program, has resulted in the reinvestment of more than $2 million in the downtown area since 1993. Mount Pleasant has twice been named one of the "100 Best Small Towns in America."

WHAT TO EXPLORE WHILE IN TOWN: The Main Street Bakery is a great place to enjoy a slice of the world-famous Laura's Cheesecake. The cakes are made right in the store and shipped around the world. Visitors to town should see the Legends and Lawless Museum and Larry Lawrence's Antiques, Cars & Parts. There is also a small museum in the basement of the local library, which is housed in the former post office building. One can also enjoy the natural beauty of Tankerlsey Gardens or take a self-guided tour of the Bluebird Trails of Texas. Information can be obtained at the Main Street offices at 501 North Madison.

GETTING THERE: Located in east Texas, Mount Pleasant is situated on US-271 just off Interstate 30 at exit 162.

FOR MORE INFORMATION: City of Mount Pleasant Main Street, 501 North Madison, Mount Pleasant, TX 75455, 903/575-4000

SAN MARCOS, TEXAS

Texas Natural and Western Swing Festival

This is a festival for all Texans—and those who wish they were. During the third weekend in May, downtown San Marcos dons denims, hats, and boots to celebrate everything Texan, from western swing music to chili and Dutch oven cook-offs. This festival highlights downtown retailers particpating in the Texas Natural program, which promotes Texas-made products and goods. The western swing music of Texas is featured during the day on the historic downtown square, along with trail rides, heritage crafts, cowboy poets, and more. Past activities have included armadillo races, gunfighters, and historical reenactments. Visit the Texas Marketplace, where products of the Lone Star state are sold, such as art, clothing, plants, leather goods, and food. Sit under the giant oaks on the courthouse lawn, or let your feet move you at this laid-back, toe-tappin' Texas good time!

Western swing musicians ensure a good time.

ADMISSION: *None*
DATE: *Third weekend in May*

The Sights and Sounds of Christmas

San Marcos begins the Christmas season with this weekend of lights, activities, food, and fun. The Wise men arrive by camel, and the traditional candlelight posadas processional is accompanied by mariachis. At the Night in Old San Marcos, you can sample biscuits baked over an open fire in a dutch oven, churn butter, make cornhusk dolls, and watch a variety of artisans at work. At the log schoolhouse, children may string cranberries and popcorn and decorate a community Christmas tree. At Old Bethlehem, authentically costumed characters preside over workshops where children can try their hand at making toys, sandals, or candles. The 5,000-square-foot Texas Marketplace offers a variety of Texas-made products for Christmas shopping. Santa and Mrs. Claus spend the evenings at Santa's Palace, taking requests, and the Sugar Plum Theater offers stories, puppet shows, and special entertainment for kids. Visitors at this three-day event enjoy starting the holiday season Texas style.

ADMISSION: *None*
DATE: *First full weekend in December*

About San Marcos

SAN MARCOS IS SITUATED at the border of the Texas Hill Country and the blackland prairie. The spring-fed San Marcos River flows through the city, providing habitat for several endangered species. Archaeologists have found evidence of Native Americans living along the river as far back as 12,000 years. The Spanish discovered the springs in 1689 on St. Mark's Day as they searched for LaSalle. The town was organized in 1851 and incorporated in 1877. Through the efforts of the Main Street program and the community, the downtown has once again become a viable business location. Through its innovative Texas Natural program, San Marcos Main Street has encouraged local businesses to carry products made in Texas, creating a market specialization for San Marcos. If you eat in a downtown cafe, the meat you enjoy is likely to have been raised in Texas. The clothing that catches your eye may be made of Texas cotton, wool, mohair, or leather, or designed and constructed in Texas. Once plagued with a declining retail market because of the development of a local mall and urban sprawl, the "heart of the city" is now home to specialty shops, galleries, and cafes as well as professional offices and service businesses.

WHAT TO EXPLORE WHILE IN TOWN: A visit to the Hill Country Humidor at 122 North LBJ Drive is an adventure. This shop has retained its original pressed tin ceiling, features Texas Travis Cigars, coffees, and art, and is noted for its popularity as a place where customers can play a game of dominos and hear the latest local news. The Cafe on the Square, at 126 North LBJ, is a local favorite for its breakfast tacos, microbrews, and Texas Ice Cream. A walking or driving tour guide is available at the Main Street offices at City Hall, 630 East Hopkins, and features the completely restored 1909 courthouse on the square.

GETTING THERE: San Marcos is located between San Antonio and Austin, just off Interstate 35.

FOR MORE INFORMATION: San Marcos Main Street Program, City Hall, 630 East Hopkins, San Marcos, TX 78666, 512/393-8430

WESTERN
STATES

California

Idaho

Oregon

Washington

California

BERKELEY, CALIFORNIA

The Jupiter Jam Jazz and Blues Festival

The Jupiter Jam is a series of four free jazz and blues concerts set within an urban street fair. Presented by the Downtown Berkeley Association, it is located in the budding arts district on Addison Street, just steps away from the Berkeley BART station. Historically, the event has attracted a diverse audience, representing all ages and ethnic backgrounds, from the Bay Area and beyond.

ADMISSION: *Donations welcome*
DATE: *First four Saturdays in August*

About Berkeley

EVERYONE OF A CERTAIN AGE knows about Berkeley, California. After its years as a hippie mecca in the late 1960s, the city has faced new issues in keeping its downtown vibrant. The Downtown Berkeley Association was formed by business and property owners concerned about the health of the central business district. Building on strengths of its history of political activism and the drawing power of University of California-Berkeley, it has developed an arts and entertainment district base to cater to the many visitors it welcomes each year. The Association has also been hard at work trying to improve its image with innovative solutions to perennial issues such as graffiti and panhandling.

WHAT TO EXPLORE WHILE IN TOWN: Downtown Berkeley features more than 100 shops, restaurants, cafes, and pubs, plus 21 movie screens—visitors won't lack for entertainment. Of special note is the Addison Street Arts District, which houses the acclaimed Berkeley Repertory Theater. A walking tour brochure is available at the Downtown Berkeley Association and at the Convention and Visitor's Bureau.

GETTING THERE: Berkeley is located 5 miles east of San Francisco on Interstate 80.

FOR MORE INFORMATION: Downtown Berkeley Association, 2230 Shattuck, Suite H, Berkeley, CA 94704, 510/ 549-2230

DINUBA, CALIFORNIA

Cinco de Mayo Celebration

This event salutes the Mexican-American culture and the diversity of this agricultural area. Mariachi music and folklorico dancing help to celebrate the Mexican Day of Independence. Food, crafts, and a good time are on the schedule for this festival held in downtown Dinuba.

ADMISSION: *None*
DATE: *First full weekend in May*

Dinuba Main Street Car Show

Don't be surprised if you're whistling the tune "Low Rider" while strolling through the myriad of vintage and modified cars at this show. This event is a hot rod lover's dream: Corvettes, Mustangs, T-birds, muscle cars, race vehicles, and street rods participate—more than 250 cars. The show, held in downtown Dinuba, includes food, events for kids, and opportunities for shop talk with car owners and enthusiasts.

ADMISSION: *None*
DATE: *First weekend in September*

Annual Raisin Festival

Dinuba honors its heritage by paying homage to the raisin with this festival. The raisin industry began here in the 1800s and continues to be a staple of the local agricultural economy. This event features food booths, crafts, and entertainment in a downtown park. The Raisin Festival parade makes its way through the Main Street district at 10:00 A.M. on Saturday.

ADMISSION: *None*
DATE: *Fourth Friday and Saturday in September*

About Dinuba

SITUATED IN THE SAN JOAQUIN VALLEY, one of the richest agricultural areas in the nation, Dinuba's life began with the arrival of the railroad in 1888 and the availability of water for irrigation. The raisin industry was introduced in the Valley in 1873 when experimental grapes were dried on the vines; five years later the raisin industry produced 500 tons, and it has grown ever since. Today Dinuba Main Street has taken a leading role in redefining the small town merchant as one who offers gracious and friendly service with competitive pricing and an upgraded mix of products.

WHAT TO EXPLORE WHILE IN TOWN: The town's new sidewalks, colorful banners, and rehabilitated storefronts were all coordinated by Dinuba Main Street. The Alta Irrigation building on north L Street has been designated a California Historical Landmark. The *Bountiful Hand* redwood carving by the renowned Carroll Barnes is part of a city park at South I and Kern Streets.

GETTING THERE: Dinuba is located 30 miles southeast of Fresno off State Highway 99.

FOR MORE INFORMATION: Dinuba Main Street, P.O. Box 672, Dinuba, CA 93618, 209/591-7000

EUREKA, CALIFORNIA

A Taste of Main Street

More than 20 of Eureka's restaurants will be preparing samples of their very best house specialties to enjoy at this culinary evening on Main Street. A ticket book buys a sampling of the North Coast's finest foods and live entertainment, followed by a big band dance. This event is a prelude to the Redwood Coast Dixieland Jazz Festival, to which shuttle bus service is provided.

ADMISSION: *$17.50*
DATE: *Fourth Thursday in March*

About Eureka

LOCATED ON HUMBOLDT BAY, Eureka and its waterfront boast an abundance of

art galleries, antique shops, and theaters. The development of its arts niche has been the foundation of the town's recent economic revitalization, thanks in large part to the Eureka Main Street program. Murals and phantom galleries—shop windows displaying local art—are some of the projects developed to encourage the arts economy. Eureka's Main Street program has played a key role in the revitalization of many of the historic downtown buildings.

Old Town Eureka.

WHAT TO EXPLORE WHILE IN TOWN: Visit the many downtown art galleries and studios, which are an important part of the local economy. Eureka's Victorian architecture is charming; walking tour guides, as well as business and restaurant guides, are available at the Main Street office. Downtown Eureka holds a farmers market every Tuesday from June to October. Cruises on Humboldt Bay are popular, and be sure to sample the local specialties: Dungeness crab, salmon, and Humboldt Bay oysters.

GETTING THERE: Eureka is located in northwest California on the coast, off State Highway 101.

FOR MORE INFORMATION: Eureka Main Street, 123 F Street, #6, Eureka, CA 95501, 707/442-9054

FAIRFIELD, CALIFORNIA

The Tomato Festival

The Tomato Festival celebrates Solano County's number one cash crop. Each year, when the time is ripe, the community of Fairfield gathers to pay homage to the fruit of its labor. On the agenda are a tomato eating contest, live entertainment, children's games, live music and a street dance, and a farmers market featuring tomatoes of all types.

ADMISSION: *None*
DATE: *First weekend in August*

About Fairfield

FOUNDED IN 1856 as the county seat, Fairfield's economy is based on agriculture. During the summer, growers from the Suisun Valley and neighboring areas converge on the downtown for the weekly Farmers Market. The improved facades of buildings downtown are due to the facade rebate program developed by the Downtown Improvement District. The area's brick sidewalks, streetlights, and benches also have been provided through the efforts of the downtown program.

The Farmers Market features plenty of tomatoes, as well as other fresh produce.

WHAT TO EXPLORE WHILE IN TOWN: The Fairfield Center for the Creative Arts, located in the downtown area, showcases local, national, and international talent. Free tours are also available at the local Jelly Belly jelly bean plant.

GETTING THERE: Fairfield is located northeast of San Francisco on Interstate 80.

FOR MORE INFORMATION: Downtown Improvement District, 625 Webster Street, Fairfield, CA 94533, 707/422-0103

FRESNO, CALIFORNIA

Sudz in the City

The Central California Micro-Brewery and Music Festival, dubbed "Sudz in the City," is the largest gathering of brewers in central California. The festival includes beer tasting under a big top tent, with entries from the West's finest brewmasters. With admission, you'll receive a souvenir glass, a guide to the brewers, and a scorecard to rate them. Also featured is live music by the best in blues, rock, and pop, with full concert staging and sound. Great food is also available to soak up the sudz. Taste the brews, enjoy the music, and relax in the shadow of the historic Fresno Water Tower downtown.

ADMISSION: *$25*
DATE: *Third Saturday in May*

Passport Fresno: International Food and Culture Festival

This colorful event spans three days, featuring food, music, dance, crafts, ritual, and costumes from the dozens of cultures comprising the Fresno melting pot. As you sample offerings from each country, you get your "passport" (either a booklet or a T-shirt) stamped. Nonstop entertainment on multiple stages, as well as food and crafts, is provided on the Fulton Mall downtown. Passport guidebooks are available for children, describing each event and the participating cultures.

ADMISSION: *Free*
DATE: *First week in October: Friday, Saturday, and Sunday*

About Fresno

FRESNO (SPANISH FOR "ASH TREE") was established in 1885 as a depot along the Southern Pacific Railroad. At the center of the San Joaquin Valley, it grew rapidly as the "capital" of the richest agricultural region in the United States. Most of the city's early-1900s buildings sprang up to house its bustling retail and department stores. After World War II, however, flight to the suburbs and a pedestrian mall downtown led to serious decline in activity. With help from the Fresno Main Street program, the city is currently working toward the rehabilitation of its buildings and facades, strengthening businesses and restoring this historic district as the area's gathering place and its center of culture, entertainment, and retail business.

WHAT TO EXPLORE WHILE IN TOWN: There are many and varied styles of architecture in downtown Fresno, ranging from the city hall's International style to the Art Deco of gas stations. One of the most notable features of the downtown Fresno area is the historic Water Tower on Fresno and O Streets. More than 100 years old, it was modeled after the Chicago Water Tower of 1867 and was in use until the 1950s. St. John's Cathedral, at Mariposa and R Streets, is the oldest Catholic church in Fresno, built in 1902 in the Gothic County Cathedral style. Several guides to Fresno's historic architecture are available at the Fresno Main Street offices.

GETTING THERE: Fresno is located in the San Joaquin Valley in central California, off State Highway 99.

FOR MORE INFORMATION: Fresno Main Street/Downtown Association of Fresno, 1060 Fulton Mall, Suite 916, Fresno, CA 93721, 209/266-9982

GRASS VALLEY, CALIFORNIA

Good Old Days Car Show

Experience a sense of nostalgia as this premiere car show breaks through the time barrier on Mill and West Main Streets in downtown Grass Valley. See 180 classic and custom cars in all their finery competing for trophies, ribbons, and bragging rights. Pack up the family in your automobile and come see these for a day of fun.

The Good Old Days Car Show in downtown Grass Valley.

ADMISSION: *None*
DATE: *Last Saturday in April*

Sierra Festival of the Arts

The streets of historic downtown Grass Valley are filled with artisans during this family event, which features sales and exhibitions of the best in regional art—jewelry, ceramics, woodworking, photography, and fine arts. Continuous entertainment is provided on stage and by strolling entertainers, and the Kids Zone offers hands-on art projects for children. During the Pastels on Pavement competition, the sidewalks of Bank Street are transformed into more than 70 concrete canvases, as artists and would-be artists use chalk and talent to color the street. Culture, color, art, and the historic Main Street combine to create this unique festival.

ADMISSION: *None*
DATE: *Last Sunday in May*

Cornish Christmas

This traditional event in Grass Valley will take you back in history to experience the sights, tastes, and sounds of Christmas past. A street fair under the stars held during the Christmas season, Cornish Christmas offers an opportunity to visit the historic downtown, sample Cornish food, and join in the gold country Christmas spirit. Strolling musicians, horse-drawn carriage rides, and an appearance by Santa Claus, who is available for consultation with children, provides a small town Christmas experience.

ADMISSION: *None*
DATE: *Friday evenings from Thanksgiving to Christmas*

About Grass Valley

IN 1850 THE DISCOVERY of gold-bearing quartz in Grass Valley established it as one of the richest gold mining regions in the state. By the 1950s this venture became unprofitable, and the mines closed. During the late 1960s, Grass Valley underwent a period of growth, which included the development of several large malls. As a result, downtown Grass Valley experienced an exodus of retail stores. However, through the efforts of the Main Street program, today Grass Valley is a strong and healthy commercial business district with a 0 percent vacancy rate, more than a half million dollars in private building rehabilitation projects, and an array of fine dining, shopping, and service businesses.

WHAT TO EXPLORE WHILE IN TOWN: A walking tour brochure, available at the chamber of commerce office, outlines more than 47 points of historic interest. One of Grass Valley's most recognized landmarks is the Holbrooke Hotel on West Main Street, restored to its glorious splendor, including the Golden Gate Saloon. The North Star Mining Museum at the end of Mill Street houses a large display of mining equipment, as well as the world's largest Pelton Mining Wheel, built in 1895.

GETTING THERE: Grass Valley is located northeast of Sacramento in northern California, accessible from Interstate 80 on State Highways 49 and 20.

FOR MORE INFORMATION: Grass Valley Downtown Association, 151 Mill Street, Grass Valley, CA 95945, 916/272-8315

LIVERMORE, CALIFORNIA

Days of Wine and Honey Festival

Downtown Livermore will be buzzing in celebration of Livermore's agricultural heritage, when the Days of Wine and Honey Festival is held downtown. Fourteen wineries are represented, as well as many local apiaries (beekeeping businesses). There are to be four stages of live entertainment, more than 200 arts and crafts vendors, great food, and fun for kids with the Bowling for Bees contest. There's even an appearance by a fellow who covers his body in bees and plays the clarinet.

ADMISSION: *None*
DATE: *First weekend in May*

Downtown Trick or Treat Night

Trick-or-treating has never been so much fun! The slogan for this event, geared toward both kids and parents, is "Say Boo to Drugs." Merchants in the historic downtown area open their doors to visitors, handing out goodies, and the local mortuaries give spooky presentations. Other activities include costume contests for adults and children, free haunted houses, pony rides, and pumpkin carving contests.

ADMISSION: *None*
DATE: *Thursday before Halloween*

About Livermore

ESTABLISHED IN 1849, the city of Livermore is situated in the East Bay region of San Francisco. Located in a valley and nestled adjacent to the Altamont hills, the historic downtown area has remained intact over the years. The Livermore Main Street Program was established in 1986 to address problems arising in the district when a large regional mall was located in the neighboring town. Downtown Livermore now boasts a vacancy rate of less than 1 percent and has successfully recruited new businesses complementary to its 14 wineries. The Main Street program has also worked hard to seismically retrofit 52 unreinforced masonry buildings against the possibility of earthquakes.

WHAT TO EXPLORE WHILE IN TOWN: Livermore's buildings reflect its California history. A walking tour booklet is available from the History Center located in the old Carnegie Library building at 2155 Third Street. Be sure to tour this great old building, built in 1911. Visitors can also see the old City Hall and Firehouse and the restored railroad depot, both dating from the late 1800s. Take a peek into Baughman's Western Outfitters, located downtown for more than 100 years. The large street clock at the intersection of First and South Livermore Avenue was a project coordinated by Livermore Main Street, raising $20,000 for its installation. The banners, planters, benches, and murals throughout the downtown are also improvements coordinated by the Main Street program. Additional visitor materials, such as hotel and event guides, are available at the Main Street office.

GETTING THERE: Livermore is located 45 miles east of San Francisco on State Highway 84 and Interstate 580.

FOR MORE INFORMATION: Livermore Main Street Project, 2310 First Street , Livermore, CA 94550, 510/373-1795

PASO ROBLES, CALIFORNIA

Paderewski Festival

The Paderewski Festival celebrates the life and achievements of famed Polish pianist and composer Ignacy Paderewski, who originally came to Paso Robles to partake of its healthful mineral baths, bought a ranch, and planted extensive vineyards. There are a variety of musical and social events throughout this festival weekend: piano competitions, evening concerts, winery tours, horse-drawn trolley tours of downtown, and a memorabilia auction,

Take a tour the old-fashioned way at the Paderewski Festival.

most of which require tickets. Contact the chamber of commerce for more information and tickets: 805/238-0506.

ADMISSION: *Events require tickets ranging from $12 to $15*
DATE: *Third weekend in March*

Strawberry Festival

The Strawberry Festival marks the peak of the season for the area's delicious, mouthwatering strawberries and is celebrated at Paso Robles' farmers market on the square. Free strawberry shortcake is featured, along with jam and baked goods, contests, live music, barbeque, fresh produce, crafts, pony rides, and a petting zoo. A good day can be had by the whole family at this free event.

ADMISSION: *None*
DATE: *Last Friday in April*

Wine Festival

The 32 vintners and grape growers in the Paso Robles area sponsor this wine festival, which is held in the downtown Paso Robles City Park. With the admission fee, visitors get a commemorative wineglass and tasting tickets. The festival also includes music, food, and other special events held at many of the local wine tasting rooms in the area.

ADMISSION: *$20*
DATE: *Third Saturday in May*

West Coast Kustom Car Show

If you prize "low riders" and classic cars, this is your dream event. Bring a folding chair and watch more than 900 restored and classic cars cruise up and down the main drag of Paso Robles. The Show'n'Shine event lets you get a close-up look at these vehicles and talk with their owners. Enjoy the farmers market on the square, along with barbeque, fresh produce, live music, and a 1950s street dance.

ADMISSION: *None*
DATE: *Memorial Day weekend*

Pioneer Day

This event with the theme "Leave your pocketbook at home" has endured since the first Pioneer Day in 1931. Here, everything is free, commercialism is banned, and merchants close their doors to join their neighbors for a relaxed, enjoyable day, free from cares of the working life. On Pioneer Day the people of the community and the surrounding areas are the guests of the Paso Robles merchants and businesses. In celebration of the first European settlers to this area, men without beards are fined $1 for a "Smooth Puss" badge, and free beans and bread are served. Families display their prized heirlooms, brought by their ancestors to Paso Robles, and a large parade is held in the morning.

ADMISSION: *None*
DATE: *Nearest Saturday in October to Columbus Day*

About Paso Robles

THE CITY OF EL PASO DE ROBLES was founded on the original trail chosen by Franciscan friars in their mission work—El Camino Real—and was known to Native Americans and the mission fathers for its hot mineral springs. Many of its most prominent buildings were constructed around the turn of the century at the town's height of popularity as a health resort. Since 1988, the Main Street program has been instrumental in bringing new business to downtown, as well as arranging for zero interest loans for building renovations and coordinating funds for seismic retrofitting studies for historic structures such as the Bank of Italy building. Paso Robles now supports 32 wineries, bed and breakfast inns, hotels, shopping, and outdoor recreation activities.

WHAT TO EXPLORE WHILE IN TOWN: A walking tour brochure is available at the Main Street office, which can direct you to the many restored historic buildings in downtown Paso Robles. Most of these, such as the Bank of Italy building and the acorn-shaped Clock Tower building, house shops, art galleries, and restaurants. Sample the ice cream at the Olde Towne Drug & Soda Fountain housed in the old Bell Theater, or sit and enjoy a cappuccino across from the City Park and Carnegie Library. Locals gather at several favorite places, such as Vic's Cafe, the Daily Grind, and the historic Paso Robles Inn. Several area wineries also give tours.

GETTING THERE: Paso Robles is located midway between Los Angeles and San Francisco, in the heart of the Central Coast on Highway 101. The city is 26 miles inland from the Hearst castle and 107 miles west of Bakersfield on Highway 46. The

Amtrak Coast Starlight stops in Paso Robles daily, just two blocks from the heart of downtown.

FOR MORE INFORMATION: Paso Robles Main Street Association, 835 12th Street, Suite D, Paso Robles, CA 93446, 805/238-4103

SAN LUIS OBISPO, CALIFORNIA

I Madonnari Italian Street Painting Festival

This two-day event celebrates the arts, as professionals and amateurs, students and children paint the downtown streets and plaza. Street painting has been an Italian tradition since the sixteenth century, and in this event chalk is used as the medium. The San Luis

Obispo Mission Plaza, the walkway in front of the Old Mission, and adjacent downtown streets are subdivided into pavement "squares," and participants are invited to become *madonnari*, or street painters, and get on their knees to fill these pavement canvases with their own inspirations. Engaging other senses, live music, children's art activities, and an authentic Italian market are also presented. Funds raised from this event benefit the Children's Creative Project, a nonprofit arts education organization that provides experiences in the arts for schoolchildren.

Artists create masterpieces in chalk on the streets of San Luis Obispo.

ADMISSION: *None*
DATE: *Last weekend in April*

The San Luis Obispo Mozart Festival

Billed as one of North America's most prestigious music festivals, the Mozart Festival in San Luis Obispo presents a diverse program of music and internationally acclaimed

artists in unique and picturesque settings. Although Mozart's music is prominently featured at the event, many other composers' works are also performed each season. The festival presents many free concerts, the popular Akademie and A*kid*emie series, and numerous social events, dinners, and parties. The events are held at various locations, including the Mission San Luis Obispo, Mission San Miguel, and several well-known wineries. For more information, call the festival office at 805/781-3008 or visit its web site at www.mozartfestival.com .

ADMISSION: *There are admission fees to some concerts; call ahead for tickets*
DATE: *Mid-July to the first week in August*

San Luis Obispo International Film Festival

Not only does this two-week film festival feature the standard fare of classic and restored films, independent features and documentaries, and tributes to outstanding filmmakers, it also features special presentations on the techncial aspects of filmmaking. The diversity of the films selected guarantees something for every age group, from kids to seniors. All events are held at venues located in the historic and beautiful downtown of San Luis Obispo. For more information, call the festival office at 805/546-FILM or visit its web site at www.slonet.org/vv/ipsloiff .

ADMISSION: *Fees for single-admission tickets and festival passes*
DATE: *Held around the last week of October through first week of November*

About San Luis Obispo

MISSION SAN LUIS OBISPO DE TOLOSA was founded by Father Junipero Serra in 1772 and is the fifth of 21 sites along California's Mission Trail. Located a few miles inland from the Pacific Coast, this is an area of natural beauty and a rich heritage spanning nearly 1,000 years. Across the centuries, it has been settled by widely varying peoples: Native American Chumash, Spanish conquerors, Swiss dairymen, Chinese laborers, Portuguese farmers, and the Victorian English, whose architecture remains heavily present today. The mission is still the focal point of the community, set amid adobes, other churches, and the magnificent vineyards whose products rival the finest offerings elsewhere. The Downtown Business Association continually works to preserve and promote the heritage and vitality of the downtown area, with initiatives in facade enhancement, street furniture, lighting, annual clean up programs, parking, and safety.

WHAT TO EXPLORE WHILE IN TOWN: In the downtown area there are a variety of attractions, including the Historical Museum, the Children's Museum, the Sauer Adams Adobe, Mission Plaza, San Luis Creek, Chinatown—including the Ah Louis Chinese Store—and the Fremont Theater with its Art Deco neon marquee. A downtown trolley can take visitors to many of these sites, and there are plenty of eateries, coffee houses, and shops in between.

GETTING THERE: San Luis Obispo is located near the coast between Los Angeles and San Francisco on State Highways 101 and 1.

FOR MORE INFORMATION: San Luis Obispo Downtown Business Improvement Association, 1108 Garden Street, Suite 209, San Luis Obispo, CA 93401, 805/541-0286

Idaho

COEUR D' ALENE, IDAHO

Classic cars cruise Main Street
Coeur d'Alene, then park for a
spectacular car show.

Car d'Lane

Car d'Lane, one of the biggest classic car shows in the Northwest, takes place in downtown Coeur d'Alene. It begins with the classic car cruise, a favorite event with the locals, when "oldies" music fills the street and classic models from every era cruise Sherman Avenue. The cars are then parked, awaiting the 10,000 or so spectators who come to gawk and vote for their favorites. A sock hop follows the show on Saturday night.

ADMISSION: *Car show and cruise free; dance tickets are $10*

DATE: *Third weekend in June*

Coeur d'Alene Downtown Street Fair

This street fair offers a chance to see and buy from more than 150 artisans who display their arts and crafts—glass, jewelry, toys, pottery, wood, silver, and ceramics. This is a juried assembly, so the quality of exhibitors is high and only handcrafted materials are displayed. In harmony with the arts theme, there are also clowns, jugglers, and poets roaming about, entertaining the crowds, and "busker" street musicians on every corner, keeping the atmophere lively. Activities for kids include a carnival, llama rides, and appearances by costumed characters.

ADMISSION: *None*

DATE: *First weekend in August*

Festival of Lights Parade

Everyone loves a parade—regardless of the weather. Every year thousands bundle up and line the streets to celebrate and enjoy the annual Festival of Lights parade. The parade begins at 5 P.M. and loops through downtown; floats, bands, and other finery start the holiday season. Fireworks over Lake Coeur d'Alene follow the parade. Children light candles and sing carols to round out this small town Christmas experience.

ADMISSION: *None*
DATE: *Friday after Thanksgiving*

About Coeur d'Alene

COEUR D'ALENE (pronounced "coor da-lane") is a land of crystal-clear lake waters and majestic mountain peaks. Through the years the region has prospered with an economy centered on natural resources, but recently Coeur d'Alene has begun to capitalize on its greatest natural assets: the recreational potential and scenic beauty of the region's lakes and mountains. Snowmobiling, skiing, golf, and other outdoor activities have earned it the title "Playground of the Northwest." The Coeur d'Alene Downtown Association has been a leader in the revitalization of the downtown area, which has included coordination of new fixtures such as lights, benches, banners, and sidewalks.

WHAT TO EXPLORE WHILE IN TOWN: Within walking distance of the downtown are several parks, the North Idaho Museum, the Centennial Trail, and boat launching facilities. Don't miss experiencing a unique "Huddy Burger" at Hudson's Hamburgers. This third-generation family restaurant boasts the same menu as when it opened in 1907. A visitor information center provides maps and guides of the downtown and area destinations. It can also book many activities available in the area: walking tours, sightseeing by bus or seaplane, and trips by lake ferry. Also available are chartered horse and buggy rides and rentals of bicycles, surreys, rollerblades, skis, boats, jet skis and snowmobiles, all complete with necessary clothing and gear.

GETTING THERE: Coeur D'Alene is at the intersection of Interstate 90 and US-Highway 95.

FOR MORE INFORMATION: Coeur d'Alene Downtown Association, 408 Sherman Avenue, Suite 203, Coeur d'Alene, ID 83814, 208/667-4040

Oregon

GRESHAM, OREGON

Spirit of Christmas

The Spirit of Christmas is a traditional holiday celebration for the Gresham community. This event includes carolers, storytellers, horse-drawn trolley rides, hands-on children's activities, music, and, of course, appearances by Santa and Mrs. Claus. Stroll Main Street and stop at the stores, where merchants will be serving hot drinks and cookies. The day is culminated with a tree-lighting ceremony and community sing-along.

ADMISSION: *None*
DATE: *The Saturday after Thanksgiving*

About Gresham

NAMED FOR PRESIDENT ARTHUR'S postmaster general, W.Q. Gresham, the city is located 15 miles east of Portland and is the gateway to the Columbia River Gorge National Scenic Area. In 1991 the city of Gresham partnered with the Gresham Downtown Development Association to improve the appearance of the downtown area, providing new sidewalks, benches, trees, lighting, and flowers. These efforts have spurred new interest in residential and commercial development downtown, which now has a 0 percent vacancy rate and a waiting list for tenants.

WHAT TO EXPLORE WHILE IN TOWN: A walk around Gresham will yield unique restaurants, shops, and architecture. The bungalow style is prevalent in the area for early residential structures, and the Truffle Hunter restaurant, at 225 West Powell, is a Craftsman bungalow-style house, listed on the National Register. The First Bethel Baptist Church located in Main City Park, built in 1866, is the oldest building in Gresham and is also listed on the National Register. In Pioneer Cemetery, one can find markers of Gresham's founding families as well as significant trees listed on the city's Tree Preservation Register. A walking tour guide and other information can be found at the Gresham Downtown Development office at 323 N.E. Roberts Avenue.

GETTING THERE: Gresham is located in northwestern Oregon, just 15 miles east of Portland. It is accessible by Interstates 5 and 84 and is situated on US Route 26.

FOR MORE INFORMATION: Gresham Downtown Development Association, P.O. Box 2043, 323 N.E. Roberts Avenue, Gresham, OR 97030, 503/665-3827

Washington

KENT, WASHINGTON

Canterbury Faire

Canterbury Faire is a community arts festival, attended by well over 30,000 people who have come to enjoy literary, visual, and performing arts. Canterbury Faire's medieval theme celebrates Kent's connection to Kent, England. The Faire also features contemporary entertainment and activities that the whole family can enjoy.

ADMISSION: *None*
DATE: *Third weekend in August*

About Kent

KENT, LOCATED IN THE PUGET SOUND REGION, was incorporated in 1890 and named for Kent, England, because hops were a major agricultural crop in the area, as they were in the original Kent. A rich agricultural land, the Kent Valley was a major supplier in the Northwest for vegetables, berries, and dairy products. In recent decades, Kent has developed into a manufacturing, housing, and distribution center. Recent decades of floods, earthquakes, and other natural disasters have destroyed many historic structures. However, the Kent Downtown Partnership has been instrumental in the rehabilitation of the few historic structures left in the community. It has also worked with developers to ensure that new construction enhances the existing structures in the historic district.

WHAT TO EXPLORE WHILE IN TOWN: There is an abundance of public art in downtown Kent, as well as diverse parks. A walking guide and public art guide are available at many downtown businesses and public buildings.

GETTING THERE: Kent is located between Seattle and Tacoma in the Puget Sound region of Washington. It is just off Interstate 5.

FOR MORE INFORMATION: Canterbury Faire, 220 Fourth Avenue South, Kent, WA 98032-5895, 206/859-3991

PASCO, WASHINGTON

Pasco Fiery Foods Festival

If you're a chili-head, this festival is for you. It celebrates one of this agricultural area's largest crops: chile peppers. More than 100 varieties are grown here, and wines and microbrews are produced in the area as well. So the downtown association put it all together and produced the Pasco Fiery Foods Festival. This is an old-fashioned street festival and farmers market, offer-

ing salsa contests, chile pepper contests, and more than 60 microbrews in a beer garden. There's also a huge kids' area with activities such as paper and pottery making. A range of fine craftsmanship by local artists, featuring jewelry, baskets, and glass blowing, will be displayed. There is continuous entertainment on two stages and, of course, lots of specialty spicy foods.

Peppers—and more—attract folks to Pasco during its Fiery Foods Festival.

ADMISSION: *None*
DATE: *First weekend in September*

About Pasco

PASCO WAS ESTABLISHED in the 1800s, first as a railroad town, later developing into a retail and agricultural center of southeastern Washington. With the arrival of a mall in the late 1960s, retail businesses left the downtown. The Main Street program (called Pasco Downtown Development Association) was begun in the early 1980s and continues its efforts to establish a vital downtown in the face of a changing retail landscape. Successful projects include the former Whitehorn Building, now called the Pasco Village Marketplace, which Pasco Downtown Development purchased, restored, and now rents space as a business incubator for new start-up businesses. It also houses the offices of Pasco Downtown Development.

WHAT TO EXPLORE WHILE IN TOWN: Visitors can explore the Ice Harbor Brewery, a microbrewery and pub, which is a Pasco favorite. Walking tour brochures of the downtown area are available at the Pasco Village Marketplace. Visit the farmers market, (the largest in Washington state) held May through November on Wednesday and Saturday mornings from 8:00 A.M. to noon at 4th Avenue and Columbia Street.

GETTING THERE: , Pasco is located in southeastern Washington, on US-395. It is just off Interstate 82; take I-182 east from exit 102 to Pasco.

FOR MORE INFORMATION: Pasco Downtown Development Association, 104 West Lewis, P.O. Box 842, Pasco, WA 99301, 509/545-0738

PUYALLUP, WASHINGTON

Meeker Days Hoedown and Bluegrass Festival

When it was first held in 1939, during the golden anniversary of Washington's statehood, Meeker Days Hoedown was designed to celebrate the pioneer spirit of Puyallup's founder, Ezra Meeker. Since then, it has grown to become one of the largest bluegrass events west of the Mississippi. It's a three-day street festival featuring musical entertainment on three stages. There's also a "Taste of Puyallup," provided by area restaurants, a farmers market, an antique car show, and a juried arts and crafts show. Kids love the "firemen's muster," the Super Cool Science Show, and the llama rides. There are lots of games for adult kids, too, as well as a beer garden serving microbrews.

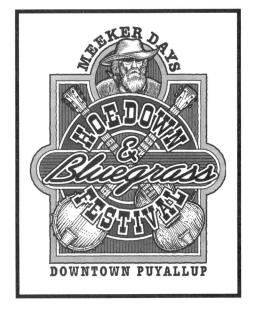

ADMISSION: *None*
DATE: *Third weekend in June*

Hometown Santa Parade

Join the whole town of Puyallup as it welcomes Mr. and Mrs. Claus, fresh from the North Pole, with an old fashioned community parade. Children of all ages can delight as floats, marching bands, horses, and antique cars parade down Main Street, heralding the arrival of the Clauses riding in an antique fire engine. After the parade, head toward Pioneer Park for the tree lighting ceremony, hot chocolate, and Christmas carolers. Later, children can whisper their wishes into Santa's ear at the Senior Center.

ADMISSION: *None*
DATE: *First Saturday in December*

About Puyallup

PUYALLUP WAS INCORPORATED in 1890, with founding father Ezra Meeker as its first mayor. Through the years the fertile valley around Puyallup has produced a wide variety of crops, such as hops, berries, small fruits, and, lately, bulbs and flowers. The Puyallup Main Street Association has helped to revitalize the historic downtown area by providing low-interest loans to building owners for rehabilitations, and pushed for a street renovation project to spruce up the downtown area. The Association worked for Landmark designation for historic Puyallup buildings, which provides tax abatement for their owners. It also developed and established Arts Downtown, Puyallup's outdoor gallery, and installed historical markers for the historical walking tour.

WHAT TO EXPLORE WHILE IN TOWN: There are many places of interest in Puyallup; first, visit the Main Street offices at 104 West Main, Suite 204, for information and walking tour guides. The Powerhouse Restaurant was previously a Puget Power substation, built in 1924 (454 East Main). Catch a movie at the Liberty Theater (116 West Main), built in 1924, an old-fashioned, single-screen movie house catering to families. If you're hungry, try coffee or lunch at Lonzo's (109 South Meridian) or at Pohlman Corner (101 South Meridian).

GETTING THERE: Puyallup is located in western Washington, outside Tacoma on State Highway 161. It is accessible from nearby Interstate 5.

FOR MORE INFORMATION: Puyallup Main Street Association, 104 West Main, Suite 204, P.O. Box 460, Puyallup, WA 98371, 206/840-2531

ILLUSTRATION CREDITS

NORTHEASTERN AND MID-ATLANTIC STATES

Page 3, Friends of Center Cemetery; **p. 7,** Downtown Carlisle Association; **p. 8,** South Side Local Development Company; **p. 9,** Robert Eddy; **p. 15,** Franklin Downtown Development Office; **p. 16,** John R. Trovato; **p. 18,** Mark Milligan; **p. 20,** Partnership for Warrenton Foundation; **p. 24,** Huntington Main Street; **p. 25,** Preston Publications; **p. 27,** Main Street Morgantown; **p. 28,** Battle of Point Pleasant Memorial Committee.

SOUTHERN STATES

Page 30, The Dothan Downtown Group; **p. 31,** Florence Main Street Program; **p. 33,** Main Street Mobile; **p. 34,** Main Street Helena/King Biscuit Blues Festival; **p. 37,** Paul Donofro Jr., Architect; **p. 39,** Washington Avenue Association; **p. 41,** Downtown Dalton Development Authority; **p. 42 (also shown on p. ix),** LaGrange Main Street; **p. 44,** Main Street Newnan; **p. 45,** Thomasville Main Street; **p. 46,** Angelene Willard, City of Toccoa; **p. 48,** Vidalia Main Street Program; **p. 49,** Ashland Main Street; **p. 50,** Robin Deaton; **p. 53,** Erin Milburn, *The Harrodsburg Herald*; **p. 54,** *The Gleaner,* Henderson, Ky.; **p. 55,** Heart of Hopkinsville; **p. 56,** Marion County Country Ham Days Committee; **p. 58,** Mt. Sterling Main Street; **p. 59,** Paintsville Main Street, Inc.; **p. 61,** Winchester First; **p. 63 (also shown on p. ix),** Whitney Atchetee, Abbeville Main Street; **p. 64,** Covington Downtown Development; **p. 67,** Morgan City Mainstreet; **p. 68,** Ruston Main Street; **p. 70,** Don Zeringue; **p. 71,** Vivian Main Street; **p. 72,** Aberdeen Main Street; **p. 74,** Logo art by the Publik Notice, Printing and Office Supply; **p. 74,** Cleveland/Bolivar Chamber of Commerce; **p. 77,** Hammons and Associates, Inc.; **p. 78,** Downtown Tupelo/Main Street Partnership; **p. 80,** Clay County Economic Development Corporation; **p. 82,** Downtown Boone Development Association; **p. 84,** Burlington Downtown Corporation; **p. 87,** Donnie Roberts, *The Dispatch*; **p. 89,** Newton Downtown Revitalization; **p. 90,** Downtown Waynesville Association, Inc.; **p. 91,** Downtown Waynesville Association; **p. 92,** Tim Conway; **p. 93,** CityScape/Kristie Phillips, photographer.

MIDWESTERN STATES

Page 98, All for Ava; **p. 99,** Galesburg Downtown Council; **p. 101,** Mildred Walther, Macomb Downtown Development Corporation; **p. 103,** Midtown Mattoon; **p. 104,** Vander Bleek Design, 102 1/2 East Main Street, Morrison, Illinois, 61270; **p. 108,** Savanna *Times Journal*; **p. 110 (also shown on p. x),** Eric Hastings, photographer, *Tuscola Review*, Tuscola, Ill.; **p. 112,** Joe Sneathen, Sneathen Sign Company; **p. 115,** Bob Corum Graphics; **p. 117 (also shown on p. x),** Downtown Partners, Inc.; **p. 118,** Ron Walloch, photographer; **p. 120,** Main Street Corning; **p. 123 (also shown on p. x),** Gary Alben, *Ogden Reporter;* **p. 125,** Holland Main Street/DDA; **p. 126,** Downtown Branson Betterment Association; **p. 128,** Hannibal Main Street Program, Inc.; **p. 129,** Hannibal Main Street Program, Inc.; **p. 130,** River City T's; **p. 132,** Missourian Publishing; **p. 133,** Chippewa Falls Main Street; **p. 136,** Main Street De Pere; **p. 137,** (upper) Dodgeville Revitalization, (lower) Dodgeville Revitalization; **p. 138,** Marshfield Area Chamber of Commerce and Industry; **p. 139,** Jon Weiss; **p. 140,** Richland Main Street/Chamber; **p. 141,** Richland Main Street/Chamber; **p. 142,** River Falls Main Street; **p. 143,** Sheboygan Falls Main Street; **p. 144,** Viroqua Chamber–a Main Street City.

MOUNTAIN AND PLAINS STATES

Page 146, Great Bend Downtown Development; **p. 147,** Fort Scott Downtown Program; **p. 151,** Willa Cather Pioneer Memorial & Educational Foundation; **p. 152,** Faye L. Kennedy; **p. 153,** Laramie Downtown Development Authority; **p. 154,** Laramie Downtown Development Authority; **p. 155,** Uptown Sheridan Association; **p. 156,** Jane J. Rice.

SOUTHWESTERN STATES

Page 159, Carlsbad MainStreet; **p. 160,** Bill Cabral; **p. 161,** Los Alamos MainStreet; **p. 162,** Main-Street Roswell; **p. 164,** (upper) John Williams, Williams Photography, 6 W. Main St., Ardmore, OK; (lower) Ardmore Main Street Authority; **p. 165,** Checotah, Oklahoma Main Street Program; **p. 166,** El Reno Main Street; **p. 167,** Tracey Montgomery; **p. 168,** Perry Main Street; **p. 169,** Bryan Main Street Project; **p. 171,** Elgin Main Street; **p. 172,** *Lampasas Dispatch Record*, Fred E. Lowe, Publisher; **p. 173,** City of Lampasas Main Street Program; **p. 175,** Main Street/Tourism Project Mineola; **p. 176,** Elaine Thomas; **p. 177,** San Marcos Main Street Program.

WESTERN STATES

Page 180, Downtown Berkeley Association; **p. 182,** Eureka Main Street; **p. 183,** Fairfield Downtown Improvement District; **p. 184,** Downtown Association of Fresno; **p. 185,** Teri Paulus, photographer; **p. 188,** Paso Robles Main Street Program **p. 190,** (upper) Jeffrey M. Greene/IMAGEWEST, (lower) San Luis Obispo Mozart Festival; **p. 192 (also shown on p. ix),** Coeur d'Alene Downtown Association; **p. 194,** Gresham Downtown Development Association; **p. 195,** Kent Downtown Partnership; **p. 196,** (upper) Craig Doupé, (lower) Craig Doupé; **p. 197,** Puyallup Main Street Association.

INDEX TO EVENTS BY MONTH

AUGUST

1st week:

Black Dirt Days, Conrad, Iowa, 119
Bluegrass in the Park, Henderson, Ky., 54
Coeur d'Alene Downtown Street Fair, Coeur
  d'Alene, Idaho, 192
Cotton Row on Parade Day, Greenwood, Miss.,
  77
Franklin Jazz Festival, Franklin, Tenn., 95
Heritage Day Riverfest, Pontiac, Ill., 105
Jupiter Jam Jazz and Blues Festival, Berkeley,
  Calif., 180
Red Hot Blues and Chili Cookoff, East Hartford,
  Conn., 2
San Luis Obispo Mozart Festival, San Luis
  Obispo, Calif., 190
Tomato Festival, Fairfield, Calif., 183
W. C. Handy Music Festival, Florence, Ala., 31

2nd week:

Jupiter Jam Jazz and Blues Festival, Berkeley,
  Calif., 180
Lampasas Quilt Extravaganza, Lampasas, Tex., 172
Red Cloud Streetcar Days, Red Cloud, Neb., 151

3rd week:

Canterbury Faire, Kent, Wash., 195
Jupiter Jam Jazz and Blues Festival, Berkeley,
  Calif., 180
Pioneer Days Festival, Harrodsburg, Ky., 53
Pure Water Days Fun Fest, Chippewa Falls, Wis.,
  133

4th week:

Civil War Reenactment, East Hartford, Conn., 2
Frisco Festival, Rogers, Ark., 36
Jupiter Jam Jazz and Blues Festival, Berkeley,
  Calif., 180
Prairie Arts Festival, West Point, Miss., 80

SEPTEMBER

1st week:

Art on the Kinni, River Falls, Wis., 142
BBQ Festival, Hopkinsville, Ky., 55
Daniel Boone Pioneer Festival, Winchester, Ky.,
  60
Dinuba Main Street Car Show, Dinuba, Calif.,
  181
Fall Festival, Wamego, Kans., 148
Marigold Festival, Great Bend, Kans., 146
New World Festival at Chander, Randolph, Vt., 9
Pasco Fiery Foods Festival, Pasco, Wash., 196
Shrimp and Petroleum Festival, Morgan City, La., 66

2nd week:

African-American Cultural Day, Culpeper, Va., 12
Arkansas River Blues Festival, North Little Rock,
  Ark., 35
Cherokee Strip Celebration, Perry, Okla., 168
Chilifest — The West Virginia State Chili Cham-
  pionship, Huntington, W.Va., 24
Diez y Sies, Bryan, Tex., 170
Okrafest, Checotah, Okla., 165

3rd week:

An Evening Under the Stars, Warrenton, Va., 20
Big River Days, Clarksville, Mo., 127
Days Fest and Fanfare, Salem, Ill., 107
Fall Fest, Fort Dodge, Iowa, 121
Historic Constitution Square Festival, Danville,
  Ky., 50
Kids Classic Festival, Beckley, W.Va., 22
Market on Main Street, Marlin, Tex., 174
Paint the Town, Morrison, Ill., 104
Poage Landing Days Festival, Ashland, Ky., 49
Somerfest Arts and Heritage, Somerset, Ky., 59

4th week:

Annual Raisin Festival, Dinuba, Calif., 181
Country Ham Days, Lebanon, Ky., 56
Fall Festival of the Arts, Washington, Mo., 131
Fall Funfest, Cookeville, Tenn., 93
Festival of St. Francis, St. Francisville, La., 69
Festival of the Singing River, Florence, Ala., 32
Madison Chautauqua, Madison, Ind., 115
Midwest Cornish Festival, Mineral Point, Wis.,
  139
Olde Boone Streetfest, Boone, N.C., 82
Pecos Valley Chile and Cheese Festival, Roswell,
  N. Mex., 162
Preston County Buckwheat Festival, Kingwood,
  W.Va., 25
Smiles Day Weekend, Rushville, Ill., 106
Taste of Ardmore and Art and the Park, Ardmore,
  Okla., 164
Taste of Sumter, Americus, Ga., 40
Trail of Tears Commemorative Event, Golconda,
  Ill., 100
Tuscola Harvest Homecoming, Tuscola, Ill., 110

OCTOBER

1st week:

Annual Fall Jubilee, Manassas, Va., 17
AutumnFest, Marianna, Fla., 37
Ava Emu and Craft Festival, Ava, Ill., 98
Battle Days, Point Pleasant, W.Va., 27
Bayfest, Mobile, Ala., 33
Centerfest, Richland Center, Wis., 140
Chili Night, Beckley, W.Va., 22
Culpeper Music Fest, Culpeper, Va., 13
Franklin Fall Festival, Franklin, Va., 14
Kentucky Apple Festival, Paintsville, Ky., 58
Louisiana Cattle Festival, Abbeville, La., 62
Passport Fresno: International Food and Culture
  Festival, Fresno, Calif., 184

2nd week:

Antique Alley Street Festival, Reidsville, N.C., 89
Arts Festival & Octubafest 18th Century
  Encampment, Carlisle, Pa., 6
Blue Bluff River Festival, Aberdeen, Miss., 72
Canton Flea Market Arts and Crafts Show, Can-
  ton, Miss., 73
Church Street Art and Craft Show, Waynesville,
  N.C., 91